THE LONG SHADOW
OF SEXUAL ABUSE

THE LONG SHADOW OF SEXUAL ABUSE
Developmental Effects across the Life Cycle

Calvin A. Colarusso, MD

JASON ARONSON
Lanham • Boulder • New York • Toronto • Plymouth, UK

Published by Jason Aronson
An imprint of Rowman & Littlefield Publishers, Inc.
A wholly owned subsidiary of The Rowman & Littlefield Publishing Group, Inc.
4501 Forbes Boulevard, Suite 200, Lanham, Maryland 20706
http://www.rowmanlittlefield.com

Estover Road, Plymouth PL6 7PY, United Kingdom

Copyright © 2010 by Jason Aronson

British Library Cataloguing in Publication Information Available

Library of Congress Cataloging-in-Publication Data

Colarusso, Calvin A.
 The long shadow of sexual abuse : developmental effects across the life cycle / Calvin A. Colarusso.
   p. ; cm.
 Includes bibliographical references and index.
 ISBN 978-0-7657-0766-6 (cloth : alk. paper) — ISBN 978-0-7657-0768-0 (electronic)
 1. Child sexual abuse—Case studies. 2. Adult child abuse victims—Case studies. I. Title.
 [DNLM: 1. Adult Survivors of Child Abuse—psychology—Case Reports. 2. Child Abuse, Sexual—psychology—Case Reports. 3. Personality Development—Case Reports. 4. Sexual Behavior—psychology—Case Reports. 5. Stress Disorders, Post-Traumatic—psychology—Case Reports. WM 167 C793L 2010]
 RJ506.C48C646 2010
 618.92'85836—dc22

                                                                    2010014044

∞ ™ The paper used in this publication meets the minimum requirements of American National Standard for Information Sciences—Permanence of Paper for Printed Library Materials, ANSI/NISO Z39.48-1992.

Printed in the United States of America

I dedicate this book to those individuals and families who have suffered for a lifetime from the calamitous effects of chronic childhood sexual abuse.

Contents

Preface

THIS BOOK HAS ONE SIMPLE PURPOSE—namely, to describe the profound interferences with normal developmental processes that occur in every subsequent developmental phase from the time of the abuse throughout childhood,
adolescence, and young, middle, and late adulthood. I hope to demonstrate,
convincingly, that the effects are lifelong.

Some of the case histories of older individuals provide truly unique clinical material to be studied and understood, because in the nearly fifty years
since the childhood sexual abuse they had never been evaluated nor told their
stories to any mental health professional. Indeed, many of them had never
talked to anyone about what they had experienced. The details are horrific
and difficult to read. It has been my experience that not only clinicians, for
whom this book is primarily written, but also educators, parents, indeed all
concerned adults often use the term *sexual abuse* but do not know in any detail what children who are victimized experience.

The book is organized as follows: a section on normal development for
each developmental phase is followed by case histories, arranged chronologically according to the age of the victims at the time I evaluated them. Then
the effects of the sexual abuse are traced from the time that the abuse took
place in childhood to the chronological present. For those individuals who
were evaluated in childhood or adolescence, the developmental histories will
be relatively short. For those who were evaluated in adulthood, including
some in their sixties, the developmental effects cover decades; indeed, half a
century. As is standard practice, all names and identifying details in the case
histories have been altered to protect the privacy of the subjects.

The following sequence of developmental phases that I will utilize is based on the ideas of Sigmund Freud (1905), Erik Erikson (1963) and Robert Nemiroff and myself (1981). Childhood, encompassing Freud's oral, anal, oedipal and latency stages, will cover the years from birth to adolescence. Adolescence will refer to the years from twelve to twenty. Adulthood will be divided into three phases: young, middle, and late adulthood, covering the remainder of the life cycle.

A board-certified child and adult psychiatrist and child and adult psychoanalyst, I've spent most of my professional life in private practice treating children and adults and teaching at the University of California at San Diego and the San Diego Psychoanalytic Institute. However, the case histories in this book are the result of my more than thirty years of work as an expert witness in civil cases. During the course of those years, while serving as an expert witness for both plaintiffs and defendants, I've evaluated approximately one hundred cases of child sexual abuse. I did not treat any of the individuals whose stories are presented here. To have done so would have been a conflict of interest. Some of the evaluations included psychological testing and a review of relevant records. Others, because the cases settled before a more thorough evaluation could be finished, are not as complete but all of them provide information that illustrates the basic purpose of this book.

This is not a book about diagnosis or treatment, although both will be addressed. DSM-IV diagnoses will be given for each individual and the obvious need for treatment will be described as I assessed it at the time that the evaluation occurred. Decisions on what kind of treatment and how much treatment will be needed will obviously be made by the mental health professional working with his or her patient at the time. But my recommendations, based on these evaluations and my forty years of experience with sexual abuse victims, do convey my belief that individuals who have been chronically sexually abused in childhood need psychiatric intervention in the form of psychotherapy and medication periodically for the rest of their lives. The efficacy of psychodynamic psychotherapy to treat childhood sexual abuse has recently been discussed in the literature (Shedler, 2009; Leichsenring and Rebring, 2008). However, one of the strongest insights that I have acquired from this work is that at our present level of understanding no amount of treatment can result in a cure for those cases in which the abuse was chronic. All we can realistically hope to do is diminish the harmful effects.

Because of the focus on the effect of the sexual abuse on developmental processes it may appear that I am attempting to describe an exclusive, cause-and-effect relationship between the sexual abuse and the psychopathology that developed at the time of the abuse and for decades afterward. That is not the case. I am suggesting that the sexual abuse had a profound deleterious effect on developmental processes and that these detailed developmental histories present unique clinical material that has not been previously presented in a format like this. However, I am fully aware that new developmental tasks and challenges that presented themselves as life progressed, other traumas, resilience and a plethora of other life experiences, among other factors, were also involved in the clinical presentation of each of the individuals at whatever age I happened to see them. Developmental processes, normal and pathologic, are enormously complex. I will discuss some of the most recent literature on the relationship between developmental processes and childhood sexual abuse in chapter 2.

I wish to state clearly that diagnostic thinking and treatment conclusions drawn from diagnostic interviews and psychological testing conducted for use in a legal process are distinctly different from opinions and conclusions that would emerge from an extended psychiatric diagnostic evaluation and/ or treatment process. But the diagnoses and treatment recommendations described do serve to relate the case material to DSM-IV, the only widely accepted diagnostic nomenclature in the field, and the literature on childhood sexual abuse.

My experience in this area is broader than these forensic evaluations. In my more than forty-five years of private practice I've treated many children and adults who were sexually abused as children. Years ago, while I was in the United States Air Force, I worked part time at the California Medical Facility at Vacaville, a prison/treatment facility, where I had the opportunity to study and treat perpetrators.

Although I have learned to tolerate the horror in these stories, I remain deeply affected by the knowledge of what adult human beings, particularly those in positions of responsibility and power, are capable of doing to vulnerable children.

My intention in this book is not to focus on or demean religion or any particular religious denomination. It is well known that the sexual abuse of children is not the exclusive domain of any religion or of religious individuals in general. Abusers come from all social strata and belief systems.

Clearly we understand very little about what motivates perpetrators to attack children. Further, as previously described, our treatment efforts are woefully inadequate to minimize or eliminate the devastating effects of chronic childhood sexual abuse. I hope that the information in this book will stimulate research and encourage mental health professionals to study and treat both those who have been abused and those who abuse.

Acknowledgments

As I APPROACHED MY SEVENTY-FIFTH BiRTHDAY I did not intend to undertake the arduous task of writing another book. Five seemed to be enough. However, I was asked by Salman Akhtar, MD, professor of psychiatry at Jefferson Medical College (my alma mater) and training and supervising analyst at the Philadelphia Psychoanalytic Center for Psychoanalysis, to speak at the 2009 Mahler Symposium. At the welcoming dinner, with his usual enthusiasm, he asked me what I was currently working on. Before I had much of a chance to respond he walked me over to Jessica Bradfield from Jason Aronson, placed my hand in hers, and declared that we should work on a book together. So, I'd like to thank Dr. Akhtar, for prodding me into what has been a most engaging, energizing effort.

Clark Clipson, PhD, Reid Meloy, PhD, and Robert Stieber, PhD, provided assistance and advice. All three are highly skilled professionals who were supportive and encouraging. They have enhanced my understanding of childhood sexual abuse.

I'd also like to thank Julie E. Kirsch, editorial director at Jason Aronson, for her excellent suggestions and willingness to patiently tolerate my lack of computer expertise and insufferable boasts about the glories of southern California weather compared to that of the East Coast.

And I must once again thank Jean, my wife of fifty years, for tolerating the many hours I spent in my "cave" working on yet another book when I should have been retired and waiting around the house for her next command regarding the proper use of my time. She has always unselfishly supported my professional activities with grace and only an occasional complaint.

I have had the privilege of working with many outstanding lawyers—too many to mention by name—during my many years of serving as an expert witness. The highly skilled individuals who asked me to evaluate the individuals in this book provided their clients with empathy, compassion and understanding and in most instances the encouragement to emotionally and legally confront the unthinkable traumas that so badly damaged their lives. They deserve all of our thanks.

1

Introduction

DEVELOPMENTAL THEMES AND ISSUES

SINCE THIS BOOK IS ABOUT THE EFFECTS of chronic childhood sexual abuse on developmental processes throughout the life cycle, a definition of *development* is in order. The definition that I find most useful was proposed by Rene Spitz (1965), who defined it as "the emergence of forms, of function, and of behavior which are the outcome of exchanges between the organism on the one hand, the inner and outer environment on the other" (p. 5). In essence, Spitz suggested that the mind evolves because of the *continuous* interactions among three sets of variables: the body (or organism) as it matures during childhood and regresses during adulthood; the mind itself (the inner environment), as it exists at any particular point in the life cycle; and external influences (the outer environment), consisting primarily of the family of origin in childhood and the family of procreation in adulthood.

For many years the predominant viewpoint held that development was a phenomenon of childhood and adolescence. Adult developmental theory, utilizing a definition such as Spitz's, suggests that development is lifelong because exchanges between the organism and the environment occur from birth to death, producing a continuous effect on psychic development. The adult is not a finished product insulated from the environment but, like the child, is in a state of dynamic tension which continually affects and changes him or her. The evolving nature of the symptoms of the adult individuals in this book, over five decades in some instances, is convincing evidence of dramatic change in the adult mind over time.

For more detailed information on adult development the reader is referred to relevant chapters in this book and to the work of individuals such as Neugarten (1979), Pollock and Greenspan (1998), Vaillant (1977), and Robert Nemiroff and myself (1981).

A definition of the word *chronic* as used in this book is also in order. Simply stated, chronic refers to multiple experiences of sexual abuse. Many of the individuals whose case histories are reported here were abused more than one hundred times. All but one, a three-year-old girl, were repeatedly abused.

The age at which the abuse began and ended is another important issue that needs to be considered in understanding these case histories. Recent clinical research (Gaensbauer and Jordan, 2009) indicates that very early trauma—before the age of four—does not support linear models of the effect of long-term carryover nor the idea that early traumatic experiences would be directly accessible in the course of therapy. As language developed, particularly by the age of three, memories were more assessable and able to be reported verbally.

This finding is in sharp contrast to the conclusion that I have drawn from the case material in this book. In most instances at least some of the memories of the sexual abuse were vivid and a clear-cut cause-and-effect relationship between the chronic sexual abuse and the devastating developmental interferences that followed throughout the life cycle was evident to both the abused individual and myself. The results of the study by Gaensbauer and Jordan on early trauma and the effect of later (in latency and adolescence) sexual abuse described in this book are not incompatible. The difference is due to the increased complexity of psychic structure and experience that develops during latency and adolescence. Children abused during later childhood and adolescence register the abuse in a much more organized way than do children who experienced trauma in early childhood. The infantile psyche responds to trauma in a much more diffuse, impressionistic manner.

The most prevalent psychoanalytic view of the effect of significant childhood trauma is confirmed by the case studies in this book of individuals who were chronically sexually abused during latency and adolescence. Namely, the ego is overwhelmed by the trauma and the effects on developmental processes and psychopathology are lifelong. The psychic helplessness of the dependent child's ego results in the violence becoming branded on the psyche, leaving its traumatic mark (Marcano, 2006). "The overwhelming of the ego induced by trauma is thought to leave indelible memory imprints (conscious or unconscious) that cause ongoing flashbacks, affective re-experiencing, traumatically driven behavioral reenactments, trauma-determined fears and traumatic dreams. . . . The trauma is seen as having an enduring organizational influence on the patient throughout the life span" (Gaensbauer and Jordan, 2009, p. 948).

However, as previously described, the effect of the childhood sexual abuse must be integrated with other life experiences and traumas that occurred as the individual moved on chronologically. The pathology of any sexual abuse victim, regardless of age, must be understood in terms of their entire life experience, not the sexual abuse in isolation.

DEVELOPMENTAL CONSIDERATIONS OF DIAGNOSIS AND TREATMENT

A central concept of psychodynamic developmental theory is that knowledge of normal development provides vital information necessary to conceptualize and treat psychopathology. Developmental knowledge and research should seek "to map the complex pathways from early childhood to later adaptive or maladaptive development which can then form the basis for interventions for both preventing and treating disorders" (Luyten, Blatt, and Corveleyn, 2005).

The concepts of *equifinality* and *multifinality* are particularly useful in understanding the complexities of the developmental process and the developmental psychopathology presented by the case studies in this book (Cicchetti and Rogosch, 1996). The principle of *equifinality* suggests that different developmental pathways may lead, depending on their interaction with other factors, to the same developmental outcome. *Multifinality* refers to the idea that one particular developmental factor such as an adverse event, depending on other factors involved, may lead to different developmental outcomes. "These issues of equifinality and multifinality force both researchers and clinicians to think in terms of the complex pathways that lead to a given end state, rather than focusing on specific disorders" (Luyten, Blatt, Van Houdenhove, and Corveleyn, 2006, 2008).

A recent study of thousands of HMO members (Anda et al., 2006) once again confirmed the relationship between early adverse childhood experiences such as childhood sexual abuse and a wide variety of psychological disorders and problems. But more importantly, the researchers also found a clear relationship between the number of adverse experiences in childhood and the degree of psychopathology in adulthood. *Earlier and more intense adversity produced a greater number of maladaptive outcomes.* "Future research should investigate the complex pathways that are responsible for both vulnerability associated with early life trauma and for resilience, as clearly not everyone with a history of early adversity is at increased risk for psychopathology or (functional) somatic disorders" (Luyten, Blatt, Van Houdenhove, and Corveleyn, 2008, p. 40).

Much more needs to be done to understand the relationship between developmental processes and resilience. A growing area of study, beyond the scope of our focus here, the resilience literature attempts to explain why some individuals from severely disadvantaged backgrounds seem to traverse developmental challenges with relative ease and eventually function as competent adults while others are incapacitated by similar experiences (Besser, Vliegen, Luyten, and Blatt, 2008). There are no examples of resilience in this book.

RELEVANT LITERATURE ON CHILDHOOD SEXUAL ABUSE

The Third National Incident Study of Child Abuse and Neglect (NIS-3) (Sedlak and Broadhurst, 1996) reported a significant increase—two-thirds higher—in the incidence of abuse and neglect since the last national incident study. In 1993, 1,553,800 children in the United States were abused or neglected under the Harm Standard. From 1983 to 1993 there was an 83 percent increase in childhood sexual abuse. Girls were abused three times as often as boys. Children were vulnerable to sexual abuse from the age of three.

A more recent ten-year research update review of child sexual abuse (Putnam, 2003) based on all English-language articles published after 1989 containing empirical data, provided current information on prevalence, risk factors, outcomes, treatment and prevention of child sexual abuse. Childhood sexual abuse was found to constitute approximately 10 percent of officially substantiated child maltreatment cases, numbering approximately 88,000 in 2000. Adjusted prevalence rates were 16.8 percent for adult women and 7.9 percent for adult men. Risk factors included gender, age, disabilities, and parental dysfunction.

When attempting to understand the effect of childhood sexual abuse on adult developmental processes it is important to recognize that child victims and adult survivors exhibit similar core symptoms of anxiety, depression, dissociation and sexual problems. "New symptoms and defenses emerge during adolescence and adulthood, such as substance abuse, somatization, eating disorders, and personality disorders. These are maladaptive attempts to cope with the anxiety and depression linked to the childhood sexual trauma, which threaten to erupt when the victims are faced with establishing intimate or sexual relationships in adolescence and adult life. These defenses often coalesce into personality traits, attitudes, and identifications that become ego syntonic and lose their connection with the childhood trauma" (Green, 1995, p. 665). The persistence of shame following sexual abuse is one of the factors that keep victims from reporting the abuse (Feiring and Taska, 2005). This was certainly true in most of the individuals whose stories are reported in this book.

Childhood sexual abuse also results in a "selective restructuring of reality" (Summit, 1983, p. 184) that, although adaptive, in some ways occurs at the expense of good reality testing. Ehrenberg (1987) suggested that survivors of sexual abuse in childhood confuse fantasy and reality as a way of dealing with all relationships—a defensive adaptation that occurs as a means of integrating abusive experiences and may continue into adulthood in the absence of continuing abuse. Traumatic stress also has damaging effects on other aspects of ego functioning, such as the capacity for representation and the capacity for self-regulation (Saporta, 2003).

Terr (1991) divided childhood trauma into two types. Type I trauma occurs when a discrete catastrophic event produces posttraumatic stress disorder. In Type II trauma, long-standing, multiple traumas lead to character pathology and the use of defenses such as denial, repression, dissociation and identification with the aggressor. Chronic sexual abuse obviously is a Type II trauma.

A variety of formal adult psychiatric diagnoses are clinically associated with childhood sexual abuse. These include the DSM-IV diagnoses of major depressive disorder, borderline personality disorder, somatization disorder, substance abuse disorders, posttraumatic stress disorder, dissociative identity disorder and bulimia nervosa disorder. Depression in adults and sexualized behaviors in children were the best documented outcomes. As a group individuals with a history of childhood sexual abuse, irrespective of their psychiatric diagnoses, manifest significant problems with affect regulation, impulse control, somatization, sense of self, cognitive distortions and problems with socialization.

A history of childhood sexual abuse has been associated with higher rates of all disorders diagnosed in women. As is evident in the clinical material in this book, childhood sexual abuse victims, male and female, are particularly prone to use dissociative mechanisms and symptoms in an attempt to cope with the trauma. The use of dissociative mechanisms, including amnesia, is particularly related to chronic abuse beginning at early ages (Chu et al. 1999; Kisiel and Lyons, 2001). Dissociation is also an important predictor of which individuals are at risk for developing posttraumatic stress disorder (Putnam and Trickett, 1997). A study by Widom (1999) indicated that slightly more than a third of the childhood victims of sexual abuse (37.5 percent) in his study met the DSM criteria for lifetime PTSD.

Sexualized behaviors have been most closely linked to child sexual abuse (Paolucci et al., 2001). These effects are most pronounced in younger children, particularly when the children are examined soon after the abusive experiences. A history of childhood sexual abuse, but not a history of physical abuse or neglect, is associated with a significantly increased arrest rate for sex crimes and prostitution, irrespective of gender (Widom and Ames, 1994).

Childhood sexual abuse is a complex life experience, not a diagnosis or a disorder. An array of sexual activities is covered by the term *child sexual abuse.* These include intercourse, attempted intercourse, oral-genital contact, fondling of genitals directly or through clothing, exhibitionism or exposing children to adult sexual activity or pornography, and the use of the child for prostitution or pornography. This diversity alone ensures that there will be a range of outcomes. In addition, the age and gender of the child, the age and gender of the perpetrator, the nature of the relationship between the child and perpetrator, and the number, frequency, and duration of the abuse experiences all appear to influence some outcomes. Thus sexually abused children constitute a very heterogeneous group with many degrees of abuse about whom few simple generalizations hold (Putnam and Trickett, 1997, p. 2).

Girls are 2.5 to 3 times more likely to be abused than boys. However, approximately 22 percent to 29 percent of all child sexual abuse victims are male (Fergusson et al., 1996; Finkelhor, 1993; Sobsey et al., 1997; U.S. Department of Health and Human Services, 1998). Boys are underrepresented in psychiatric samples, especially older boys who are often reluctant to admit to being sexually abused. *Research indicates that mental health professionals rarely ask adult males about childhood sexual abuse* (Lab et al., 2000).

The risk of being sexually abused rises with age (Finkelhor, 1993; U.S. Department of Health and Human Services, 1998). Data from 1996 indicated that approximately 10 percent of victims were between the ages of zero and three years. The percentage almost tripled (28.4 percent) between the ages of four and seven years. Twenty-five percent of cases occurred between the ages of eight and eleven. Children twelve years and older accounted for the remaining third (35.9 percent) of cases (U.S. Department of Health and Human Services, 1998).

A six-year follow-up study of 93 of 108 boys who were sexually abused by a single perpetrator in a school setting, compared with 93 age-matched controls, is particularly relevant to the developmental focus of this book. The number and frequency of reported health problems were similar in the two groups but the abused boys were more likely than controls to have symptoms that persisted for more than one year (Price et al., 2002). This pattern persisted after the abuse had stopped and the perpetrator had been imprisoned. The authors note that research that focused on sexual abuse of boys has not been as thorough as the research on girls because of the belief that abuse of boys is rare and does not result in significant sequelae, a conclusion unwarranted by the evidence to the contrary in the case studies in this book. "This longitudinal study with concurrent controls provides a snapshot of this group as they pass through adolescence, and reminds providers that the residual effect of sexual abuse may persist long after the abusive encounter" (Jay and Dell'Angela, 2002).

Sexually abused children have an increased suicide risk. Survey data from 83,731 students in the sixth, ninth, and twelfth grades revealed that four percent of students reported sexual abuse by a non-family member, 1.3 percent by a family member, and 1.4 percent by both. Youth with a history of childhood sexual abuse were at increased risk for suicide behaviors compared with other youth but the risk is reduced when protective factors are in place. "Family connectedness, teacher caring, other adult caring, and school safety were associated with lower levels of suicidal ideation and attempts for both male and female adolescents. Family connectedness appeared to have a particularly strong protective association with the outcomes" (Eisenberg et al., p. 485).

Sexually abused children are also at risk for eating disturbances. A controlled study of twenty sexually abused girls between the ages of ten and fifteen (Wonderlich et al., 2000) revealed that the abused children had higher levels of weight dissatisfaction and purging and dieting behavior than the controls. Furthermore, abused children reported eating less than control children when they felt emotionally upset. Abused children were less likely than control children to exhibit perfectionistic tendencies but more likely to desire thinner bodies. The results support previous findings with adult subjects which indicated that a history of childhood sexual abuse is associated with weight and body dissatisfaction, along with purging and dietary restriction.

In a study of suicide in Australian adolescents (Bergen et al., 2003) sexual abuse was associated with suicidal thoughts and actions, both directly and indirectly, through hopelessness and depressive symptoms. Hopelessness was associated with high suicide risk only, whereas depressive symptoms were associated with high suicide risk and attempts. Hopelessness was more strongly associated with sexual abuse in boys and depressive symptoms were more strongly associated with sexual abuse in girls.

Thus, from this selective review of the literature it is clear that childhood sexual abuse causes various disorders in childhood including depression, anxiety, behavioral problems, sexualized behaviors and posttraumatic stress disorder (Saywitz et al., 2000). But it is also clear from the case studies in this book and the literature that individuals who have been abused as children are at risk for serious problems in adulthood such as substance abuse, impaired social relationships, depression and suicide attempts and sexual inhibition and acting out (Brent et al., 2002; Nelson et al., 2002). Indeed research is indicating that abused children with posttraumatic stress disorder symptoms may have smaller total brain and corpus callosum volumes and lower IQs than carefully matched controls. These differences were correlated with age of abuse onset and longer duration of PTSD symptoms (DeBellis et al., 1999). "Thus there is strong evidence that CSA, and in particular CSA-related PTSD, places children at increased risk for suffering potentially life-long difficulties" (Cohen et al. 2004, p. 393).

2

The First Decade of Life

NORMAL DEVELOPMENT

ALTHOUGH MOST OF THE INDIVIDUALS IN THIS BOOK were seen when they were in adolescence or older, most of them were abused during the first decade of life. The first case study in the book describes the abuse of a three-year-old girl who was seen by me when she was five years of age. The second case study tells the story of an adolescent girl who was sexually abused during the latency years. Many of the older women and men in their fifties and sixties were also abused during the elementary school years. For this reason an understanding of the normal developmental processes of the years from birth to adolescence is essential to understanding their pathology.

The review of normal development in this chapter and the others in the book are not meant to be exhaustive. They are intended to provide a baseline for comparison between normality and the enormous developmental distortions and pathology that resulted from the childhood sexual abuse. For more detailed information on normal developmental processes the reader is referred to the yearly volumes of *The Psychoanalytic Study of the Child, Psychoanalytic Theories of Development* (1990) by Phyllis and Robert Tyson, *Child and Adult Development* (1992) by Calvin Colarusso, and *Adult Development* (1981) by Calvin Colarusso and Robert Nemiroff.

The Emergence of Self and Other: The Theories of Spitz and Mahler

The theories of Rene Spitz and Margaret Mahler, both clinicians, provide ideas on early development that are readily conceptualized and compared, thus forming a grid on which to build a more comprehensive picture of the first years of life. They are emphasized here because they explain how the child develops a cohesive sense of self and awareness of others that is at the core of all human relationships. Chronic sexual abuse severely warps attitudes toward the self and others. Evidence of severely damaged self-esteem and relationships with others will be painfully obvious in each of the case histories in this book, hence the focus on this topic.

Rene Spitz

I will begin with the theory of Rene Spitz (1965) because his work preceded and influenced Mahler's. Spitz used the term *psychic organizer* to explain the importance of the smile response, the eighth-month anxiety, and negativism. He borrowed the term from embryology where it is used to describe a set of agents and regulating elements which influence subsequent change. Before the emergence of the organizer, for example, transplanted cells will assume the form and function of the tissue into which they are placed. After the emergence of the organizer they will retain the form and function of the tissue from which they came.

In an analogous way, the smile response, stranger anxiety, and negativism are indicators that a new form of psychic organization and complexity has occurred which cannot be reversed. "If the child successfully establishes and consolidates an organizer at the appropriate level, his development can proceed in the direction of the next organizer" (Spitz, 1965, p. 119).

Spitz described the *smile response* as the first active, directed, intentional behavior. Through his research Spitz learned that the infant will respond to a gestalt of the human face—forehead, eyes and nose seen straight on and in motion. Under normal circumstances a genuine smile in response to mother's, or father's, face occurs by four to six weeks of age, always by three months of age. The appearance of the smile in response to the human face indicates that a number of important mental processes are beginning to form. They include the differentiation of internal from external stimuli, reality from fantasy, past from present and conscious from unconscious.

Spitz called the second psychic organizer *stranger anxiety*. By the middle of the first year, sometimes earlier, children become acutely apprehensive in the presence of a stranger and respond by turning away or crying. The appearance of stranger anxiety indicates that the infant has developed the capacity to distinguish one human from another and to recognize the importance of a specific person for his or her well-being. The child is beginning the process of forming relationships. This is the beginning of what is formally called object (people) relationships.

The third psychic organizer is *negativism*, expressed by the toddler in the second and third year of life as "no." Spitz places great emphasis on the importance of locomotion as a stimulus to psychological development. Once the toddler begins to walk, at approximately one year of age, the basic nature of his or her relationship with the world changes. During infancy the interaction between mother and child was organized by tactile and visual contact, particularly in the context of feeding. In the second year of life their relationship is increasingly shaped by the toddler's ability to create a physical distance between them. As he or she begins to venture away, verbal communication becomes a necessary part of their relationship.

This newfound ability of the toddler to walk, climb and explore forces mother and father to repeatedly curb the child's initiative out of concern for his or her safety. Increasingly they must say "no," shaking their heads from side to side. These prohibitions cause frustration which the healthy toddler doesn't readily tolerate. He or she responds to these limitations by developing the defense mechanism of identification with the aggressor and turning the "no" against the restrictors. Once the mechanism is established the stubbornness of the second year begins in earnest.

Margaret Mahler: Separation-Individuation Theory

For a more extensive exposition of Mahler's theory please refer to *The Psychological Birth of the Human Infant* (Mahler, Pine and Bergman, 1975). Mahler described the first three months of life as the *pseudo-autistic stage*. The term addressed the relatively undeveloped state of mental functions at that time. The relationship between the infant and mother is the key to normal developmental progression because the infant is dependent upon the mother not only for survival, but also for physical and emotional stimulation and relief from states of intolerable instinctual or environmental stimulation.

When mother engages the infant physically and emotionally the infant progresses to the *second subphase* of the separation-individuation process, called the normal symbotic phase and gradually becomes aware of a "need-satisfying object" who responds to his or her smiles and cries and relieves hunger and other instinctual and environmental pressures. Both Spitz and Mahler are describing the infant's gradually developing awareness of someone outside of the self and of the nature of their relationship, but self and other are not yet distinct and separate.

Mahler's *third subphase*, confusingly called the separation-individuation subphase, covers the period from twelve to thirty-six months. Like Spitz, Mahler and her colleagues view locomotion as a great catalyzing influence on the development of the ego. As walking exposes the infant and toddler to deliberate bodily separation from mother, psychological separation and individuation inevitably follows. Only a fair degree of emotional acceptance and "communicative matching" on mother's part is necessary for this to occur. When parental acceptance is present the toddler is at the "peak of elation" and is free to explore the world while still sharing in mother's magical powers. Mahler considers the toddler's negativism as a healthy expression of the drive toward autonomy.

When the separation-individuation process progresses normally the result, at approximately age three, is the critical achievement of *object constancy*. This is the capacity that is at the core of all human interactions for the rest of life. The term may be defined as the capacity to maintain mental representation of mother and other important persons for extended periods of time in their absence. So equipped, the young child is capable of providing himself or herself with emotional sustenance and relatedness. In the preschool years object constancy is jeopardized by prolonged absences from the primary caretakers. *Self constancy* is the complement to object constancy. By the middle of the second year, toddlers begin to think of themselves as separate beings. As the capacity for mental representation increases and the separation-individuation process proceeds, the sense of self grows until a stable core of identity is firmly established.

Many other developmental tasks of the first five years of life, such as feeding and weaning, toilet training and cognitive development, will not be addressed here because they are not central to an understanding of childhood sexual abuse; but should abuse occur during these early years of life newly acquired capabilities, such as bowel and bladder control, which are not yet firmly established, may be lost.

SEXUAL DEVELOPMENT DURING CHILDHOOD

Sexual awareness in the first year of life is not very evident to the observer, yet the infant is developing what Robert Stoller (1968) called *core gender identity*—the basic sense of oneself as male or female, which is the basis on which later sexual attitudes and understanding are built. This complex phenomenon results from a confluence of biological, environmental and psychological factors and attitudes. The process begins in utero, stimulated by the admixture of male and female hormones which influence the development of the body and brain and determine the appearance of the external genitalia. When the external genitalia are clearly of one sex or the other the child is declared to be a boy or girl, and powerful conscious and unconscious forces are set in motion in the primary caretakers which cause them to determine the environmental assignment of gender. Stoller reached his conclusions, which are widely accepted, by studying infants born with indiscriminate genitalia. Infants could be successfully assigned to one gender or the other when surgery was performed by eighteen months of age. After that time the core gender identity could not be changed.

During the second and third years of life a new element is added to the undefined sense of gender identity, namely the *awareness of the existence of two different types of genitals*. In the process of this discovery the boy and the girl further define their own gender identity by developing a more complex understanding of the appearance and workings of their sexual equipment. This discovery by toddlers does not appear to be an isolated event. In their observations of children during the second year of life, Galenson and Roiphe (1976) were struck by the determination of toddlers to observe their parents' genitalia and elimination processes, as well as those of peers and their own.

Infantile Sexuality

Freud's notion of the child's focus during the oedipal years builds on core gender identity and the awareness of genital difference. It refers to the nature of sexual thought and action as experienced and understood by the child of approximately ages three to six. Some adults, unfamiliar with the development of cognitive and emotional processes in early childhood, assume, incorrectly, that the child has the same physical and emotional sexual experiences as they do. Preschool children are intensely curious about the nature of the genitals—theirs, their parents', other children's and adults' and animals'. Based on the pleasure that they experience from stimulation of their genitals by themselves, and inadvertently by adults in the process of diaper changes and baths, three-year-old children are acutely aware that there is something very special about this area of their bodies. The essence of infantile sexuality is both physical and psychological. Children in this age group actively masturbate, producing powerful, pleasurable sensations; and because of the achievement of object constancy they have the ability to relate these pleasurable genital sensations to the stable images and memories of their parents and other significant people that are available to them intra-psychically. Themes of envy, competition and concerns about retaliation from the much bigger and more powerful parents for the child's competitive wishes and fantasies dominate the intrapsychic world.

The oedipal-aged child has acquired the same two components of sexuality that all older children and adults have: sexual sensation in the genitals that is related to thoughts and feelings about others, in both the child's fantasies and in real relationships. The difference is that the young child experiences these sensations in an immature body and mind. When development proceeds normally, and the child is not introduced to sexual involvement with mature bodies and adult control, infantile sexuality adds a new dimension to the developmental line of sexuality and prepares the child for further elaboration of sexual identity in the latency years (ages six to eleven).

The Elaboration of Sexual Development in Latency

During latency masculinity and femininity are considered within the environment outside of the home, adding a subjective cultural dimension. Because of the need to maintain the repression and avoidance of infantile sexual preoccupations which dominated the oedipal phase, the latency focus is on same-sex activities and active avoidance of the opposite sex. Boys play with boys and hate girls and vice versa. In the rush to be more masculine or feminine, nearly every activity is assigned to one sex or the other. This subjective determination is influenced primarily by family values and peers. Children identify strongly with the parent of the same sex, internalizing what it means to be masculine or feminine in that family. This arbitrary division is also very strong in the peer group where there is constant vigilance against the demonstration of interest in the opposite sex and the desire to participate in coed activities and games. Broader culture attitudes are added through interest in and identification with figures from sports, literature, and the popular media. This normal, phase-limited need to exaggerate the difference between the sexes begins to disappear during preadolescence and is gone forever during adolescence, replaced by the biologically driven need for heterosexual interaction.

Sexual abuse during latency destroys the muting of sexual interests and excitement which are characteristic of this phase and disrupts the establishment of same-sex identifications which provide the basis for readiness to engage the tumultuous sexual upheaval that is at the center of adolescent development.

Other Major Developmental Tasks of Latency

Like all other developmental phases, latency is characterized by the presence of several issues, unique to these years, that must be engaged and mastered if normal developmental progression is to occur. Although they will not be discussed in detail, an awareness of them is important because like all other aspects of this and every phase, they are compromised by sexual abuse.

Freud (1923) described *conscience formation,* or the internalization of the superego, as an outcome of the resolution of the oedipal complex. Once internalized the superego becomes a positive stimulant to further development by freeing the child of oedipal preoccupations and becoming the vehicle for the internalization of moral values. In addition, the superego becomes a major source of self-esteem as the child thinks and acts in ways that meet the expectations of parents, peer group and the broader culture.

Friendships, Peer Relationships

Rangell (1963) suggested that friendly feelings have their roots in the gratifying relationship between infant and mother. As the toddler and pre-schooler gain experience outside of the nuclear family, relationships with others become increasingly important. This movement outside the home becomes a significant part of the child's experience when formal learning begins. For the first time, the child forms relationships which are not dictated by or controlled by the parents. Progression along the developmental lines of conscious formation, separation-individuation, sexual identification and physical and cognitive maturation are required if one is to be accepted by the same-sex peer group. The latency-aged peer group acts as a rough diagnostic instrument, ostracizing and attacking those who have not taken the necessary developmental steps needed to fit in. Acceptance by the peer group is an important indicator that development is progressing smoothly.

Adjustment to School and Formal Learning

Just as acceptance by the peer group is a good indicator of normal developmental progression, so is successful adjustment to elementary school. The school acts as an assessor of early developmental progress because it is the first social agency outside of the nuclear family which intensively and realistically evaluates the child. The transition from home to school may seem simple since most children accomplish it without great difficulty, but successful adjustment indicates that development is progressing normally along multiple developmental lines. The child who adjusts to kindergarten or first grade must be able to control bowel and bladder and sit still; demonstrate the cognitive maturity for reading readiness activities, the forerunners of reading and writing; separate from parents and be able to relate to strange adults, sharing their interest and affection with others; relate to peers and accept the rough-and-tumble interactions within the peer group; and accomplish all this with a considerable degree of impulse control and a minimum degree of regression.

Latency falls within Piaget's (1969) stage of concrete operations. In essence, the latency-aged child is capable of formal learning because he or she can think rather than act, consider variables, similar and dissonant, and begin to understand time. Erikson (1963) focused his consideration of latency on the child's ability to acquire useful skills. The desire to acquire knowledge of the tools of his or her culture and how to use them is called industry. Not learning how to feel productive results in feelings of inferiority.

Sexual abuse during this phase disrupts the adjustment to school and the learning process. A sudden drop in the child's grades or significant change in behavior in the school setting should cause parents, teachers and others to consider the possibility, along with many others, that the child is being sexually abused.

Late latency, ages eight to ten or eleven, is often referred to as *the golden age of childhood*. This term refers to the equilibrium that exists between the slowly growing body and the developing psyche's ability to comfortably manage biological impulses and drives. The result in healthy children in this age group is a state of emotional calm, a cooperative attitude toward parents and other adults, and the ability to comfortably focus on formal learning and peer relationships. This was in evidence in Tara, the nine-year-old girl whose case study is the second one in this chapter, until she was sexually assaulted. Even after the assault the ability to maintain some ego functions was evident. The inexperienced clinician might come to the erroneous conclusion that the sexual assault was less damaging than it actually was. In a case like this, psychological testing can be particularly useful in uncovering the full extent of the psychological trauma.

Preparing for Adolescence

During latency children separate from parents, enter the community, internalize the conscience, develop peer relationships and acquire formal learning and hobbies. All of these positive developmental steps are not only important in their own right, they are also essential in creating a solid foundation, a reservoir of strength to help weather the psychological upheaval of adolescence which lies just ahead.

CASE STUDY: LENA

Lena was five years old when she came to my office, accompanied by her mother and grandparents, for a child psychiatric evaluation in connection with her civil lawsuit. The information which follows was obtained from mother, grandfather and Lena herself.

It is customary for a child psychiatrist, particularly with a very young child such as Lena, to obtain historical information from the significant adults in the child's life as well as from the child. Records were obtained from the therapist who had treated Lena for several months and from the hospital that performed a sexual abuse evaluation after the assault, which occurred when Lena was three years old. The therapist and examining physician believed that Lena was repeatedly sexually abused. The perpetrator was discovered, tried and convicted and was in jail at the time of my evaluation.

Mother and grandmother were invited to sit in on the two diagnostic sessions with Lena. In order to give the child time to be comfortable with me the first session focused on general subjects and interests. Lena and I sat on the floor as we talked and played with various toys and puppets. During the diagnostic interview with mother a developmental history was taken and Lena's response to the sexual abuse was described. Then Lena was seen for a second time without family members being present. Finally Lena's grandfather asked to give his observations of his granddaughter.

First Diagnostic Interview with Lena

Lena presented as a bright, talkative five-year-old. She was dressed casually and immediately engaged me. Lena chose blocks in the forms of numbers and letters and spelled out her name. Then she took the blocks and built a big house and a tower. Lena brought a doll to the interview. When asked, Lena volunteered her birth date and that she was in kindergarten. She knew her teacher's name and described a number of friends. As she built towers it was clear that Lena had excellent fine motor coordination.

When asked about her favorite TV show, Lena mentioned cartoons. She enjoyed knocking down the towers after building them. I asked who lives in her house. Lena mentioned her mother and father. Her grandparents lived nearby and she sees them almost every day. Of course, she added, she also lived with a cat and a dog. When I asked about dreams Lena said that she had scary ones about ghosts and animals. She was not interested in revealing further details. Toward the end of the interview we talked about her dolls. Lena volunteered that she had a baby sister. Sometime she played with her sister pretending that she was a doll. When asked for three wishes Lena listed a baby sister, a baby brother and another dog.

Diagnostic Interview with Mother

Mother was in her late twenties. She had full-time employment and was thankful that her parents were available to watch Lena and her sibling while mother worked. Mother noted that the sexual abuse "had changed all of our lives. We worry constantly about the possibility of another attack and whether Lena will be normal again."

Father was also in his late twenties. Gainfully employed, he felt very guilty because he had not been able to protect his daughter. Father became enraged at the perpetrator when he appeared in court at the criminal trial and had to be restrained from attacking the man. Grandfather and grandmother were healthy and vigorous. They had been actively involved in Lena's life from birth to the present.

Mother heard about the abuse when her parents called. Lena had just had her third birthday. She said that a "big boy" at school had touched her "couci" (vagina) and her "butt." When asked, Lena told her mother the same story. Mother immediately took Lena to a hospital where an examination was performed. Redness was observed around the vagina but not around the anus. Mother took Lena out of school and informed the police. The investigation centered on a male employee of the school. He had been in Lena's classroom for approximately three months before the abuse was discovered.

When mother asked Lena how often the man had touched her she replied every day at naptime. She said that he pulled down her panties while she was napping, touched her and asked her to touch his "boy part." Mother doesn't know if Lena did as requested.

Lena has been in therapy for several months. The therapist, who attempts to approach the subject of the molestation on every visit, is teaching her where one can be touched and where one should not be touched. Lena tells mother she only wants to talk about the molestation to mother and grandmother. Mother feels the therapy is helping because Lena is more open about her thoughts and feelings. Mother had difficulty finding a therapist for Lena. Several individuals refused to treat her because they didn't want to become involved in a lawsuit.

Symptoms

The following symptoms occurred after the sexual abuse began. None were present before that time. At the time of the sexual abuse Lena had dreams approximately four to five times per week. At the time of the evaluation, nearly two years after the sexual abuse ended, dreams about the abuse disturbed sleep approximately one to two times per week. Lena reported that the "big boy" is chasing her or trying to wake her up and grab her panties. Nightmares were not present prior to the sexual abuse.

Lena was fully toilet trained by thirteen to fifteen months of age. She began to wet nightly at three years and one month of age. This was approximately one month after the perpetrator began to work at the preschool and before the sexual abuse was discovered. The enuresis was still occurring at the time of the evaluation, approximately two to three times per week.

Lena becomes frightened when she sees a strange man, particularly men who are about the same size and race as the perpetrator. She also does not want anyone to see her nude. Mother has tried to help her understand that it is okay to be nude when dressing or bathing. Lena becomes very clingy when confronting a new situation or person. This was particularly true when she went to a new school after the sexual abuse occurred. She asked if the big boy was going to be there. When in a public place such as a mall or a restaurant Lena is glued to her parents' or grandparents' side.

Lena refuses to sleep alone. If forced to be in bed by herself she will scream for hours. Sooner or later Lena ends up in her parents' bed. Naptime is a major problem at home and school. Lena doesn't want to sleep. Mother feels that naptime is particularly distressing because that's when the sexual abuse took place. Lena is also afraid of the dark. The perpetrator turned off the lights at the school during naptime. Grandfather observed this on several occasions when he went to the school to pick up Lena.

Developmental History

Mother's pregnancy with Lena was full term. She was healthy through-out. The delivery was vaginal and there were no complications. Lena was a healthy and vigorous infant. Lena was breast fed for approximately six months. Mother was home full-time during this interval. Then she returned to work and parents and grandparents shared the childcare. Developmental milestones occurred within a normal time frame or were early. There have not been any lengthy separations from parents or grandparents. Lena has not had any operations or serious illnesses.

Second Diagnostic Interview with Lena

After playing for a while I asked Lena if she had any worries. First she said no but after a few moments changed her answer to yes. She has "imagination problems." Her grandparents are afraid of the dark. Sometimes she is too. She doesn't like spiders.

I asked her to tell me about her old school. She was hesitant and anxious but began to talk about the "big boy" who touched her "couci" at naptime. This happened every day when it was dark. He also touched other children. He would pull down their pants. Lena would be asleep and he would say something and she wouldn't answer. "I don't like him. He did that bad thing to me."

When asked why she sleeps with her mother and father Lena said that she cries every night if she has to sleep alone. She is afraid of the dark. Lena does have dreams about the big boy. Sometimes he is disguised as a monster. He does things like he did at school. Lena doesn't like to take naps by herself. She doesn't like the dark because she might see the big boy. He might come back. Lena volunteered that he should be in jail.

Discussion with Grandfather

Grandfather asked to speak with me. He felt that Lena's repeated attempts to put her tongue in his mouth and unbutton his shirt to lick his chest must be connected with the sexual molestation. She had never done anything like that before. He set limits on the behavior and it stopped. Because of his experience in a mental health setting he understood this behavior to be a sign of sexual abuse. Grandfather also noted that Lena became cruel to a small family dog at about the time that the molestation was discovered. This was very uncharacteristic of her because she had always loved animals.

He went on to describe his observation of a man acting suspiciously in regard to his granddaughter when he came to pick up Lena at school shortly before the sexual abuse was discovered. Lena described the man as a teacher and later told her grandfather that a boy at school was pulling down her underwear and touching her.

Diagnosis

The *Diagnostic and Statistical Manual of the American Psychiatric Association* is the only widely recognized diagnostic nomenclature in the field. I am using it as a basis for formulating diagnoses throughout this book. When using it the diagnostician is asked to divide his or her diagnostic impressions into five subdivisions, called Axes. Using this nomenclature I made the following diagnosis in regard to Lena:

Axis I: Major diagnoses are to be listed here. Sexual Abuse of Child V61.21, Focus on the Victim 995.54.

Axis II: Character disorders, long-standing patterns of maladaptive behavior are to be listed here. None were present.

Axis III: Any medical conditions that directly relate to the diagnosis on Axis I are listed here. Physical examination revealed redness in the vaginal area.

Axis IV: Psychosocial and Environmental Problems: From a list in the manual the diagnostician is asked to list any factors that amplify an understanding of the diagnosis on Axis I. Problems related to interaction with the legal system/crime: victim of crime and litigation are specifically listed as stressors.

Axis V: Global Assessment of Functioning Scale: On a scale from 1, profound, to 100, absent; the diagnostician is asked to describe the severity of the patient's symptoms.

I rated Lena's symptoms in the 41–50, serious range.

The five axes will not be described in the diagnostic discussions to follow throughout the remainder of the book.

Treatment

The treatment Lena was receiving was helpful. However, it is being provided by a student rather than a highly experienced child psychiatrist or child psychologist. Treatment of childhood sexual abuse is best attempted by an experienced clinician who has a thorough understanding of the nature of such abuse and a mature understanding of his or her own sexuality. With this reservation in mind I recommend that Lena participate in individual psychotherapy twice per week, for a period of at least one year. During adolescence a course of individual psychotherapy, once per week for one year, is indicated to help Lena deal with physical/sexual maturity and dating. Although, as stated in the preface, therapy recommendations in the distant future would need to be determined by a clinician at that time, it is likely that a third course of individual psychotherapy will be indicated when marriage and children are being contemplated.

These treatment recommendations are based on the premise that sexual abuse, even in a child as young as Lena, who clearly has knowledge and memory of what happened to her and continues to have symptoms two years after the sexual abuse ended, will have pervasive pathological effects well into the future. By helping Lena deal with current symptoms and in the future with the developmental tasks of integrating physical and sexual maturity, dating, and eventually marriage and parenthood, the harmful effects of the sexual abuse will be muted, and healthy, normal development promoted.

Prognosis

The prognosis for diminishing—but not eliminating—the effect of the sexual abuse on Lena's future development, if the program of treatment outlined above is followed, is good. Lena is bright, verbal and able to relate to a therapist. Further, she has a strong support system in the form of knowledgeable parents and grandparents who are able to understand the emotional and developmental consequences of the sexual abuse and willing to support efforts at therapeutic intervention. As will become clear in many of the case examples to follow, treatment is often strongly resisted by both the abused individuals and their families.

CASE STUDY: NINE-YEAR-OLD TARA

This case study is somewhat different from others in the book because there was only a single instance of abuse, which was accompanied by violence. It is meant to demonstrate that attempted abuse in a threatening setting can have serious psychological consequences. The evaluation consisted of a diagnostic interview with Tara's parents, two with her, psychological testing and a review of records. Tara grew up in an intact family. She lived with her parents and younger brother. Almost ten at the time, she was at home with her mother when the assault occurred.

Parental Interview

The family lived in an upscale apartment complex. Tara was playing with a friend on the lawn several doors down from her home when a strange man approached, picked Tara up and began to touch her as he carried her toward the family's apartment, which he had apparently been observing. Mother was in the kitchen when she heard Tara scream. As mother ran into the front room the perpetrator fled. Tara told her mother that the man had touched her privates and digitally penetrated her vagina. The perpetrator was caught several hours later and admitted the abuse. Tara was taken for a sexual abuse examination.

Informed of the abuse, father rushed home and found Tara screaming. She repeated that the man had touched her private parts and her breasts. When she took a bath after the assault the water was pink with blood. The perpetrator was tried, pleaded guilty and was sentenced to prison. Tara was taken to a therapist a few months after the assault. At the time of my evaluation she had been seen approximately twenty times. The parents were told that the diagnosis was Posttraumatic Stress Disorder.

According to her parents, after the assault Tara began to have nightmares, intrusive images, fear and distrust of men and a refusal to be alone. The preoccupation with the assault and the resulting symptoms were most severe during the first six months afterward. At the time of my evaluation, which was conducted eighteen months after the assault, Tara continued to be clingy, fearful and moody.

Developmental History

Mother's pregnancy and delivery with Tara occurred without difficulty. Mother was the primary caretaker and breast-fed Tara during the first year of life. Father worked a nine-to-five job and was a constant presence in Tara's life from birth onward. Toilet training was achieved without difficulty and Tara enjoyed preschool. She had not had any serious illnesses, operations or emotional difficulties prior to the assault.

Tara is a fine student. Well behaved, she has lots of friends. Her grades suffered for the first six to nine months after the assault and then returned to As and Bs. Tara enjoys sports, reading and piano.

Diagnostic Interview with Tara

I asked mother to accompany Tara into my office and stay for a while because of the child's fear of men. She looked uneasy when mother left but was reassured by mother's explanation of why she and I were meeting. As the interview progressed it became clear that this attractive, latency-aged girl was intelligent and had a fine vocabulary. Her speech was fluent and understandable but very muted and difficult to hear when she talked about the assault later in the interview and was able to describe her detailed memories of the assault.

Because she was apprehensive at first, I asked Tara to tell me what she did for fun. She liked to play with her friends, go on vacations and visit her family. Tara volunteered that next year she would be in her last year of elementary school. She was looking forward to being a "senior."

Tara loved to do gymnastics. She was particularly good at tumbling and had been practicing since she was six. Tara enjoyed her family except for her brother who was a "pain." Father took her to the movies and mother sometimes let her stay up late. When I asked her to tell me three wishes, a common practice in diagnostic evaluations of children, Tara volunteered that she wished the sexual assault hadn't happened. In addition she wanted to make the Olympics and wished that all the good stuff weren't fattening. Her knowledge of gymnastics was impressive. She knew the names of all the teenage girls who were on the last Olympics team.

After some time I asked her to tell me about the man who had hurt her. With some anxiety and embarrassment Tara told me that the man forced her into the house. Their apartment was on the ground floor. "He pushed me on to the couch. I screamed. I tried to bite him but he put his hand over my mouth. His other hand went under my shirt and down my pants." After a long pause and a deep sigh she continued, "His finger went inside me. He told me I was beautiful. He said he would hurt me if I didn't shut up. That's when my Mom came and he ran away. I thought I was going to die. I was afraid he would take me away. After he left I never wanted to go outside again." Tara worried that the man would come back so she stayed in her room after school.

I asked Tara how she had changed since the attack. She noted that she didn't want to go outside for the first few months and was afraid of men. For a while it hurt when she peed. Later Tara told of not being able to sleep for several months because she was scared and had nightmares, maybe fifteen of them. With a sign of relief she mentioned that the nightmares had stopped. Intrusive thoughts about the assault occurred every day for at least six months. Tara still thinks about the man almost every day. "I don't want to be alone with anyone other than my parents."

Psychological Testing

"This youngster still shows many troubling signs of the traumatic impact of her sexual molestation. My impression is that she is suffering from PTSD, with prominent symptoms of anxiety. She also is burdened by feelings of irritability, shame and she struggles with depression."

Tara tended to underreport and tried to deny or to minimize her worries. "In spite of her defensive efforts, her scores on the scales (of the Trauma symptom Checklist for Children) of sexual concerns were grossly elevated to a point not previously seen by this examiner. . . . Her scores indicate that she is struggling with abnormally high levels of sexual anxieties, thoughts, feelings and inner emotional conflicts related to sex." Tara's IQ was in the superior range. "Her adaptive ability suffers significantly when the task at hand is not a clearly structured objective problem."

Evidence from the Rorschach pointed to "the fragility of her coping mechanisms. In significant ways, her efforts to calm her distress are actually interfering with her emotional development, because they rest so heavily upon denial, avoidance and isolation as key mechanisms to 'blind' her to her inner confusion, very limited affect tolerance and projected worries. . . . Her fears of being attacked and her inner struggles with angry feelings make her very anxious and as she becomes anxious she comes to feel extremely vulnerable and sometimes confused."

A prominent feature of Tara's stories on the Thematic Apperception Test was "her on-going struggle to overcome feelings of depression. . . . Close to consciousness are feelings of shame and guilt associated with the worry that she has done something wrong and that she is now being or will later be punished for it."

"Conclusion: It is clear that in spite of Tara's earlier treatment and the passage of time, she still suffers significantly from the psychological impact of her molestation. She is in need of the kind of psychological treatment that is most likely to provide her with the self-understanding and with the emotional tools that are necessary for her to resolve her symptoms and resume the course of normal development."

Therapist's Final Report

Tara was seen approximately thirty times in individual psychotherapy which ended about a year after the abuse. The therapist concluded that the goals of treatment had been met by using cognitive behavioral techniques, psycho-education, safety skills training and supportive techniques. Posttraumatic Stress Disorder was ruled out and a diagnosis of Adjustment Disorder with Mixed Anxiety and Depressed Mood was made.

Diagnosis

Using DSM-IV I made diagnoses of Sexual Abuse of a Child V611.21; Clinical Focus on the Victim 995.53 and Posttraumatic Stress Disorder, Chronic 309.81. At the time of the evaluation I rated Tara's symptoms in the 51–60, moderate range. Obviously, I feel that Tara's therapist did not understand the severity of the trauma or its consequences. The therapist's opinions on both diagnosis and treatment might have been different if psychological testing had been obtained.

Treatment

Tara's therapist's final report indicating that therapy was successful, concluded after a year of once-per-week individual psychotherapy, illustrates one of the major themes of this book. The effects of chronic sexual abuse, or in this instance a single violent episode, extend far beyond the months, or even years, following the attack. Therapy needs to be thought of with the extended life cycle in mind. The case studies toward the end of the book of those individuals who were abused fifty years ago and are still dealing with the effects in the present clearly illustrate this point. The consequences of child sexual abuse are lifelong and the approach to treatment needs to be also.

In regard to Tara, I would recommend an immediate course of individual psychotherapy, two times per week for twelve to eighteen months, with a clinician with extensive experience with victims of child sexual abuse. After the completion of the first course of therapy Tara should be followed periodically during adolescence. A second course of therapy will likely be needed in mid- to late adolescence. Evaluation in young adulthood will determine what therapeutic interventions will be needed at that time.

DISCUSSION OF THE SEXUAL ABUSE OF LENA AND TARA

There is little doubt that Lena was sexually abused. All of her symptoms and the story she tells are typical and similar to those presented by other abused children. Further, it is likely that the abuse occurred one or more times per week for at least two, and possibly three, months. The information provided by the grandfather, particularly Lena's attempt to put her tongue in his mouth and lick his chest, indicates that the abuse may have included involvement of the perpetrator's body and sexual acts that Lena did not or could not describe.

The sexual abuse occurred when Lena was three years old. Having been raised in a loving manner during the first three years of her life she had established a firm sense of self (separation-individuation processes) and was beginning to develop the capacity to be comfortable outside of the home in a preschool setting cared for by non-familial adults. This critical developmental process, necessary for emotional and academic success in elementary school, was, and still is, arrested. Lena is unable to feel safe and secure outside of her parents' presence, let alone outside of her home. The fear of being attacked again has also produced a significant regression in the ability to sleep alone, another important indicator of the ability to move beyond the comforting infantile closeness with mother toward self-comforting and self-generated emotional security.

Lena had clearly established a core gender identity—the internal perception that she was female. She had just entered the phase of development when children begin to observe the relationship between the sexes (primarily through observing their parents) and begin to contemplate their role in such a relationship. The conceptualizations that three-year-olds construct are, under normal circumstances, based on their fantasies, which are devoid of knowledge of adult sexuality or sexual interaction with adults. Lena was exposed to adult male genitalia, very likely in a state of erection; and was sexually (and painfully) stimulated in ways that the three-year-old body and mind are unable to integrate or understand.

The consequence of the traumatic stimulation is evident in her sexually explicit, adult-like behavior with her grandfather. One of the clearest indications that a child has been sexually abused is the presence of adult-like sexual behavior which is totally foreign to the child's physical and intellectual level of development, for example, attempts at French kissing or descriptions of semen following some form of contact with an adult male penis.

Further, Lena developed a basic mistrust of adult males. The foundation on which healthy sexual relationships are built during adolescence and adulthood is close, nonsexual interactions with men throughout early childhood. After this sense of basic trust in males is internalized during the first decade of life the adolescent girl integrates her burgeoning physical and sexual maturity with the earlier sense of trust and security with males and is ready to begin the dating process.

A basic premise of this book, even with children who are abused before age five as was the case with Lena, is that such children almost undoubtedly will have long-lasting effects developmentally, particularly in regard to sexual development in adolescence and during young adulthood when marriage and parenthood occur, hence the recommendations for a course of psychotherapy in each of those developmental phases. The fact that Lena has parents and grandparents who are sensitive and understanding of the effects of sexual abuse on young children will increase the chances that she will get the treatment she needs, during adolescence in particular, even though she may have repressed the sexual abuse and be resistant to therapy. As will be evident in all of the case histories in this book, childhood sexual abuse inevitably leads to compromised development and significant inhibition and suffering in adolescence and throughout adulthood.

Tara: There is no doubt that Tara was sexually assaulted. The assailant was tried and convicted and is in prison. Eighteen months after the assault Tara continued to have symptoms, which although diminished in intensity and frequency, are still prominent. The intensity of the traumatic effect on her latency-age development is most evident on psychological testing, which indicates that she continues to suffer significant anxiety and depression and a sense of guilt. That sense of guilt is particularly instructive because even though the sexual abuse resulted from an attack by a stranger Tara still feels that somehow she is responsible. I have never met a child who was sexually abused, once or hundreds of times, by a stranger or someone known, who did not feel responsible and guilty. Understanding this concept is key to working with abused children in therapy.

Based on both clinical presentation and psychological testing it is clear that Tara is still suffering from symptoms of posttraumatic stress disorder eighteen months after being attacked. Her internal mental state is frequently dominated by feelings of anxiety and depression.

Although Tara is relatively comfortable in regard to academic performance and peer relationships, the relative calm of late latency seen in most healthy children—and Tara's development was proceeding in a healthy direction in all areas before the assault—is soon to be disturbed by the biological and psychological upheaval of adolescence. The underlying trauma and conflicts, which were readily apparent on psychological testing, indicate that considerable emotional, intellectual and developmental regression will likely occur during the adolescent years. Dating and beginning sexual involvement will be particularly difficult. Despite her intactness prior to the assault and the diminished level of overt symptomatology, Tara's future development, particularly during adolescence, is at risk.

The developmental difference between ages five and nine in regard to intellectual functioning, cognitive understanding and the use of sophisticated
defense mechanisms is significant. In addition, the difference between the
repeated abuse in Lena's case and the single assault in Tara's case helps explain
why Lena's symptoms are more obvious and severe.

3

Adolescence:
Ages Twelve to Twenty

NORMAL DEVELOPMENT

THIS CHAPTER ON NORMAL ADOLESCENT DEVELOPMENT is presented here because although the sexual abuse in the next case study occurred during the latency phase of development the abuse was not discovered until late in adolescence. Hence, a knowledge of both phases of development is helpful in understanding the clinical material.

Adolescence begins with a well-defined, maturational event—puberty—and ends in a more nebulous manner. Chronologically adolescence ends at age twenty, but the mastery of the psychological tasks of adolescence continues well into young adulthood.

Puberty may be narrowly defined as the first ejaculation in the boy and the first menstrual period in the girl. These biological events are the beginning of a profound physical change which renders the latency-age mind inadequate to the task of managing the physically and sexually mature body. Adolescence could be defined as the years in which the mind develops the ability to integrate these changes in relationship to self and to others (Erikson, 1956). Much of the information in this chapter is extracted from the classical text *On Adolescence* by Peter Blos (1962). The reader is referred to this work as a starting point for obtaining a more detailed understanding of adolescence.

Adolescence requires a major reworking of all aspects of earlier development, in the process exposing and amplifying preexisting psychopathology. This is particularly true for children who were sexually abused before and during adolescence because the integration of physical and psychological sexuality is such an integral focus of the adolescence developmental process.

The Developmental Tasks of Adolescence

Accepting the Physically and Sexually Mature Body

The process of physical and sexual maturation occurs over a number of years. Because this process is uneven and uncontrollable, it is accompanied, even in the most attractive adolescent, by periodic losses in self-esteem and injured narcissism. Legs, arms, and noses are too long; pimples too gross and obvious; and in private thought or conversation with best friends, breasts and penises are too small or too big.

The slowly growing, comfortable body of the latency years is gone, replaced by one of great, and potentially disastrous, unpredictability. Boys experience spontaneous erections at the most embarrassing times. Girls worry that a period will begin in a public place and be noticed by others. Wet dreams occur with increasing regularity, announcing to mother that her son is, as one boy put it, "either masturbating or wetting the bed. I don't want her to know anything about me."

As these changes are accepted and integrated, the body may gradually become a source of pride and pleasure. Hours are spent examining body parts, primping in front of the mirror and choosing clothing which will display the body to others. Feelings of doubt and desires to exhibit are often in conflict with each other but there is nothing quite so grand as the fifteen- or sixteen-year-old proudly displaying his or her body for all to admire.

Establishing an Active Sexual Life

The course along this developmental line should be gradual. In pre and early adolescence the task is to accept the sexually mature body, particularly the growth of underarm and pubic hair and the enlargement of the genitals and breasts. New sexual abilities, such as increased vaginal lubrication and ejaculation, are explored through masturbation. The middle adolescent makes tentative steps toward involvement with a sexual partner but handles most sexual feelings through fantasy and masturbation. By late adolescence most individuals are psychologically prepared for an active sexual life which includes intercourse.

The absence of progression along this developmental line often indicates the presence of significant psychopathology. So does too-early involvement. Evidence for these conclusions is found in every case study in this book. Nothing interferes more with adolescent sexual development than sexual abuse prior to or during adolescence. The range of psychopathology following childhood sexual abuse ranges from inhibition and disgust to hyper-sexuality and promiscuity.

Separating Physically and Psychologically from Parents

Referring to Margaret Mahler's separation-individuation theory, which describes developmental processes in the first three years of life, Peter Blos (1967) described adolescence as the "second individuation." Just as the infant must separate and individuate from mother, so must the adolescent physically and psychologically separate from parents and home in order to become an autonomous, independent young adult. The attainment of physical and cognitive maturity allows the adolescent to approach self-sufficiency. The onset of sexual maturity makes it imperative that he or she direct sexual feelings outside of the family. At the beginning of adolescence the child is dependent on his or her family of origin and is sexually immature; at the end of it, the late-adolescent/ young adult is relatively independent and sexually active, ready to eventually establish a family of procreation and take a place in the adult world.

Preparing to Work

It is ironic that adolescents must make major decisions about work and career (by exclusion or choice) that affect the rest of their lives at a time when they are so preoccupied with dramatic and disconcerting physical, sexual and social changes. The ability to successfully manage this difficult developmental task during adolescence is dependent on various emerging mental functions such as the ability to delay gratification, channel impulses, sublimate, utilize intellect, visualize the future and begin to conceptualize oneself as an adult at work rather than a child at play.

The degree to which work during adolescence stimulates or impeded the expansion of developmental potential varies from individual to individual and culture to culture. For some, particularly those who are planning to enter a trade or non-college-related work, experience on the job during adolescence may be highly valuable and gratifying. For those who are college bound, studying may be the most beneficial form of work during these years. Others avoid dealing with the issue of work during the adolescent years entirely and engage this developmental task during young adulthood.

Peer Relationships and Friendships

From elementary school onward, throughout the rest of life, friendships play a central role in human experience because they are shaped by the need to engage and resolve phase-specific developmental tasks. In adolescence friendships facilitate the engagement and resolution of such critical developmental tasks as psychological separation from parents and the beginning integration of attitudes toward work, play and sexuality.

Girls begin their maturation spurt one to two years before boys and in early adolescence are often more developed and taller. These "young Amazons" often belittle their male peers and are attracted to older boys. Within the same-sex peer group they are often cruel to each other, shift loyalties on a day-to-day basis and openly attack competitors and enemies. Because early adolescent girls are physically developed and often present a pseudo-mature posture, they sometimes rush toward mid- and late-adolescent social and sexual behavior for which they are unprepared psychologically. This pseudo-maturity makes them highly vulnerable to premature involvement with older adolescent boys—and sexual predators. Parental understanding of these early adolescent developmental processes, the setting of appropriate limits, and an acute sensitivity to the inordinate interest of older males in their daughters are extremely important factors in preventing adolescent sexual abuse.

Pre- and early-adolescent boys are quite threatened by their more mature counterparts and cover their emerging sexual feelings and fears with bravado, boasting and even physical attacks. They continue to maintain, for the most part, the prevailing latency attitude of "hating" girls and are most comfortable in same-sex peer groups.

By mid-adolescence both sexes are more comfortable with the sexually mature body and boys catch up to girls physically, usually surpassing them in height and weight. Friends remain a major source of support as both sexes begin dating and sexual activity. They are available to compare experiences, answer questions and provide comfort and support when relationships end.

Through involvement in sports and extracurricular activities peers share in the acquisition of skills and also provide boosts to self-esteem. Most importantly, peers, and sometimes their families as well, provide loving relationships that help cushion the emotional and physical withdrawal from parents, a subject we will now consider.

Relationships with Parents

Early adolescence brings with it an uncomfortable change in the relationship between parent and child. Gone is the easy openness and mutual admiration of late latency, replaced by avoidance, secretiveness and public embarrassment ("Mom, will you please drop me off here. I don't want my friends to see you!") on the part of the adolescent; and bewilderment, sadness and anger on the part of the parent. Often these attitudes alternate with the long-established closeness and mutuality that formed the basis of the normal latency-phase relationship between parent and child.

The emerging powerful, hormonally driven sexuality affects all relationships, including those with parents. What was a comfortable, easily managed emotional interaction just a few months ago is suddenly complicated by an unwelcome sexual component. Hugs and kisses, indeed any form of physical contact, may produce feelings of discomfort and stimulate conscious or unconscious sexual feelings and fantasies. The body can no longer be counted on to respond to closeness in predictable ways since a fleeting touch or extended hug may produce an erect penis or nipples. Bedroom and bathroom doors are suddenly locked tight to keep parents away from the pubescent body.

Aspects of this conflict are often observed in relationship to the adolescent's bedroom. Signs on the door that say "Parents—Keep Out!" although unnerving, underline the need to separate and individuate. Insistence on wild décor, suggestive posters, and the absence of neatness and cleanliness are all indicators of the intense need to create a semblance of independence from parental space and values, while remaining in their secure, protective midst. When confined to the home, such behavior, although not conducive to parental peace and equanimity, facilitates the developmental process and is self-limiting.

One father, objecting to the presence of "pictures of Bruce Springsteen's crotch all over my daughter's bedroom walls," was mildly placated by the comment that they were, after all, only pictures. His daughter was practicing a form of safe adolescent sex—fantasy! He was also reassured by the recognition that his daughter's behavior and surly attitude were reserved for him and his wife. Neighbors, friends and teachers spoke of her in glowing terms, indicating the presence of judgment and responsible behavior in the midst of developmental regression and turmoil.

The Adolescent Crush

During middle adolescence, following the acceptance of the physically and sexually mature body, there is a gradual turn toward a real, sexually driven relationship. These early efforts to engage the opposite sex are both thrilling and frightening. When one's affections are returned, the result, immortalized in song and verse, is the experience of falling in love, more properly called adolescent infatuation. A necessary prerequisite of, but quite different from, mature adult love, infatuation furthers developmental progression by loosening the emotional ties to the parents. But in a sense, the adolescent falls in love with the idealized parent of childhood, characteristics of whom are projected onto the boyfriend or girlfriend. This necessary developmental step in the process of emotional separation of sexuality from the parents makes it difficult to see the new loved one in a realistic light. This explains why the sense of disillusionment in the boyfriend or girlfriend is so strong when the projected idealization is withdrawn.

Because of the tenuous nature of these relationships, there is a great fear of rejection, often actualized, and the inevitable experience of narcissistic injury. The ability to engage in a number of infatuations is a sign of strength and resilience, since despite the pain involved when they end, each relationship leads to greater separation and individuation. Healthy adolescents have many sources of narcissistic gratification and supply to cushion the pain of loneliness and rejection and fill the time between infatuations. Elaboration of latency-aged interests, a focus on school work and athletics and the pursuit of hobbies provide non-sexualized pleasure and facilitate sublimation and the acquisition of valuable skills and abilities that will serve the adolescent well into adulthood.

As will become readily apparent in the cases to follow on sexual abuse during adolescence, *the adolescent who is developmentally ready for adolescent infatuation is extremely vulnerable to sexual predators.* Adults, especially those in positions of power who have frequent contact with the adolescent, such as coaches and teachers, are very often the subject of adolescent crushes. Vivid examples of the manipulation of adolescent infatuation in order to sexually abuse vulnerable adolescent girls by teachers and a coach will be presented in chapters 4 and 5. Mature adults understand the developmental process involved and protect the adolescent against themselves. Perpetrators use the development process to ensnare and abuse the vulnerable teen.

By late adolescence, most individuals have accepted the body as a sexual instrument, partially replaced the parents as primary love objects, and begun an active sexual life. For others, these themes continue to evolve well into young adulthood where they fuse with the developmental demands of young adulthood. Many of the older individuals whose case studies appear later in the book never achieved a healthy sexual life at any point in their adult lives as a result of the childhood sexual abuse.

The following case studies illustrate pre- and elementary school sexual abuse manifestations in adolescence. Three boys were abused by a church official, with the awareness of his wife, at a religiously oriented pre- and elementary school. The boys varied in age from four to nine at the time that the abuse began. The religious organization denied that the abuse had occurred until similar allegations against the same missionary were made public years later. I evaluated the boys when they were ages twelve, fifteen and nineteen.

CASE STUDY: GEORGE

George was evaluated when he was twelve years old. At the time of the evaluation he had just completed elementary school and was living with his parents. George presented as a very quiet, pre-pubertal youngster who sat quietly throughout our two interviews and avoided looking at me. Despite his discomfort he was able to tell me his story, commenting that he was "tired" as he related the details of the abuse. Affect was depressed and there was no evidence of a thinking disorder.

First Diagnostic Interview with George

I asked general questions about his life as he focused his attention on the games and cards that I provided. George became a bit more animated as he talked about his interest in sports. He liked all sports and was on a baseball team at school. He played second base. The team had a four-and-four record and George was batting .300. Before making the school team he had played Little League baseball since he was a little boy. His favorite teams were the Cubs and the Red Sox.

I asked about school. "It's cool." George was an "average student." He liked math the best and didn't have problems with his teacher. George had friends, including a best friend, William. They played board games and had sleepovers. When I asked about what his family did together George volunteered that they went on hikes and out to eat. He liked watching TV with his father.

Eventually I asked George to tell me about his experience with the perpetrator whom we shall call Mr. S. George remembered playing baseball on the playground at school. He thinks he was about three years old when he first went there. Mr. S drove the children on field trips, took them to the pool and supervised the playground. When asked what Mr. S did, George answered, "He would have me sit on his lap and stick something up my butt." George was unsure what Mr. S put in his butt. This occurred in the bathroom after swimming at a pool. Both George and Mr. S were naked. George wasn't sure how often this happened but he thought about ten times. "It hurt!" Mr. S would push the thing in and out. "He would just do it."

Mr. S would also "clean" George's penis. George made a masturbatory motion as he described the cleaning. He thinks his penis got hard when Mr. S rubbed it. He later learned about masturbation but he didn't know what was happening at the time. "I was too young to understand." The masturbation also occurred "a lot, I think more than ten times." George saw Mr. S's penis but doesn't remember being asked to touch it.

He never talked to the other children about what Mr. S did to him or the similar things that he saw Mr. S do to the other children. George volunteered that after the anal penetrations "my poops would be hard and I would get constipated for a long time."

Interview with Mother

George's mother confirmed that her son was at the preschool between the ages of four and six. Mr. S's job was maintenance, transportation and child care before and after school. During the summer he took the children to a nearby swimming pool on a regular basis and on occasional field trips.

When George was taking a bath he told his mother how Mr. S would "clean" his penis. He demonstrated the up and down masturbatory movement that Mr. S used. Mother became alarmed and talked to the school director. After a period of time the director denied that Mr. S would do something like that. She did not believe George. Mother was sure it was true and removed George from the preschool and eventually consulted an attorney. A few years later the director met with mother and father and informed them that the police reported that Mr. S had been accused of abusing two boys at a boarding school where he had previously worked. The director apologized and offered counseling for George. George was seen by a social work student for a short period of time. Mother saw little change in George as a result of the therapy. Mother didn't know about the anal penetration until George mentioned it a few days ago, in her presence, to the attorney. She was shocked and dismayed.

Symptoms

During the summer before his sixth birthday, while he was still attending the preschool, George told mother that his bottom hurt. After he repeated this a few times mother looked and found a laceration. She did not take George to a physician because she thought the tear was due to a large bowel movement. George stopped complaining of his bottom hurting soon after he stopped going to the preschool. He was constipated during that summer and for several months afterward. Mother told him to drink water and gave her son stool softeners. George is still occasionally constipated. Before attending preschool George had had regular bowel movements.

George had always wanted to go to preschool, particularly during the summer. In the middle of his last summer there he began to resist going to school. George was not able to tell his mother why he didn't want to go.

Nightmares began shortly after mother removed George from the pre-school. They continued for approximately two years after the abuse ended. George's pediatrician prescribed antidepressants, which seemed to help. George was unable or unwilling to tell his mother about the content of the nightmares. Approximately eighteen months before he was removed from the preschool George became very fearful. He insisted on having a night light and refused to go to the bathroom alone. George still wants a night light on because he is occasionally afraid to be alone.

George was toilet trained by age two and a half for both bowel and urine. After being dry for about two years George began to wet the bed. Between the ages of six and twelve he wet the bed every night. More recently the bed-wetting has diminished to once or twice a week.

During his last summer at the preschool George began to smear feces on the wall. This continued for approximately a year after he left the preschool. Mother thinks that George "plays with himself in his rear." He gets up on his knees and has his hand near his rectum. Mother tries to get him to stop when she sees this behavior but suspects that it occurs when George is alone.

Developmental History

Pregnancy, labor and delivery were normal. Early developmental milestones occurred on schedule. George walked at one year and was talking in short sentences by age two. Mother was at home as a full-time caretaker. There were no significant separations from either parent. George had no difficulty separating to attend preschool and enjoyed the experience before the molestation.

George achieved average grades throughout elementary school. He has friends and is not a disciplinary problem. Very active in sports, George is usually easygoing and obedient. Part of a large extended family, George spends a lot of time with his cousins. He is close to his father, who is very involved in George's athletic activities.

Second Diagnostic Interview with George

During the second diagnostic interview I asked George to expand on his reactions to the abuse. He did remember telling his mother when he was in the bathtub that Mr. S had cleaned his penis but didn't know why he didn't tell her about his butt hurting. When asked about the content of his nightmares, he replied "of him doing it again." The nightmares had continued "for a while" but he hadn't experienced any recently. George was afraid at night "of him being in the bathroom and doing something to me again. I stopped being afraid once he was in prison." George still likes the night light on. "I got used to it." Bed-wetting began during the abuse. George indicated that he stopped a few weeks ago.

Psychological Testing

George scored in the average range of intellectual functioning. The psychologist commented on George's performance on My Worst Experience Scale "George responds to this instrument in a consistent manner. He endorses being sexually assaulted as the worst experience he ever had. He denies any other history of trauma exposure. He denies that he is still bothered by this experience, but at the time it 'upset me a lot' . . . He reports that he continues to think about 'things he could do to get back at the person who hurt me.'"

Traumatic Symptom Checklist for Children

"The minor reports being overly preoccupied with sex for someone his age. For example, he reports having intrusive thoughts about sex and touching his private areas too much. He also demonstrates a tendency to be over-reliant on fantasy to the exclusion of the 'real' world and its demands. This dissociative symptom serves to reduce George's painful internal experience and is not likely to be perceived by him as problematic or unwanted."

Millon Pre-Adolescent Clinical Inventory

"George indicates that he continues to experience intrusive thoughts on this instrument, and admits he has thoughts about killing himself . . . He lacks a clear sense of identity and values himself in terms of his relationships with others. He is at risk of becoming a member of a social group that, while providing a sense of identity and self-esteem, may also lead him into behavioral difficulties."

Rorschach

"George attempts to maintain a psychological equilibrium by keeping stressful experiences at a minimum and avoiding disturbing thoughts and feelings. He may subsequently avoid new and challenging situations. When under stress, he may become unduly distressed, lowering his tolerance for frustration and decreasing his impulse control . . . He has little tolerance for uncertainty and ambiguity and prefers situations that are clearly defined and well-structured . . . George generally thinks in a logical, coherent manner, and there is no evidence of thought disorder . . . George demonstrates several trauma indicators on the Rorschach. In general, he feels helpless and fears feeling out of control. The world is experienced as a dangerous place by him. He has a rather idiosyncratic way of seeing the world that may be influenced by his victimization . . . He tends to be withdrawn from others as he feels that people are not safe, and feels that he is unable to count on people for support."

The psychologist suggested a diagnosis of Posttraumatic Stress Disorder, noted dependent personality traits and rated George's symptoms in the moderate range of severity. "It is highly recommended that George become involved in individual psychotherapy to treat posttraumatic symptoms. Both trauma-specific and cognitive-behavioral interventions are indicated . . . Treatment should also address his sexual concerns as he enters adolescence and begins to confront these developmental issues. Referral to a psychiatrist for medication management of his posttraumatic symptoms is strongly recommended . . . He may wish to participate in psychotherapy on occasion throughout the course of his life as needed when issues related to intimacy, trust, stress, or additional trauma exposure arise."

Therapist's Notes

George was seen shortly after the abuse was reported by a social work intern for approximately a dozen times. A psychiatrist prescribed antidepressant medication and made a diagnosis of Depressive Disorder, NOS.

The therapist talked of nightmares and pressure on the parents' marriage related to the abuse. In addition reference was made to George touching another child in an inappropriate manner. George's teacher heard him talk about "humping" another child on repeated occasions. George denied that he had done so. He was encopretic during the course of treatment. George reported multiple sexual abuse experiences with Mr. S. They were similar in nature to those that he reported to me and others.

Diagnosis

Using DSM-IV I made diagnoses of Sexual Abuse of Child V61.21; Clinical Focus on Victim 995.53; Posttraumatic Stress Disorder 309.81, and Depressive Disorder NOS 311.00. Dependent personality traits were noted on Axis II. On Axis III I noted anal penetration, fecal smearing, constipation and enuresis. I rated George's symptoms in the 41–50, serious range.

Therapy

George would benefit from individual psychotherapy with a clinician experienced with childhood sexual abuse, two to three times per week for three to five years. In addition, as George entered adolescence, he might benefit from group therapy with other male victims of sexual abuse. Antidepressant medication may be indicated during the course of therapy and possibly afterward. Additional courses of psychotherapy in the decade of the twenties, and possibly beyond, will likely be required. If outpatient treatment is unsuccessful psychiatric hospitalization may be indicated in adolescence or young adulthood.

Discussion

Such severe sexual abuse at such an early age resulted in very significant interference with developmental progression. During and following the abuse George regressed and loss control of bowel and bladder. Fecal smearing, an extreme symptom, occurred for at least a year after the abuse ended. Occasional bed-wetting was still present at the time of the evaluation. George's latency years were compromised by the above symptoms and significant levels of depression, low self-esteem, interference with formal learning, compromised peer relationships, a fear of men, an inability to be comfortably alone and sexual acting out.

On the verge of entering adolescence, it is highly likely that he will have major difficulty integrating sexual maturation and the pressures for sexual activity which result from the outpouring of sexual hormones. Already prone to inappropriate sexual behavior, he is at great risk for sexual interactions which could result in involvement with legal authorities. Further, his sense of sexual identity is already confused as he enters adolescence. Developing a comfortable sense of masculinity during adolescence will be extremely difficult, even with intensive therapy.

George's fear of being alone and requiring his parents' presence will interfere with the separation-individuation process during adolescence. Difficulty in developing the confidence to achieve academically, participate in peer activities such as much-loved athletics and relating to male peers and adults should be anticipated.

Prognosis

The prognosis, even with the intensive treatment regime outlined above, is guarded.

CASE STUDY: LUIS

First Diagnostic Interview with Luis

Luis shuffled into my office with a shy grin and a hesitant handshake. A well built, big fifteen-year-old, he looked older than his actual age. After explaining the purpose of our meeting I asked Luis to tell me about himself. He was interested in sports. Because of his size he was asked to try out for the football team. He played on the line and guessed that he was pretty good. He also threw the discus and hammer on the freshman track team. When he was younger he had played Little League baseball. School was "ok" but PE was his favorite subject. Later Luis indicated that his grade point average was so low that he could only practice with the football and track teams. He couldn't actually compete until his grades improved. He was working hard to get a 3.0 average.

Things were good at home, kind of "laid back." He enjoyed spending time with his brother and his parents. He had to do his homework first but he particularly liked going to the movies with his father. They both liked action movies.

The Abuse

Luis knew that we were here to talk about Mr. S "and what he did to little kids." He described Mr. S as quiet and "kind of big." Luis thought he was about seven years old when he started with Mr. S.

Mr. S would drive the kids around. The little ones would sit on his lap and steer the car. Luis saw him reach into the kids' pants. He would move his hands up and down. This happened many times whenever they went to the pool or on a field trip. Mr. S had Luis sit on his lap, at least three or four times. Mr. S put his hand on Luis's penis and massaged it. Luis didn't remember if his penis got hard or what he thought at the time. Mr. S never said anything and Luis didn't tell anyone.

At the swimming pool in the changing room Mr. S would be naked. As he undressed the kids Mr. S would put his hand on the boys' penises. Luis could see Mr. S's penis too. It was big and hard. Luis's older brother, Alfredo, would try to keep Luis away from Mr. S. Luis remembered seeing Mr. S have little girls sit on his lap. His hand would be in their pants. They would make noises like they were being hurt. Sometimes they would cry. Mr. S's wife was there sometimes. She would look away.

When his mother first asked him if he was abused Luis said no. When Luis was in fifth or sixth grade his brother asked him if he was touched. Luis said yes. Alfredo told Luis that he had to tell his mother and he did.

Diagnostic Interview with Mother

Mother had no idea about what had happened to Luis. He never talked about it until shortly before Mr. S's trial over a year ago. Alfredo, Luis's older brother, denied being abused for a long time. Luis was with Mr. S from about age seven to nine but he had been at the school for several years before that. He might have been abused then too. Mother seemed to be coming to terms with what happened, and for how long, for the first time.

Symptoms

Mother related that when Luis was about seven "there were signs." Luis would eat the skin off his hands. He chewed his fingernails until they bled. This behavior diminished at about age ten, after Mr. S was gone. Playing sports helped Luis stop chewing his nails. Luis would isolate himself. He still doesn't relate well to other kids. Luis tries hard to be part of the group but he gets aggressive and the other kids push him away. Sometimes he explodes and throws things. He tries to be the bully. Luis has some friends at school but no one calls. He never gets invited to other boys' homes or to birthday parties.

Luis's grades have always been extremely poor despite spending time with tutors. The school did testing and didn't find any evidence of a learning disability. The school would call and say Luis always had to go to the bathroom. Luis gained a lot of weight during the time he was in elementary school. Mother estimated that he was fifty pounds overweight at the time of the evaluation.

When Luis was about seven years old he refused to be alone. He slept with his parents until he was ten. Luis still prefers to be with someone, particularly at night. He seems very sad. His temper seems less violent since he talked to the attorney about the abuse.

Developmental History

Pregnancy, labor and delivery occurred without difficulty. Luis was a healthy infant, a good eater, who said single words by eleven months and walked at a year of age. Mother was home for the first year and then went back to work. Luis was a strong-willed toddler who was determined and independent. He was toilet trained by age two. Close to both parents, Luis did not have any significant illnesses or operations in childhood.

The sexual abuse occurred during the latency years. Luis was interested in sports from an early age. He achieved average grades in elementary school and got along well with the teachers. In retrospect mother feels that as the abuse continued Luis became mildly disruptive in school and combative with friends. Luis went through puberty at about age twelve. He seemed to enjoy growing up, particularly his voice changing. He did not verbalize any unusual sexual behaviors and curiosities. Luis seems interested in girls but he has not had a girlfriend. He is just beginning to talk to girls on the phone.

Second Diagnostic Interview with Luis

I asked Luis to tell me how he felt the sexual abuse by Mr. S had affected him. "It changed my life," he said. "I try not to think about it. I only think about it when I'm asked. Then I just go into a stare. I just figured it out a couple of years ago, that I was touched." Luis was unaware that the perpetrator, at his trial, had identified him as one of the children that he molested. Luis began to figure out that he was molested after his mother and brother asked him. He didn't recall any memories before that time. "Then I remembered sitting on his lap in the van and being at the pool with him. It makes me feel violated, just knowing that it happened to me, that I was taken advantage of when I was little. I wish I had told somebody about it when it happened."

I brought up the various symptoms that mother had mentioned. Luis did not remember severe nail-biting but did acknowledge that he does bite his nails. When asked about friends Luis said, "I don't have any friends outside of school. There aren't many kids where I live. They're younger." Luis did not remember being very angry when he was in elementary school or going to the bathroom a lot. He had no idea why he gained so much weight in fourth and fifth grade.

Luis was never abused by anyone other than Mr. S. He had not had any sexual experience with girls since becoming a teenager. When he masturbates he thinks about girls and makes sure that he never thinks about the sexual abuse. Luis emphasized that he doesn't have sexual thoughts about guys.

Psychological Testing

The psychologist made the following observations about Luis after completing the testing. "During the interview Luis became evidently agitated, shaking his leg and breathing more rapidly, when discussing his victimization."

Luis scored in the average range of intelligence.

On My Worst Experience Scale

"Luis endorses being sexually assaulted as the worst experience he ever had. He denies any other history of trauma exposure. He states that he is still bothered by this experience and at the time it 'upset me a little.' He meets the criteria for PTSD in his responses to this test, indicating that he is plagued by intrusive thoughts, has avoidant symptoms (tries not to talk about what happened, avoids the place where he was abused, harder to make himself do things, couldn't remember some things that happened to him during the abuse), and has significant symptoms of hyperarousal (attention difficulties, hypervigilance and exaggerated startle response). He demonstrates clinically significant problems in the area of hypervigilance (which continues today) and general maladjustment. These latter problems are typical of children who are young at the time they are traumatized, and include regressive behaviors such as enuresis, agitation, thumb-sucking, and nail-biting. Outside of nail-biting, Luis indicates that he no longer demonstrates these other regressive behaviors."

Luis responds to the Millon Adolescent Clinical Inventory in a highly defensive manner on this instrument, indicating that he tends to minimize and deny problems . . . Predominant personality patterns indicate that despite his ability to make a good first impression, Luis tends to be unreliable, impulsive, resentful, impatient and moody. He is somewhat immature, defiant and self-dramatizing. He tends to act without thinking, sometimes getting into trouble with others unnecessarily. Irresponsible and undependable, he is prone to relying on acting out behaviors as a means of defending against uncomfortable feelings. He tends to deny having any personal problems or internal conflicts. Any social problems he has tend to be rationalized, and he is prone to blame others for his problems . . . He is fearful of being perceived as indecisive, soft-hearted or weak. An undercurrent of defensive vigilance rarely subsides. He admits a history of being sexually abused on this instrument."

Luis was quite guarded in his approach to the Rorschach. "He attempts to maintain a psychological equilibrium by keeping stressful experiences at a minimum and avoiding disturbing thoughts and feelings. He may subsequently avoid new and challenging situations. When under stress, he may become unduly distressed, lowering his tolerance for frustration and decreasing his impulse control. He is a rather emotionally over-controlled individual who has difficulty relaxing emotionally, being spontaneous, showing his feelings, and relating to others on a casual, informal basis. He is also prone to being oppositional, indicating the presence of underlying anger and resentment. He avoids self-examination and lacks self-awareness, and is not psychologically minded."

Diagnosis

The psychologist suggested ruling out Posttraumatic Stress Disorder and Oppositional Defiant Disorder. He related Luis's symptoms in the mild range of severity. But he added, "It would appear that when he was younger, Luis met the criteria for PTSD because of the typical regressive behaviors he demonstrated following his molestation by Mr. S (enuresis, agitation, nail-biting, thumb sucking). At the present time, he continues to demonstrate problems with trusting others and with being hyper-vigilant with regards to possible threat and danger, but does not seem to demonstrate the other symptoms of PTSD at the level of severity required for the diagnosis. On the other hand, there is evidence from the test data that Luis tends to be quite guarded and to under-report his psychiatric symptoms and personal problems. Because he had once met the criteria for PTSD, he is at greater risk for both trauma exposure and for developing this disorder if faced with another trauma during the course of his life. Symptoms may also be triggered by situations that involve intimacy and/or sexuality. Without adequate treatment, he is (at the very least) at risk of having chronic interpersonal difficulties and developing problems with substance abuse."

Treatment

"It is highly recommended that Luis become involved in individual psychotherapy to develop increased resilience and ability to cope with stress. Helping him improve his interpersonal skills, promote assertiveness and improve his ability to more accurately perceive the environment in terms of danger cues is also indicated. Cognitive-behavioral interventions may be helpful in reducing chronic tension and allowing Luis to relax more, particularly in social situations. Helping him develop increased self-awareness and tolerance for his emotional experience through insight-oriented work may also be helpful. After a period of time, participation in a group for adolescent victims of sexual abuse may be helpful. There is no current indication of a need for psychotropic medications at the present time. He may wish to participate in psychotherapy on occasion throughout the course of his life as needed when issues related to intimacy, trust, stress, or additional trauma exposure arise."

Diagnosis

Using DSM-IV I made the following diagnoses: Sexual Abuse of Child 995.53, Clinical Focus on Victim 995.53, Dysthymic Disorder 300.4 and during the first year after the abuse, Posttraumatic Stress Disorder. As noted by the psychologist, and evident on clinical examination, some symptoms of PTSD remain but not enough to meet the diagnostic criteria in the *Manual*. I rated Luis' symptoms in the 41–50 range until approximately age ten and at the time of the evaluation in the 51–60, moderate range.

Treatment

Luis would benefit from an immediate course of individual psychotherapy, two times per week for three years. At some point in the future group therapy with male victims of sexual abuse would be helpful. During periods of stress antidepressant medication may be indicated. A second course of individual psychotherapy, once per week for one to two years, is indicated during the decade of the twenties to deal with issues of intimacy, marriage and parenthood. Further treatment needs can be determined at that time.

Prognosis

The prognosis, with the treatment program described above, is fair to good.

Discussion

Luis does not appear to have been subjected to the extreme degree of sexual abuse as George had been. However, he may have repressed experiences that could be uncovered in therapy. The perpetrator definitely named him as one of the children who were abused. Certainly his older brother, whose experience will be described next, tried to protect him from Mr. S.

During the abuse, which occurred during latency, Luis exhibited signs of anxiety such as nail-biting and thumb-sucking and regressive symptoms such as enuresis and temper tantrum–like behavior. Instead of becoming more autonomous and self-soothing he began to sleep with his mother and brother. In addition he became isolated from peers and fearful of being alone. Difficulties with learning were present before the abuse but they became accentuated during and afterwards. Clearly, the major developmental tasks of latency were significantly compromised.

Now in mid-adolescence, Luis is preoccupied with the abuse which "changed my life." Attempts to integrate his physically and sexually mature body are complicated by memories of the abuse and intense shame, embarrassment and sexual confusion. At a time when peer relationships should be prominent, except for sports, he remained isolated from peers and had not yet developed a typical mid-adolescent relationship with a girl.

As the psychologist noted, Luis is at risk for responding to future trauma with a return of posttraumatic symptoms. As with all child abuse victims of either sex, the young adult issues of intimacy, marriage and parenthood will be conflicted. If Luis becomes the father of a boy he is likely to experience anxiety when touching his son's body and overprotective and anxious about the possibility of his child or children being abused as he was. As will become evident in the case histories of those in their fifties and sixties that are presented toward the end of the book, concerns about becoming a parent or protecting one's children become lifelong and a source of major anxiety.

CASE STUDY: ALFREDO

Diagnostic Interview with Alfredo

Alfredo presented as a tall, overweight, well-groomed late adolescent. He was somewhat shy but cooperative and friendly. Alfredo made good eye contact and seemed to have a need to tell his story. He initiated conversation spontaneously, had a good vocabulary and spoke with feeling. Alfredo's affect was somewhat constricted and he often appeared anxious as he talked.

Alfredo was nineteen at the time of the diagnostic interview. A high school graduate, he was working as a retail clerk while living with his younger brother, Luis, and his parents. After time spent talking about his interests in sports and TV programs Alfredo was ready, almost eager out of a sense of pressured anxiety, to talk about the abuse by Mr. S. Alfredo went to public school but from first through fifth grade he also attended an after-school program at a church-related school. The abuse occurred during the fourth and fifth grades, and possibly before, at a swimming pool and on field trips. Alfredo didn't tell his parents what was occurring until a year later.

In the pool Mr. S would offer to help the children swim. He would get behind Alfredo and push his pelvis against Alfredo's backside while he put a hand in the boy's shorts. Mr. S's hand would remain on Alfredo's penis for five to ten minutes. Alfredo would think "this wasn't right" and would try, unsuccessfully, to move away; but he was afraid to say anything. He wasn't sure if he got erections during the abuse in the pool. On some days this happened several times. Mr. S's wife would be at poolside. She looked hurt when she saw her husband holding a boy in the water.

After spending time in the pool Mr. S would take the boys into the shower. He would be naked and wash the other boys. Alfredo saw Mr. S touch the other boys' genitals as he washed and dressed them. Alfredo refused to shower with Mr. S and also kept his brother, Luis, away from the perpetrator. Alfredo and Luis never talked about the abuse when they were alone. Alfredo has a vague memory of being at Mr. S's home. He recalls seeing the bedroom but cannot recall details of what happened. The memory is accompanied by anxiety and pain.

Alfredo remembers telling his parents that Mr. S was "weird" but all he could verbalize was that he didn't like being around Mr. S. "His touching me and seeing him naked, I hid it for a year." When Alfredo was in high school he was called to the school office to meet with a female police officer who asked him if he had been abused by Mr. S. Alfredo was shocked by the question because he hadn't talked to anyone about the abuse before. He was very embarrassed and didn't want to go into details. As the legal proceeding against Mr. S got underway Alfredo gradually told his parents what had happened to him.

Symptoms

"I had trouble sleeping. It would take me a while to fall asleep. I wanted to sleep with my parents or my brother. I think it was due to being alone in the pool with him. When I was alone at night I didn't like it." The symptom began before Alfredo told his parents about the abuse and continued for approximately three years after the abuse ended.

"I got fat." Before the abuse occurred Alfredo described himself as skinny. After the abuse he began to gain weight until his present weight was well over two hundred pounds. "I stopped doing things after he abused me. I didn't want to go anywhere and I guess I started to eat."

"I still don't want to be alone. I'm afraid to go upstairs alone. Someone might be there and they might pull me away, take me away and kidnap or kill me" (this from a nineteen-year-old man who weighs over two hundred pounds). This symptom began soon after the abuse started and, although diminished in intensity and frequency, continues to the present. If Alfredo is alone he is more likely to think about the abuse. "I zone out, I have to shake it off."

"I used to be a great student." Alfredo was in accelerated classes before the abuse. From then on his grades went "downhill." Throughout the school years after the abuse Alfredo always passed his courses, but with mediocre grades. As he spoke a sense of sadness permeated his thoughts as he recognized that he had not been able to realize his academic potential. Alfredo felt that the abuse was related to the drop in his grades but he couldn't say why. He also felt badly about having avoided activities and dances in high school. "I never told anyone what happened except my parents and the attorney, and now you."

Developmental History

Developmental history was obtained from both Alfredo and his mother. During the elementary years Alfredo had lots of friends, was well behaved and before the abuse really enjoyed learning. After the abuse Alfredo avoided the kids who had also been abused by Mr. S. Occasionally one of them would ask if anything weird had happened to him. Alfredo always said no.

Puberty occurred at age thirteen. Alfredo started noticing girls in sixth grade and began dating soon afterwards. He had his first serious girlfriend in ninth grade and another in senior high school. Alfredo had intercourse with both of these girls. He denied having fantasies about the abuse during intercourse. As his sexuality developed Alfredo began to understand what it meant to be abused and began to relate his symptoms to the abuse. He had not had any homosexual experiences.

Alfredo has not used drugs or alcohol to excess nor had any problems with the police. He does not have a psychiatric history and has never been in therapy. Mother related that she wanted to get therapy for Alfredo but it was difficult to get Victim of Crime funding.

Diagnostic Interview with Mother

Mother began by mentioning that when Alfredo was ten years old he complained that a man at school, Mr. S, was "weird." He did strange things. Alfredo worried that he would get in trouble for talking about Mr. S. When mother inquired Alfredo told her about Mr. S putting his hand between Alfredo's legs under his bathing trunks. He refused to give further details, again because he was afraid that Mr. S would find out and punish him. Alfredo did not tell mother about the sexual abuse of others at that time. Only after it became know two years ago that Mr. S had abused other children was Alfredo able to reveal other details.

Mother told Alfredo that she would have to call the principal of the church school. The principal said that Alfredo's story couldn't possibly be true but she would talk to Mr. S. The principal called back the next day and said that Mr. S said it was unintentional. Mother decided to let it go. The principal said that she would report the accusation to CSPP but she never did. Alfredo felt very guilty and wanted to write an apology letter to Mr. S.

Six years later, when Alfredo was sixteen, the principal contacted mother and asked to come to the family's home. She apologized over and over again because it had become known that Mr. S had abused others as well. The principal offered to pay for a psychologist. A few weeks later the educator reported that Luis had also been abused. Mother had asked Luis if he had been abused when Alfredo told her about Mr. S but Luis said no. Until very recently Luis continued to insist that he had not been abused.

Symptoms

Mother described the following symptomatic behavior in Alfredo as a result of the abuse.

"He developed a severe fear of being alone." This fear began before Alfredo told his parents about the sexual abuse. They were puzzled by this significant change in behavior. "He was like my shadow." This behavior lasted for three or four years, stopping when Alfredo was about thirteen to fourteen years of age. This fear was exaggerated at bedtime. "He had to sleep with us or his brother all the time." Alfredo said he was afraid of being alone but could not describe what he was afraid of. This behavior also lasted for three or four years and stopped when Alfredo was in middle school.

"He got very depressed." Alfredo became very negative, sarcastic and withdrawn. He would close himself up in his room, which he painted black. This behavior began after the parents were told by the principal that Mr. S was a molester when Alfredo was in mid-adolescence. It lasted for more than a year.

"His grades dropped." Alfredo had been identified in second grade as a GATE child— one with superior academic potential and a high IQ. Mr. S would pick Alfredo up after the public school day and take him to the after-school program. Mother reasoned that the abuse began when Alfredo was in third grade. Up to that point Alfredo made all As. In fourth grade when he had to reapply to the GATE program he failed the examination and his grades dropped to Bs and Cs in regular classes. Alfredo never achieved outstanding grades again. When he began to fail in senior high school Alfredo's parents pulled him out of school and provided home schooling. He did manage to graduate, but just barely.

"He gained a lot of weight." Alfredo was thin and lanky through the ninth grade. Then he began to gain weight. At the time of the evaluation he was obviously overweight, almost obese. After the abuse became public Alfredo paid less attention to his appearance. He said that he didn't need to care because he was fat anyway.

"Alfredo has difficulty getting close to men. He is not close to any male family members. There is a wall, no trust there. His girlfriend relationships don't work out. There's no connection, no emotional attachment."

Psychological Testing

On the Behavioral Symptoms Index, a measure of Alfredo's overall problem behaviors as rated by his mother, there were significantly more symptoms related to a mood disorder than to acting out or disruptive behavior. He was often reported as being nervous, worried, fearful and concerned about making mistakes.

On the DAPS, a self-report measure of trauma exposure and posttraumatic response, Alfredo met the diagnostic criteria for PTSD. "His symptoms have caused significant impairment in his relationships and in social situations. At the present time, he reports having dissociative symptoms, including feelings of unreality and depersonalization."

On the TSI, another self-report measure of posttraumatic symptoms, Alfredo endorses several items related to dysfunctional sexual behavior, including having sex to keep from feeling lonely or sad, having sexual thoughts when he felt he shouldn't have them, wishing he could stop thinking about sex, wanting to have sex with someone he knew would be bad for him, and having sex that had to be kept secret from other people.

The psychologist noted that Alfredo "is most hampered in his interpersonal relationships . . . he has difficulty in more intimate relationships. That is, he is fearful of being hurt or taken advantage of by others, and so has difficulty allowing himself to be vulnerable and acknowledge weaknesses and needs that would foster closeness with others."

A diagnosis of Posttraumatic Stress Disorder, Chronic, Mild was suggested. Alfredo's symptoms were rated in the moderate range. The psychologist concluded that Alfredo's symptoms "are chronic in nature and cause clinically significant distress and impairment in social and adaptive functioning . . . Alfredo's life has been negatively affected in numerous other ways. His self-confidence and self-esteem were damaged, and he continues to struggle with having a realistic self-image that is not reliant on an inflated, overly positive view of himself. He continues to have difficulties in the area of trusting others in general, particularly male authority figures. Perhaps he is most affected in his ability to establish an intimate relationship, as he fears being hurt so much that he will not allow himself to be vulnerable in the way that would facilitate closeness with another person. Indeed, it is the conclusion of this examiner that Alfredo's life has been dramatically altered as a result of the experience of childhood sexual abuse by Mr. S."

Individual psychotherapy, two to three times per week for several years' was recommended along with group therapy with other male victims of childhood sexual abuse and medication. "He will likely require ongoing psychotherapy throughout the course of his life, particularly when he has difficulty in his intimate relationships."

Diagnosis

Using DSM-IV I made diagnoses of Sexual Abuse of a Child V61.21, and Posttraumatic Stress Disorder, Chronic, Moderate 309.81. Dissociative symptoms were evident on psychological testing.

Treatment

Alfredo is in need of individual psychotherapy, twice per week, for at least three to four years. Anti-anxiety and/or antidepressant medication may be

indicated during the course of therapy as the abuse is explored, particularly
if repressed memories are recovered. As recommended by the psychologist,
group therapy with victims of childhood sexual abuse may be helpful during
or after the initial course of individual psychotherapy. It is highly likely that
Alfredo will need additional psychotherapeutic intervention as he approaches
marriage and parenthood. As with almost all sexual abuse victims, developing
intimacy within a committed relationship will be difficult for Alfredo. Should
he have children, particularly a male child, issues of over-protectiveness and
reliving the trauma when his son reaches the ages at which he and his brother
were abused will need to be addressed.

Prognosis

The prognosis, with treatment as outlined above, is fair.

Discussion

Alfredo was nineteen years of age at the time of the diagnostic evaluation.
Normal development was compromised throughout the adolescent years. Alfredo had difficulty in separating from his parents, indeed he needed to sleep
with them for several years after the abuse and was afraid to be alone in his
own home. Academic performance was significantly compromised. Alfredo
was performing well in accelerated classes before the abuse. Afterward he
struggled academically and achieved mediocre grades, at best. Body image
and self-esteem were significantly affected. Alfredo became very heavy and felt
unattractive. His sexual development was compromised with doubts about
his masculinity. In addition, according to his mother he became significantly
depressed during and after the abuse.

On the verge of young adulthood, Alfredo will struggle with the developmental task of combining sexuality with intimacy. Marriage and parenthood
will be sources of conflict and anxiety. This young man has the intellectual
capability to achieve a higher education. This realistic goal may not be realized. Further, the need for psychotherapy will extend through at least several
years of the decade of the twenties and thirties, facilitating the engagement of
the developmental tasks of young adulthood and hopefully promoting developmental progression.

SIMILARITIES AND DIFFERENCES IN THESE THREE CASES

Childhood sexual abuse tends to undermine the growing, latency age, cognitive capacity for introspection and curiosity about the self. When memories produce pain, anxiety and fear thinking and feeling become something to be avoided, not relished. Strong defense mechanisms such as repression, isolation and dissociation are set in motion in an attempt to maintain emotional equilibrium. This defensive posture has a significant effect on formal learning, which is a prominent developmental task during latency, i.e., the elementary school years. All three boys struggled academically. George was an average student. Luis' grades were extremely poor. Alfredo went from being a GATE student prior to the abuse to a very poor one for the remainder of his elementary and high school years. Of course, the sexual abuse was not the only factor in the learning difficulties of these three boys; but the drop in academic performance after the years of abuse, particularly in Luis and Alfredo, seems clearly related to the sexual abuse. Any sudden drop in academic performance or desire to avoid school in a child who had previously enjoyed going should alert both parents and educators that the changes should be thoroughly investigated. Sexual abuse should be on the list of possibilities.

Very young children are more likely to tell someone that they are being sexually abused than older children and adolescents are. This tendency is due to the fact that the young child truly does not understand what is happening, has little or no knowledge of adult sexual behavior, does not feel responsible and therefore does not experience shame.

George was five years old when he was abused. He told his mother soon after the abuse began. Luis and Alfredo were well into latency and beyond when they were abused. Both were aware of their own sexual feelings and knew that the genitals were special areas in regard to touching. They also had an immediate sense, although they didn't fully understand why, that what Mr. S was doing to them was wrong. Neither of them volunteered that they were being abused although both expressed negative feelings about Mr. S which their parents did not investigate. As they got older, particularly during adolescence, both came to a much fuller understanding that they had been abused and experienced intense shame because of a sense—extremely common in most victims—that somehow they should have been able to resist and avoid further involvement.

All three boys developed nightmares and significant fears of being alone. All began to sleep with their parents or siblings. These are striking symptoms, particularly in the two older boys. Since the normal latency-age push is toward increased involvement with peers and other adults such as teachers and coaches, the regressive tendency to remain physically and emotionally attached to parents is particularly detrimental to normal developmental progression. The need for close physical and emotional contact with parents continued in the two older boys into adolescence. George is likely to exhibit the same behavior when he reaches adolescence.

In a similar manner, instead of becoming increasingly involved with peers and boosting self-esteem through extra-familial relationships, Luis and Alfredo resorted to regressive self-soothing through overeating. Alfredo, in particular, is clearly obese. As the body sexually matures in adolescence and becomes a vehicle for participation in sports and other activities, it becomes a significant source of self-esteem in healthy boys. Luis and Alfredo, both of whom are very interested in sports, are not integrating a body image that is infused with pleasure and pride.

In these cases, and many others later in the book, dissociative tendencies (and in some instances, diagnoses) are prominent aspects of the psychopathology. Dissociative defense mechanisms are most commonly seen in individuals who have been subjected to extreme trauma. They are also very common in sexually abused children, particularly young ones. All three boys utilized dissociative mechanisms to one degree or another. These were particularly evident on psychological testing. Significant gaps in memory, which again will be described frequently in a number of cases to follow, may be an indication of dissociation. For example, Alfredo remembered going to Mr. S's home but does not remember what happened there.

George, the youngest, manifested hypersexual behavior in the form of anal stimulation and attempted sexual involvement with peers. The openness of this behavior indicates the pressure to repeat the abusive experiences. In formal terms, he was using the repetition compulsion and activity over passivity in an attempt to master the traumatic stimulation. The two older boys, more aware of and more concerned about the reaction of others, did not manifest such behavior. They managed to contain the over-stimulation at an intrapsychic level. Alfredo, in particular, was preoccupied with unwanted sexual thoughts.

4

Three Adolescent Case Studies

THE FOLLOWING CASE STUDIES of three adolescent girls illustrate the effects of chronic sexual abuse on female development in adolescence in a complementary manner to the case studies of the three adolescent boys presented in chapter 3.

In addition, in two of the case studies in this chapter, the sexual abuse began in adolescence. The girls' emerging sexuality and the development of the normal adolescent phenomena of crushes on authority figures made them particularly vulnerable to the two teachers who took advantage of them.

CASE STUDY: NADINE

Nadine was a casually dressed adolescent girl when she entered my office for the diagnostic interviews in connection with her civil lawsuit against the perpetrator. Her excellent vocabulary and obvious intelligence made her appear older than her stated age of fourteen. She sat quietly throughout the diagnostic interviews, responding at first hesitantly to my questions and then gradually volunteering details. Nadine's affect was flat throughout the interviews but a strong sense of depression was present whenever she addressed the sexual abuse and its consequences. Thinking was logical and goal directed and there was no evidence of delusions or hallucinations.

The evaluation consisted of more than three hours of interviews with Nadine and her mother, psychological testing performed at my request by an experienced forensic psychologist, and a review of therapy, legal and school records. All of the following information was provided by Nadine and her mother.

Diagnostic Interview with Nadine

Nadine was a ninth-grade student at a public school. Her parents were divorced when she was in elementary school but remain on good terms. Nadine lives with her mother but sees her father frequently.

I began the first interview by asking Nadine general questions in order to give her time to become comfortable with me. She enjoyed spending time with her friends, shopping and sports. In the fall she hoped to try out for the girls' basketball team. At present Nadine's grades ranged from A to D. She didn't know her GPA. Nadine and her mother got along well. They have mild battles over things like making the bed and curfews. Nadine also enjoys being at her father's home nearby.

After this introductory period I asked Nadine to tell me about her experiences with the teacher who molested her. She spoke quietly, with some trepidation. Because of her obvious intelligence and command of English Nadine was able to describe her experience in a sober but straightforward manner. I continually had to remind myself that I was listening to a fourteen-year-old girl, not someone much older. Due to the sensitivity of the material I did not push for details at this point because it was clear from the legal proceedings what had occurred, but Nadine soon volunteered details.

Mr. L was Nadine's teacher during the eighth grade. She was thirteen at the time. The sexual abuse started in the fall semester and continued until the end of the school year. "I was sexually harassed." The abuse began with "kissing. Then he made me touch him. Then he touched me. Later on he had me do oral things on him. Then he raped me. It was spread out over eight months and went on and on."

At the beginning Nadine was "in shock and disbelief. I didn't know what to do or how to react." She had not had any prior sexual experience other than a kiss from a boy when she was twelve years of age. "I tried to block it out. I got really sad. Then I got really mad. I was kind of numb toward the end." Nadine did not tell anyone about the abuse. Mr. L never hit her but he did hold her down while he raped her. He told her not to tell anyone. "If I go down, you go down with me." The perpetrator did not show her pornography or involve others in the sexual abuse. The teacher told Nadine that he loved her and wanted to marry her. She never cared for him, "other than hatred."

The abuse was discovered when Nadine's father heard her cell phone ring and looked at an explicit text message from Mr. L. Father and mother talked to her about the abuse on the way to the police station. The police had Nadine call Mr. L and invite him to her home. When he arrived the police arrested him. Nadine testified at the pretrial hearing. After Mr. L was arrested and spent a few days in jail he posted bail and was released. He was free at the time of our evaluation. Nadine worried that he would approach her. "He is going to go to jail for a long time so what would he have to lose?" The trial was set for several months in the future.

The sexual abuse occurred on nearly a daily basis, more often than was described in the court proceedings. There were four or five occasions of forced vaginal penetration. All occurred on the floor in the perpetrator's home or in the back seat of his car. The court proceedings described a number of occurrences of fellatio. Nadine thinks there were at least four times as many as described in the court documents. Sexual touching and masturbation occurred at least thirty or forty times. Mr. L ejaculated on most occasions. Mr. L covered his sexual interest in Nadine by telling her parents that he thought she was an exceptional student whom he wanted to help. "He manipulated them. What he did was terrible." Nadine did not understand how school officials didn't notice Mr. L's continuous interest in her. "I didn't see how they couldn't know. He was always looking at me and around me."

Diagnostic Interview with Mother

During the hourlong interview with Nadine's mother I took a developmental history and asked mother to describe her observations about how the abuse had affected her daughter.

Mother's pregnancy with Nadine was planned. There were no problems during the pregnancy. Mother did not use drugs or alcohol. The child was breast- and bottle fed. Nadine was weaned at approximately one year of age. Mother was home as the primary caretaker. Nadine was a good eater and slept through the night by six weeks of age. Developmental milestones occurred within normal limits. Speech development was early. Nadine was easily toilet trained. She made an excellent adjustment to preschool and kindergarten and has not had any major illnesses or operations.

During elementary school Nadine was well behaved, had lots of friends, and made excellent grades. She was a leader who loved sports and reading. Nadine reacted strongly to the parental divorce which occurred during these years. She became angry and disobedient for a short time. Her excellent academic performance continued. Nadine had her first menstrual period shortly before her eleventh birthday. She made a good adjustment to junior high school, and then the abuse began.

After the abuse began Nadine cried every night. Mother asked why she was crying but her daughter didn't provide any clear information. "Some days she would be in a ball, so clammed up." Nadine began pulling out her hair. She had never done that before. Nadine became very depressed. She cried all the time and slept on the floor. When she stopped doing homework her once excellent grades slipped. After Nadine lost her appetite mother took her to the family physician, who prescribed antidepressant medication and recommended therapy, which began soon after.

Continuing her discussion of the effects of the sexual abuse on Nadine, mother said, "She is a different child. She is forever changed. She stopped talking about the future." When mother asked Nadine if she was thinking about suicide she gave a noncommittal answer. "She may not even pass this year. She was in all honors classes and involved in sports and extracurricular activities."

Second Diagnostic Interview with Nadine

During this second diagnostic interview with Nadine I asked her to describe her sense of how the sexual abuse had affected her, and she replied, "It made me lose who I am. It slipped me into a deep depression and caused trust issues." Nadine was less confident, paranoid and jumpy. "It put me in counseling for god knows how long. I'm on an antidepressant." Her outlook on people had changed because people treated her differently. Friendships that she once had ended after the sexual abuse became known.

She continued, "It put more stress on me than a lot of adults have. It caused me to not really care about my grades. They went down drastically." Nadine noted that she had withdrawn from many social and extra-curricular activities. Further, she was afraid of Mr. L. "He isn't in jail. I don't get to go to the mall with my friends as I did." Her parents had become much more protective. At this point Nadine anxiously rushed from topic to topic.

"I don't remember what I was like before. I don't know what I want. I didn't want to live anymore. I didn't want to be around people." Nadine had suicidal thoughts but did not act on them. "I didn't care if I lived. I used to trust everyone until they gave me a reason not to. Now it's the other way round.

"I'm afraid of men, particularly strong men. It's affected my experience with all of my teachers. I won't go to them for help. I don't want to talk to them." Before the abuse Nadine described herself as a straight A student. Last semester she received Cs, one D and two or three Fs. "People who know treat me differently. They seem to be really cautious around me. Kids at school know. So do my friends and family. My dad doesn't know how to relate to me. I lost a lot of my friends. They ignore me." During the abuse she was "numb.

I guess you can say I wasn't really there. It's affected every single aspect of my life."

Psychological Testing

Nadine scored in the superior range of intellectual functioning.

On the MVVES, a self-report measure of trauma exposure and posttraumatic response, "she scores in the well above average range in terms of her overall level of distress, indicating that her most significant trauma involved her history of sexual assault. The degree of her reported distress remains clinically significant at the present time."

On the TSCC, a self-report measure of posttraumatic distress, "she responds to the TSCC in a manner that is quite typical for an adolescent with a history of sexual abuse. Endorsed critical items on this measure include being afraid of men, not trusting people because they may want sex, and being afraid someone will kill her."

On the PAI-A, a self-report, objective measure of personality functioning in adolescents, "her anxiety is of a degree that is unusual even in a clinical sample of adolescents, such that her life is probably quite constricted by her psychological turmoil. Although she tries to control her anxious feelings, these efforts have little effect on preventing her anxiety from intruding on her experiences and affecting her daily functioning."

The MACI is a self-report measure of personality functioning in adolescents. "Significant psychiatric symptoms include a dysthymic (depression) disorder marked by agitated and erratic qualities. She is likely to demonstrate sequential periods of self-deprecation and despair, anxiety and futility, bitter discontent and demanding irritability. Thrown off balance by an upsurge of moods and conflicts that she can neither understand nor control, she periodically turns against herself, voicing anger and self-loathing."

The Rorschach is a projective measure of personality functioning. "Avoidant symptoms predominate on this instrument, as Nadine presents as emotionally constricted, inhibiting her emotional expression and feeling burdened by irritating feelings. She actively avoids her emotions, and experiences a degree of psychic numbing . . . Overall, these results suggest that Nadine is a resilient individual with many personal strengths who is struggling to cope with the painful thoughts and feelings associated with her traumatic exposure to sexual assault through a maladaptive pattern of avoiding the experience and expression of her emotions, keeping her problems to herself as she tries to maintain a façade of competence that she used to experience prior to her victimization."

Using DSM-IV, the psychologist made a diagnosis of Posttraumatic Stress Disorder, Chronic.

Review of Records

The police report described the investigation and arrest of Mr. L for sexual abuse. Nadine, a fourteen-year-old white female, is described as the victim. A discussion with the campus resource officer indicated that Mr. L was very interested in Nadine. He was always touching and rubbing her arms and shoulders. When asked, Mr. L said that Nadine was an excellent student and he was only interested in helping her academically. The campus resource officer also spoke to Nadine about his concerns about her relationship with Mr. L. She put her head down and said that she would deal with it.

The court proceedings describe three counts of rape in the first degree, ten counts of forced oral sodomy, and eighteen counts of indecent or lewd acts with a child under sixteen. There was sufficient evidence to hold Mr. L for trial on all counts.

Nadine and her parents were seen at a local treatment center. A diagnosis of Major Depressive Disorder, Single Episode, Moderate was made. Nadine did not feel that the therapy helped. Various school records confirm that Nadine's grades were markedly affected by the sexual abuse. She was not achieving up to the level that would be expected of a teenager with a superior IQ and an excellent academic record.

Diagnosis

The following provides a second example in this book of how diagnoses were explored in detail in order to meet the criteria required for DSM-IV diagnoses. A similar determination was made in regard to every diagnosis in the other case studies in this book but will not be provided in subsequent case studies because of the primary focus on development, not diagnosis.

Axis I: Sexual Abuse of Child, V61.21, Clinical Focus on Victim 995.53. Posttraumatic Stress Disorder, Chronic 309.81. Nadine's abuse experience clearly meets the criteria for this diagnosis. She "was confronted with an event . . . that involved actual or threatened death or serious injury, or a threat to the physical integrity of self or others." Her response "involved intense fear, helplessness or horror."

The traumatic event was persistently reexperienced by "recurrent and intrusive distressing recollection of the event," "recurrent distressing dreams of the event," "flashback episodes," "intense psychological distress at exposure to internal or external cues that symbolize or resemble an aspect of the traumatic event," and "physiological reactivity on exposure to internal or external cues that symbolize or resemble an aspect of the traumatic event."

"Persistent avoidance of stimuli associated with the trauma and numbing of general responsiveness" as evidenced by "efforts to avoid thoughts, feelings or conversations associated with the trauma," "efforts to avoid activities, places or people that arouse recollections of the trauma," "markedly diminished interest or participation in significant activities," "feeling of detachment or estrangement from others," and "restricted range of affect."

"Persistent symptoms of increased arousal" are evidenced by "difficulty falling or staying asleep," "irritability or outbursts of anger," "difficulty concentrating," "hypervigilance and exaggerated startle response." The duration of the symptoms is more than one month. "The disturbance causes clinically significant distress or impairment in social, occupation, or other important areas of functioning." The Posttraumatic Stress Disorder is Chronic, indicating that the duration is more than three months.

Major Depressive Disorder, Single Episode 396.23 (severe without psychotic features).

This diagnosis is indicated due to "depressed mood most of the day, nearly every day," "markedly diminished interest or pleasure in all, or almost all, activities most of the day, nearly every day," "fatigue and loss of energy nearly every day," "feelings of worthlessness or excessive or inappropriate guilt nearly every day," "diminished ability to think or concentrate . . . nearly every day," and "recurrent thoughts of death."

Treatment

Nadine is in dire need of individual psychotherapy, three times per week, for three to four years. This treatment should be provided by an experienced child psychiatrist or psychologist. Antidepressant medication should be considered as an integral part of the therapy.

Because of the profound, extended nature of the sexual abuse, additional therapy will be required when Nadine is in her twenties and thirties. The purpose of the second and third courses of psychotherapy will be to help her deal successfully with the young adult issues of dating, sexuality, intimacy, marriage, raising children and career development.

Additional courses of psychotherapy may be needed in middle and late adulthood.

Prognosis

The prognosis, with treatment as outlined above, is fair. The prognosis without appropriate treatment is very poor.

Discussion

Nadine entered adolescence bright, accomplished, fully engaged in life and happy. There is no indication that she had any significant problems or psychopathology prior to the sexual abuse. At the age of thirteen she was severely traumatized by multiple experiences of fellatio and rape, over the course of a school year, by an authority figure.

All major developmental tasks of adolescence had been severely compromised. Her first sexual experiences, for which she was totally unprepared, were forced on her by an adult. The aggression involved in the multiple experiences of fellatio and rape made an indelible impression on the early teen and will contaminate and compromise future sexual activity with an appropriate partner. Further, Nadine is mistrustful of men and frightened of their intentions. Dating and beginning sexual experiences will likely be very delayed and highly conflicted rather than pleasurable. Intimacy in young adulthood will be most difficult if not impossible.

Peer relationships were severely affected. Nadine lost many friends due to her emotional withdrawal and the attitude of her peers once they became aware of the sexual abuse. The adolescent peer group can be extremely cruel, particularly regarding sexual matters, which are a source of anxiety and self-doubt while dating and first sexual experiences are occurring. This anxiety is often managed by attacking and joking about sexual behavior in others.

Nadine's relationship with her parents has been compromised. She was unable to tell them about the abuse for many months. When they did learn what had happened she became concerned that her parents would see her as degraded and damaged instead of as a teenager with a great future. Learning about the sexual abuse that happened to their daughter confronted the parents with the need to deal with pain and regret. Should they have been aware? Could they have protected their daughter? Would she ever be the same again? Nadine is aware of and greatly troubled by their suffering.

Academic progression was severely impacted. Nadine went from being an outstanding student to a poor one who was uncertain of passing into the ninth grade. The loss of self-esteem related to academic achievement, indeed to being thought of as an outstanding person and student, will be a factor for the remainder of Nadine's high school years. Further, unless her academic achievement returns to the pre-abuse level, college admission and career planning will be severely affected.

Nadine is suffering from two major psychiatric diagnoses, Posttraumatic Stress Disorder and Major Depressive Disorder. Because of her intelligence, mature bearing, excellent vocabulary, and tendency to withdraw into herself and present a bland exterior, she appears to be more intact than she really is. However, as evidenced by the many quotes about her thoughts and feelings regarding the abuse, it is evident that the harmful effects have been pervasive and devastating.

The severity of the sexual abuse that Nadine experienced will continue to have a deleterious effect on her for the remainder of her life. It is difficult to overstate the psychological damage she has suffered and will continue to suffer because of the cruel and aggressive sexual abuse by Mr. L.

LATENCY/ADOLESCENT CASE STUDY: SALLY

Sally was eighteen years of age when I evaluated her in connection with her lawsuit against a neighbor who began sexually abusing her when she was seven years of age. The abuse continued until approximately age twelve. However, the molestation was not discovered until Sally was almost seventeen years of age. Her adolescent development, as will become clear as this chapter continues, was profoundly affected, to the present. The evaluation consisted of two diagnostic interviews with Sally and one with her mother. In addition a full battery of psychological testing was performed by an experienced psychologist, and therapy, school and court records were reviewed. The perpetrator was convicted and was in jail at the time of the civil suit.

First and Second Diagnostic Interviews with Sally

Soon after Sally entered my office it became clear that I was talking to a young woman in great distress. Despite being eighteen years of age, her meekness, inaudible vocal productions and somewhat disheveled dress gave the immediate impression that she was much younger and not very intelligent. Sally began by telling me that she had graduated from high school within the last year and was looking for work. Living at home with her parents and thinking about going to junior college, Sally was having difficulty deciding what to do with her life now that high school was over.

Mental Status Examination

Although Sally was able to address the subject of the sexual abuse and its effects, her sentences were often vague and unfinished, as though she could not bring the proper words to express herself into consciousness. Her affect was extremely flat and although she was able to relate to me, I had the impression of a young woman emotionally suffocated by an extreme need to avoid thoughts and feelings about the sexual abuse. There was no evidence of delusions or hallucinations but great difficulty in organizing thoughts and speaking spontaneously was continually present. The somewhat disjointed presentation of the information that follows is an attempt on my part to give the reader a sense of how disorganized and fragmented Sally's thinking was on the subject of the sexual abuse.

"The abuse affected me more than I realized when it started. It also affected my mom. I know it's a big deal but I just want to block it out. It's in the past. I just want to forget it." Recently Sally and her parents moved away from the neighborhood they had lived in for years to avoid the perpetrator's family and the memories associated with the abuse. However, Sally often needs to drive by the old neighborhood. "My family trusted them (the neighbors, whom we will call the Zs). It was an abuse of trust. I was very shy in middle school. I was always thinking about the abuse. I was hiding it from everyone." My sense as I listened was that withdrawal would be a more accurate description of Sally's lack of ability to communicate with peers and teachers. The abuse was discovered approximately two years ago when a friend told a school counselor that she thought Sally was being sexually abused. "I only hinted to her what was going on. I wanted to tell my mother for a long time but I couldn't find the words."

The Zs would call and offer to take Sally to the mall or shopping. Although she didn't want to go and knew Mr. Z would abuse her, she couldn't bring herself to say no.

"I always got nervous when I was with him. I kinda shut down. I wanted to resist him. I'd get worked up and shut down. When I was with him I'd stand there. He'd do things to me. I just shut down." As her thoughts continued in a disconnected way, Sally noted that after the abuse was discovered "people told me that I didn't have to feel bad. I do feel a little bit of guilt."

When I asked about friendships in high school Sally said, "I was a loner. I didn't have a lot of close friends. I try to be outgoing now but I'm still pretty much alone." Sally began to talk to boys in her junior year in high school. She had a boyfriend for a few months. "We made out but we didn't do the things that happened with Mr. Z."

The Abuse

Sally was unable to speak coherently about the details of the sexual abuse. It was told in bits and pieces. Apparently Mr. Z would take Sally upstairs in his house. He had her sit on the bed then made her undress and took pictures. "He kissed me a couple of times" (she could not continue). Sally nodded in agreement when, using information obtained from legal documents, I mentioned that he had her masturbate him and perform fellatio. Later she added that sometimes he gave her drugs and alcohol.

Therapy

When I asked about her psychotherapy Sally said the therapist tried to approach the sexual abuse but they hadn't gotten very far. Sally had been going for about a year. It was once a week for a while, then every other week. "I haven't seen her for a while. Maybe it was a month ago."

As I reviewed the diagnostic criteria for Posttraumatic Stress Disorder with Sally she revealed the following additional information. Intrusive thoughts about Mr. Z and the sexual abuse were present many times each day. Sally has dreams about the sexual abuse. It was difficult for her to describe details although some dreams dealt with specific sexual experiences with Mr. Z. Dreams occur less frequently than they did while the abuse was occurring but they are present numerous times each year.

Flashbacks occur frequently, to the present. Again, Sally had difficulty describing the content. Some were stimulated by interviews during the criminal proceedings. Sally is unable to avoid thoughts and feelings about the abuse. When she is preoccupied with details of the abuse she cannot think or concentrate. Participation in age-appropriate activities has been markedly diminished from the time of the abuse to the present. Sally has extremely strong feelings of detachment and a pronounced restriction of affect. She described herself as irritable and angry and had obvious difficulty in concentrating. "My mind is always watching out for Mr. Z or some other man like him."

Diagnostic Interview with Mother

Mother described Sally as very anxious and depressed, eating irregularly and lacking in confidence. She began to notice a difference in her daughter in third or fourth grade. Sally began wetting herself at school. An evaluation by a pediatrician failed to discover an organic cause. The wetting, always during the day, continued occasionally throughout middle school and high school and still occurs. Elementary school teachers began to comment that Sally spent her time daydreaming. She was not paying attention and did not seem able to concentrate. In middle school Sally "really started to fall apart. She shut down and couldn't cope." The school suggested special classes and extra help in completing assignments. "That's the only reason why she graduated. She didn't have the normal coping skills to deal with anything. She would go off by herself and zone."

Mother was particularly distressed when Sally began neglecting her hygiene. She wouldn't take showers for days on end unless forced to do so. On other occasions she stayed in the shower forever. Sally has difficulty leaving the house and rarely initiates any activities. "Sally missed out on all the normal things kids her age do, close friends, dating, having fun. There is no bond with friends."

Mother spoke of Sally's "maddening" disorganization. Sally overanalyzes everything and takes too long to get ready for everything. "She's much more anxious. She has periods of depression too. I had no idea what was going on. She won't get a job. All she wants to do it be with the family. It's a nightmare that doesn't go away." The therapist was very frustrated too. "Sally didn't want to talk and she was late all the time. I don't know how much was accomplished." Mother discovered the pervasive nature of the sexual abuse by reading legal documents. She was shocked by the accounts of masturbation, oral sex and the use of drugs and alcohol to enable Mr. Z to dominate Sally.

Mother provided the following developmental information. Sally was the product of a planned pregnancy which went to full term. There were no problems with the pregnancy, labor or delivery. The infant was breast fed for several months. Mother was home on a full-time basis and was the primary caretaker. Sally has not had any major illnesses or operations at any point in her life. She was toilet trained easily and from approximately the age of three until she began to wet during the day after the sexual abuse began there was no loss of bowel or bladder control.

Sally was a very easygoing, loving, happy child who separated easily when attending kindergarten. She was considered to be a rapid learner who had a fine memory. Sally was very successful academically in the early elementary grades and had numerous friends. She loved to dance and swim. The family took frequent vacations. Then dramatic changes occurred during the fourth grade.

Puberty occurred when Sally was approximately thirteen years of age. The enormous psychological, social and academic deterioration that occurred during the later elementary, junior and senior high school years has been described in prior sections of this case study.

Psychological Testing

In addition to clinical interviews with Sally and her mother the psychologist administered a Mini-Mental State Examination, Detailed Assessment of Posttraumatic Stress, Trauma Symptom Inventory, Multiscale Dissociation Inventory, Beck Depression Inventory, 2nd Edition, Adult Manifest Anxiety Scale, OCD Screener, Personality Assessment Inventory and Rorschach and Thematic Apperception Tests. Mother completed the Behavioral Assessment System for Children, 2nd Edition.

There was no evidence on the testing of any type of cognitive deficit.

After administering the Detailed Assessment of Posttraumatic Stress the psychologist reported the following: "Sally reports having significant re-experiencing and avoidant symptoms. She reports being plagued by recol-lections of the traumatic event, along with feeling that she cannot control these intrusive thoughts and feelings. She makes conscious attempts to avoid people, places, conversations and situations that might trigger intrusive re-experiencing symptoms, and also avoids her feelings. In addition, there is evidence of significant withdrawal, apathy and emotional numbing. She is reluctant to discuss her problems with therapists or others, and may have problems with treatment adherence. This avoidance pattern is often associ-ated with a more severe and chronic course . . . at the present time, she reports having developed significant dissociative symptoms following the trauma that remain present at this time."

In discussing the results of the Rorschach the psychologist commented that Sally "perceives herself as inadequate in relation to others . . . She is at con-siderable risk for being flooded by affect and overwhelmed by more emotion than she can tolerate. The threat of emotional overload interferes with her ability to think before she acts, and also interferes with her ability to maintain attention and concentration . . . Cognitively she demonstrates no evidence of a thought disorder."

The stories on the Thematic Apperception Test were filled with "themes of loss, sadness and not being able to have what she wants."

The psychologist suggested as diagnostic possibilities Posttraumatic Stress Disorder, Chronic, with Anxiety and Obsessive-Compulsive Features, Dys-thymic Disorder and dependent personality features. He rated her symptoms in the moderate to severe range.

School Records

High school records indicate four years of marginal grades, frequent incompletes, excessive absences, little effort and failure to meet standards. Special class placements and tutoring allowed Sally to meet the minimal stan-dards for graduation. She graduated at the bottom of her class.

Therapy Records

Sally was seen by a social worker. She was treated with antidepressant medication and psychotherapy. The therapist's diagnosis was Major Depres-sive Disorder, Single Episode, Moderate and Anxiety Disorder. Therapy notes indicate a continuous sense of being overwhelmed and experiencing anxiety and fear on a daily basis. Toward the end of her senior year Sally had significant problems with attendance. She was also very stressed by the legal proceedings and hearings related to the criminal investigation and trial.

Sally was able to tell the therapist that she felt very vulnerable when naked or when taking a shower. The absence of clothing brought back strong memories and feelings of being abused by Mr. Z. On occasion, Sally went a week without bathing. She repeatedly asked the question, "why me?" Sally felt intense shame when remembering the sexual acts that took place with Mr. Z. She had thoughts of harming herself but never acted on these impulses. The therapist made frequent references to disorganized thinking, particularly if there was any mention of the sexual abuse. Sally's presentation in the therapy sessions sounds exactly like the manner in which she looked and talking during my diagnostic evaluation.

Diagnosis

Using DSM-IV I made the following diagnoses:
Sexual Abuse of a Child V61.21, 995.53; Clinical Focus on the Victim, Post-traumatic Stress Disorder, Chronic 309.81; and Major Depressive Disorder, Single Episode 296.22.

A diagnosis of Dependent Personality Disorder was indicated on Axis II. Sally had significant problems with severe dependence feelings toward her parents and discomfort in leaving home. She was unable to relate to peers and isolated herself from appropriate age-related activities. The ability to concentrate and learn was extremely compromised, as was the ability to work. Sally's symptoms were in the 41–50, serious range

Treatment

Sally's response to the chronic sexual abuse that occurred in latency and early adolescence is one of the most severe that I have seen. She is badly in need of intensive psychotherapeutic intervention. Individual psychotherapy, two to three times per week for at least three or four years, is indicated immediately. Antidepressant and/or anti-anxiety medication should be utilized as an integral component of the treatment plan. A therapist with extensive experience in treating victims of sexual abuse should conduct the treatment.

Outpatient therapy may not be sufficient to manage the profound developmental interferences which are preventing this young woman from engaging comfortably in age-appropriate activities and relationships. An intensive day treatment or inpatient program should be provided if individual psychotherapy on an outpatient basis is unsuccessful.

Two additional courses of individual psychotherapy, assuming that the initial treatment outlined above is successful, will be needed at the time of courtship and marriage and later if and when Sally's children are nearing the ages at which she was abused.

Prognosis

The prognosis is very guarded.

Discussion

All of the major developmental tasks of the latency and adolescent phases of development were severely impacted by the chronic sexual abuse by Mr. Z that occurred repeatedly over a four- to five-year span between the ages of seven and twelve.

From third or fourth grade onward this bright girl, who had been a promising student in the early elementary grades, began to underachieve in school. She gradually became intensely preoccupied and withdrawn in class and increasingly uninterested in learning. As Sally withdrew, involvement with peers in friendships and group activities became extremely limited. Prior to the sexual abuse Sally was an outgoing, happy child who enjoyed playing with friends and participating in group activities. Her interests in hobbies, lessons of various kinds and participation in sports also diminished significantly. Sally expressed little or no interest in these activities and only participated when forced to do so by her parents.

Latency is the phase of development when children of both sexes learn what it means to be a boy or a girl in their culture. This process takes place through relationships and identifications with parents and mentors who provide examples of what masculinity or femininity means. These interactions take place, normally, in the absence of any sexual involvement with peers or adults. Sally's repeated sexual encounters with Mr. Z flooded her mind and body with emotions and experiences that she was completely unable to integrate. This intense sexual preoccupation and fixation totally prevented Sally from developing a healthy latency-age, or adolescent, sexual identity.

Early adolescents must cope with the developmental task of integrating the emerging presence of a sexually mature body into their identity and mental life. After the onset of puberty (narrowly defined as the first ejaculation in the boy and the first menstrual period in the girl) the individual of either sex must become accustomed to the rapidly changing physical body and the powerful sexual urges that flood his or her body. This integration takes place normally through discussions with peers, in sexual education classes and with parents—but entirely in the absence of any sexual involvement with adults. As the teen gradually becomes accustomed to the sexually mature body experimentation with peers begins, leading to the beginning establishment of pleasurable sexual relationships in middle and late adolescence.

Sally was repeatedly introduced to such adult experiences as mutual masturbation, oral sex, and very likely other sexual acts that occurred when she was drugged, before puberty occurred. The developmental process of gradually becoming comfortable with the physically and sexually mature body was totally derailed, as was the process of beginning to date and develop relationships with age-appropriate peers in middle and late adolescence. At nineteen, she is intensely ashamed of her nude body and has no meaningful experience with relationships. Without intensive treatment it is highly unlikely that she will be able to tolerate dating and eventually courtship and marriage during young adulthood.

While many adolescents experience mood swings and inconsistent behavior as they engage the adolescent developmental processes, Sally became depressed, withdrawn and isolated from peers and parents. This pattern continued throughout the adolescent years and will continue into young adulthood without significant therapeutic intervention.

The severity of Sally's psychopathology is clearly indicated by the presence of the inability to control urination during the day, a developmental task that is usually mastered by age three or four. Daytime wetting, which began during the years of the sexual abuse and continues to the present, is a very unusual and highly significant symptom in an adolescent/young adult.

The ability to think abstractly increases significantly during adolescence and becomes a central factor in formal learning. It is clear from the clinical interview and psychological testing evaluation that Sally is of at least average intelligence and capable of abstract thinking, but the ability to think is so compromised by intrusive sexual thoughts and affects that she often appears to be disorganized, fragmented and incapable of coherent thought. As a result of this pathology Sally was only able to graduate from high school with intensive help and since high school has not been able to use her intelligence in the service of pursuing higher education or employment. Like the other major developmental tasks of adolescence, the ability to choose a career path is severely arrested.

CASE STUDY: CAREY

Carey was thirteen years of age and in eighth grade when she first met Mr. S, a teacher at her school. He seemed friendly to everyone and she thought that it would be nice to have him as a teacher. During the ninth-grade year, when he did teach her, she developed a crush on Mr. S. He was handsome, friendly and very smart. She worked hard to get a good grade in his class and Mr. S began to pay attention to her. Carey began to fantasize about what Mr. S's life was like. Was he married? Did he have any children? One day she got brave enough to ask him if he was married. "Yes, but not necessarily happily married," he responded with a wink and a laugh. Later Carey learned that Mr. S had been well aware of her romantic interest in him.

As the academic year progressed they talked a lot. Carey enrolled in the extra-curricular club that Mr. S supervised. Several times she stayed after the other students left to help him clean up the club room. Mr. S began to ask Carey to help out with club activities. On a few occasions he drove her home after the club meeting. During the following academic year, while driving Carey home after a club meeting, Mr. S. put his arm around her. A few months later on a similar drive he stopped the car and kissed her. As Mr. S began to show an interest in her Carey went, as she put it, "from infatuation to love." She was fifteen years of age. As kissing progressed to petting Mr. S asked if they could take their relationship "to the next level" when she turned sixteen. By that he meant intercourse. Carey was a virgin who had been on a few dates but had never had a boyfriend or any sexual involvement other than kissing.

They had intercourse for the first time a few months later, shortly after her sixteenth birthday. Carey's parents were aware of their daughter's interest in Mr. S but assumed that he was a caring teacher acting as a well-intentioned mentor toward one of his bright students. They had no awareness of the sexual relationship between student and teacher until several years later.

"I was really in love with him. I felt really guilty. It was stressful. I felt guilty coming home each time. I thought we were unique and society's rules were wrong. He was very admiring of me. He said he was in love with me." Mr. S said that there were problems in his marriage but he loved his kids.

During junior year the relationship continued. One day Mr. S drove Carey to his home where they had sex on his bedroom floor. Carey felt terrible afterwards and tried to end the relationship. Mr. S pursued her and their interactions became more frequent, often leading to intercourse two or three times per week. "I still felt always conflicted but deeply attached to him. He understood me better than anyone in the world. I thought our love redeemed any moral issues. My friends suspected and pulled away. He and I talked all the time. It was really consuming." The fact that Mr. S and Carey had a special relationship was obvious to some of Carey's friends and possibly to other teachers but no one ever reported their suspicions to school authorities.

During her senior year Mr. S began to talk about divorcing his wife and marrying Carey after she finished college. By this point Carey's life was completely centered on Mr. S. She had little contact with friends and was totally preoccupied with thoughts and feelings about him and their future. Despite having excellent grades and the probability of getting into whatever college she chose, Carey debated about leaving Mr. S. She finally settled on a college nearby so they could see each other frequently. The relationship continued during the first two years of college. Over the years Carey had continued to tell her parents that Mr. S was a teacher who had become a friend. She invited him to her graduation party and Mr. S had occasional conversations with Carey's parents about how she was doing at college. Despite this they were totally unprepared when their daughter and Mr. S announced that they loved each other and wanted to be together in the future. When her parents reacted with shock and dismay, particularly after they learned that the sexual interaction began when Carey was fifteen, Carey felt "horribly uncomfortable." "I didn't know who to comfort first, Mr. S or my parents. I started to get different views. My parents told me what we had done was horribly wrong, that Mr. S was irresponsible. Five days before my father said that I thought I was going to get married."

The parents confided in a teacher/friend who told them they must call the police. The police asked to interview Carey, who was still at college. "I arrived at the sickening conclusion I shouldn't be with Mr. S anymore. I told him that but I kept changing my mind. I had to talk to the police. I knew all along that what we were doing was illegal." Mr. S was charged, tried and sent to prison. As the months of investigation and trial proceeded Carey continued to feel that she was in love with Mr. S. But as time passed, "I thought it was right that there be legal consequences but I didn't want him to go to jail." She worried about what would happen to his family if he were incarcerated.

During the time Mr. S was in prison, with the assistance of professional help, Carey gradually understood how Mr. S had taken advantage of her and began to feel anger and resentment alongside continuing feelings of love and attachment. She estimated that they had intercourse more than one hundred times.

Developmental History

Why did such an intelligent teenager fall victim to this abusive teacher? There is little in her background that helps us understand. Carey was physically healthy throughout her life. Mother was the primary caretaker and very involved in raising her daughter. Developmental milestones such as walking, talking, bowel and bladder control and participation in preschool were easily achieved. From the first day at preschool it was clear that this was a very bright child.

Her parents separated when Carey was in elementary school but remained on good terms and shared the custody of their daughter after the divorce. During the elementary school years Carey was well liked by teachers, had lots of friends and got excellent grades. Hobbies included reading, drawing and music lessons.

Carey had her first period during sixth grade. She had been prepared by mother and seemed to adjust to the physical changes of adolescence easily. Carey experienced her first kiss when she was in eighth grade. She and the boy went "steady" for one week and then broke up. During senior high school Carey had dates with two boys her age. Mr. S encouraged these interactions. Neither relationship got beyond the first date. "They weren't the right people for me. I preferred Mr. S."

As previously described, Carey's high school years were entirely centered on Mr. S. She continued to achieve academically but had little involvement with friends or school activities and functions. "I didn't need anything or anyone else, I had Mr. S." Once in college Carey continued to excel academically. However, her mental and emotional life remained focused on Mr. S both before and after the discovery of their relationship by her parents and eventually the authorities. After the breakup Carey's involvement with males consisted of several one-night stands, a clear reflection of the inner turmoil and developmental interference which resulted from the years of abuse. She had never been sexually or physically abused prior to meeting Mr. S.

Developmental Interferences and Symptomatic Consequences of the Chronic Adolescent Sexual Abuse

Carey was first seen approximately one year after the sexual abuse had ended. Her lawsuit against the perpetrator was in process. Very intelligent and verbal, she expressed the following observations, developmental interferences and symptomatic consequences.

"I became isolated from people my age. I felt this experience marked me and made me different from people my age but I thought that any other relationship would feel immoral." Carey felt guilt because "I seduced him. It was my fault." Because of the absence of any significant relationship with boys her own age during high school she felt that only older men were attracted to her. "I feel very mistrustful of my feelings of love since I've been so messed up by them. I felt there was something sick when people were attracted to me. In the beginning I really missed Mr. S."

Carey felt depressed and disconnected from herself. "I didn't have time to know who I was. I was upset and confused. I can't connect with people. I'm lonely." In an attempt to deal with her loneliness and lack of power in the relationship with Mr. S, Carey initiated casual sex with men. "It wasn't satisfying. Now I've decided to be alone until I figure it out. There seems to be danger in being wrapped up in somebody else. I haven't had any real dating relationships." When college men have approached Carey she either rejected them because they were not attractive or they seemed too intense. "It seemed like the last guy wanted to drain my life." Recently Carey began to restore relationships with girlfriends. "Connecting with people is hard. I feel different. They can't understand where I was coming from."

Carey frequently dreams about Mr. S. "He is trying to be affectionate. Sometimes I say 'what do you think you're doing.' Other times we have sex."

Attempts at Therapy

Carey saw a therapist at school for a brief period. "I stopped seeing her. She was sympathetic and it was annoying. She agreed with everything I said. She wanted to talk about Mr. S and I wanted to talk about other things." Carey was about to begin therapy with another, very experienced psychiatrist but she had significant doubts that the therapy would do any good. She preferred to avoid thinking about Mr. S and just wanted to move on with her life, this despite the dawning awareness that the chronic sexual abuse had had a significant effect on all areas of her life. Like most child abuse victims, regardless of age, she preferred to avoid rather than confront the experience.

Psychological Testing

An experienced psychologist administered a full battery of objective and subjective tests. Some of his findings follow. Carey's IQ was in the very superior range.

"The effects of this lengthy exploitative, abusive and destructive relationship have produced major disruptions and significant impairment in nearly all areas and aspects of Carey's development and psychosocial functioning. While areas of intellectual functioning and achievement have been thus far robust, aspects of her self-image, sexuality, interpersonal relatedness, social functioning and the normative development of a comfortable identity and the burgeoning capacity for intimacy have been grossly impaired and greatly negatively distorted."

"During the abusive relationship Carey experienced high levels of anxiety and guilt. She felt embarrassed and isolated from friends based on her 'secret life.' The 'huge secret' also resulted in constant lies and concealment producing distance and detachment from parents and friends."

"Carey had no history of significant heterosexual relationships and sexual involvement prior to the abusive relationship. The relationship was understandably extremely intense, confusing and eventually painful and traumatic. Carey has not engaged in any developmentally appropriate or normative efforts to initiate or maintain a significant intimate relationship subsequent to the abusive relationship. She describes a complete lack of any heterosexual involvement that includes feelings of genuine closeness, depth, connection or empathy. Sexuality and sexual behavior are extremely conflict-laden for Carey." She presently lacks any real capacity to positively, comfortably and realistically engage in more significant relationships.

"She employs intellectualized and avoidant defensive maneuvers in an attempt to minimize and limit awareness of painful and disruptive thoughts and feelings . . . She is guarded, fearful and suspicious regarding the intentions and motivations of others. Emotional stimulation is strictly limited and avoided. She often feels judged, criticized and self-conscious. She yearns to feel appreciated and special, but simultaneously anticipates exploitation and/ or rejection."

Using DSM-IV the psychologist made diagnoses of Sexual Abuse of Child and Major Depressive Disorder, Single Episode and addressed the need for intensive, long-term treatment.

Follow-up Interview

I saw Carey again approximately a year after our first meeting. She talked more easily and openly about her life after Mr. S. "It upsets me to think about what he did to me [sighs] and the difficulties I'm having now because of it. It makes me sad." The loving feelings toward Mr. S which were present a year before were replaced by resentment and anger.

When I asked how she was doing she volunteered the following: "It's really hard to conceive of a healthy romantic relationship. I have no understanding of positive sexuality. I only know how to relate to a guy through sex. I haven't formed any lasting relationships. It doesn't make me feel good." Her friendships were also affected. "I was so isolated in high school it was hard to break into groups in college. I'm struggling to get over that.

"My relationship to myself is difficult. I feel damaged and tainted. I judge myself." Carey went on to describe intense anxiety accompanied by rapid heart rate, sometimes for days at a time. The anxiety can be set off by minor things or in anticipation of dating. "I feel low, not immersed in my life. I'm never sure how I will be. I'm less hopeful. I retreat more. I have less energy."

A few more one-night stands had occurred since I saw her a year ago. Carey tried dating without having sex but was unsuccessful. "I don't know how to act to achieve a relationship without sex. I must be doing things that signal the guy. I don't even know I'm doing it. Both younger and older men are attracted to me but it seems purely sexual. I feel like I understand better that I didn't seduce him. He seduced me."

At the time of our diagnostic session a year ago and for several months afterward Carey continued to have frequent dreams about Mr. S. Either they would get back together or Mr. S would approach her sexually and she would get disgusted. Recently the dreams have lessened in frequency and intensity.

Carey has continued to see the therapist she met with for the first time a year ago. They often meet once per week but vacations and the pressure of work have reduced the frequency of the sessions. Carey still found therapy very difficult and oftentimes had to force herself to go. She felt that she was getting something out of the therapy sessions but it was clear there was still considerable internal resistance to looking at the sexually abusive relationship and its enormous consequences for her present and future.

Diagnosis

Using DSM-IV I made the following diagnoses: Sexual Abuse of Child V61.21; Clinical Focus on Victim 995.53; Major Depressive Disorder, Single Episode 296.25; and Parent-Child Relationship Problem V61.20. Symptoms of Posttraumatic Stress Disorder were present but not enough to satisfy the criteria in the *Manual.* Carey's relationship with her parents was complicated by lying and significant deception. She was estranged from friends and unable to integrate adolescent sexual development. During the years of the abuse her symptoms were in the 41–50, serious range. At the time of the follow-up evaluation I rated them in the 51–60, moderate range.

Treatment Recommendations

In the immediate future Carey is in need of individual psychotherapy, two to three times per week for three to four years. In the decade from the mid-twenties to the mid-thirties (depending on the timing of marriage and children) individual psychotherapy two times per week for two to three years. Antidepressant medication is indicated.

Prognosis

The prognosis, with the treatment outlined above, is fair.

Discussion

Effect on Adolescent Development

The sexual abuse began when Carey was in mid-adolescence. It affected all aspects of adolescent development and continues to have a significant negative effect on the developmental tasks of young adulthood.

As described in the chapter on normal adolescent development, adolescent girls are particularly vulnerable to the sexual designs of older men, particularly those with whom they have a relationship who are in positions of authority, such as high school teachers, because they develop crushes on them. Still in the process of dealing with the powerful sexual and emotional feelings which occur following the onset of physical and sexuality maturity, they need time and a safe environment in which to integrate the tremendous physical and emotional changes which are rapidly taking place.

The emergence of crushes facilitates the normal developmental process by providing, in fantasy, a safe place to direct sexual feelings which are not ready to be acted on. As adolescence progresses and sexual feelings and thoughts are integrated crushes diminish in frequency and intensity and are replaced by age-appropriate relationships with peers.

But crushes are also developed toward adults with whom the adolescent girl does have a relationship. This is particularly true of schoolteachers because of the nearly daily contact during the school year. This phenomenon is well recognized and understood by those who teach junior high school students. Teachers learn to gently set limits on these relationships without destroying self-esteem. But others, such as Mr. S, use this normal developmental process to groom underage girls for their sexual purposes.

Carey was clearly infatuated with Mr. S and let him know her feelings by working hard in his class, joining his extracurricular club and demonstrating feelings of admiration and awe, in addition to her sexual interest in him. As he groomed her by nurturing her crush and by inappropriately returning her interest and failing to set appropriate limits on their relationship, he prepared Carey to be sexually abused.

As Carey's infatuation with Mr. S deepened and their relationship progressed, she pulled away from her friends. Her interests, activities and thoughts were increasingly directed toward Mr. S and away from friends and potential boyfriends. Friendships are vital relationships which facilitate the normal adolescent developmental process in the following manner. Friends of the same sex, who are experiencing similar sexual and relationship issues, are available to compare and share experiences. Beginning romantic relationships with age-appropriate peers provide opportunities to gradually gain sexual experience with others at the same level of experience and development.

Carey lost the opportunity to compare notes with her girlfriends due to her withdrawal from them and the need to keep the relationship with Mr. S secret. She missed the opportunity to be gradually introduced to sexual activity within an age-appropriate caring relationship, at a pace of her choosing. Instead, her first sexual experiences occurred within an abusive relationship initiated by an adult who took advantage of her for his own sexual purposes. Totally under Mr. S's physical and emotional domination, she had no way of understanding the devastating effect that the sexual abuse would have on her self-esteem in the future.

Over the course of the adolescent years there is gradual movement away from dependence on parents toward independence and autonomy. As the adolescent struggles against parental limits and restraints and begins to date and have independent relationships and activities, both parent and child redefine their relationship. Although withholding information from parents about one's activities and relationships is to be expected, most major issues in the adolescent's life are known by and negotiated with parents. Dating relationships would certainly fall in that category. But Carey, like most victims of child sexual abuse, did not, could not, tell her parents about the abuse. The relationship with Mr. S prevented the gradual adolescent process of separation and individuation from parents from occurring.

Effect on Young Adult Development

As she moves into young adulthood Carey is experiencing significant problems because of the effects of the chronic adolescent sexual abuse.

As they leave home and go off to college or work, late adolescents gradually make the shift from being dependent children to becoming self-sufficient young adults. When Carey left for college she was deeply involved with Mr. S on an emotional and sexual level. Her dependency on him for a sense of identity and well-being significantly compromised her ability to enter college as an individual, ready to stand on her own two feet, meet new people and accept the academic challenges of college. The separation-individuation process of young adulthood did not begin in any significant way until after the abusive relationship became known, Mr. S went to prison, and Carey began to think of her self as an individual, on her own for the first time, no longer dependent on her parents or Mr. S.

During adolescence individuals of both sexes first become familiar with the sexual nature of their physically mature bodies and then gradually become involved with peers. Dating and early sexual encounters are primarily self-focused and in the service of learning how to function sexually with another person.

In young adulthood, after some degree of comfort has been achieved in regard to sexuality the developmental task is to gradually develop the capacity for intimacy—namely, the ability to genuinely care for the partner at least as much as the self and to elevate emotional closeness and relatedness to an equal level with sexual satisfaction.

At the time of the follow-up interview, approximately one year after the sexual abuse ended, Carey had no ability whatsoever to engage in a caring, intimate relationship with a young man. In an attempt to master the trauma of the sexual abuse she sought out a number of one-night stands which were emotionally devastating. She cannot conceptualize herself in a loving relationship and feels that men are interested in her only for their own selfish sexual needs, as she now believes was the case with Mr. S.

Carey is experiencing strong feelings of frustration, futility and depression, doubting that she will ever be able to have what she characterized as a normal relationship with a man. She cannot conceive of a relationship which would culminate in marriage and parenthood. It will take a major therapeutic intervention to change this damaging self-perception, which is the direct result of having been chronically sexually abused.

Carey has made some progress in rebuilding relationships with family and friends. She now has an honest, open relationship with her parents and has made considerable efforts to be less isolated and more involved with friends.

In her present mental state Carey is likely to have significant difficulty traversing the young adult years. It is questionable at this moment whether she will be able to achieve a life that includes love, work and a family, accompanied by an inner sense of equanimity free from major interference from the memory and effects of the years-long sexual abuse.

ADDITIONAL COMMENTS ON THESE THREE CASES

The degree of disorganization in thinking and feeling that Sally experiences at age eighteen, five years after the sexual abuse ended, demonstrates how symptoms can actually become intensified after the sexual abuse ends. It also underscores the need for early discovery and treatment of victims such as Sally. An unanswered question is why some victims, such as Sally and the three boys in the previous chapter, experience such a significant interference with thinking and formal learning, while others, like Carey, continue to achieve academically. Some of the older victims whose stories are presented in later chapters also were able to complete college and work productively throughout their adult years. A possible answer may lie in the use of formal learning and work as a refuge from thoughts and feelings about the sexual abuse which could not be avoided when the mind was less focused.

It is worth mentioning again that *any* unusual interest in a child/adolescent, by anyone, be it family member, friend, teacher or coach should raise the suspicion index in regard to sexual abuse. Why didn't these parents, indeed, most of the parents in this book, understand what was going on? Should they have suspected? Without knowledge of and experience with the almost incomprehensible behavior of perpetrators, which is so totally foreign to the thinking of healthy adults, very few parents link a known adult's interest in their child with sexual abuse. Certainly parents, educators, and children are more aware than ever before, but the perpetrator behavior presented throughout this book is so disgusting to the average layperson that it tends to be pushed out of consciousness as quickly as possible.

Another warning sign of sexual abuse is a withdrawal from friends and peer group activities. The friendships of all three of these girls became superficial and peripheral. Nadine and Carey, both of whom were involved with teachers, gradually withdrew from their friends as they became more involved with the perpetrators. Sally, who was abused during latency, never developed normal friendships in either latency or adolescence. I have always used comfortable acceptance and involvement in the peer group as an excellent indicator of the presence or absence of psychopathology of any kind. In the many cases of sexual abuse by teachers and coaches that I have seen over the years, friends and acquaintances in the peer group always knew, or strongly suspected, that the involvement was more than platonic. Very often, a peer was the first to inform parents or authorities of the sexual abuse.

The moodiness, inconsistent behavior and relative withdrawal from family and friends that are observed in sexually abused adolescents are also seen in normal adolescents as they struggle to master the great physical, sexual and psychological changes confronting them. When in doubt parents and educators should opt for a thorough diagnostic evaluation by an experienced child psychiatrist or child psychologist in order to chart the appropriate developmental course for the adolescent in question.

These three cases convincingly demonstrate the devastating developmental effects in the years immediately following the end of the sexual abuse. Adolescent and young adult development was severely compromised. The cases, toward the end of the book, of men and women in their forties, fifties and sixties, show similar effects over not just a few years but over decades. As the years and decades after the abuse ends increase in number the individual's symptom picture becomes more complicated as new developmental tasks are compromised and old ones remain unresolved.

5

Young Adulthood

THE TRANSITION FROM ADOLESCENCE
TO YOUNG ADULTHOOD

The transition from adolescence to young adulthood is based on the real and psychological separation from the family of origin and the engagement of the phase-specific tasks of young adulthood. Peter Blos (1979) described the process as "the shedding of family dependencies, the loosening of infantile object ties in order to become a member of society at large, or simply, of the adult world" (p. 142). The length of time it takes to make the transition from dependent child to independent adult—alone in the world and enjoying it, but not yet ready for permanent attachments to a significant other and children—varies from person to person. Levinson et al. (1978) suggest that the transition from late adolescence to young adulthood occurs between the ages of seventeen and twenty-two. During these years, the individual resolves the issues of childhood dependency sufficiently to establish self-reliance. The goal is "to explore, to expand one's horizons and put off making firmer commitments until the options are clear; and to create an initial life structure, to have roots, stability, and continuity" (p. 80).

Another important intrapsychic aspect of the transition is a redefinition of the childhood and adolescent past. For the first time an entire phase of life is consigned to the past. This process, which is gradual and painful, brings closure to childhood and forces a redefinition of the self. The late-adolescent can no longer think of him- or herself as a child and must face the sometimes daunting task of becoming a young adult.

Developing a Young Adult Sense of Self and Other

For most young adults the gradual emotional detachment from parents is followed by a new inner definition of themselves as comfortably alone and competent, able to care for themselves and eventually for others. This shift away from the parents continues long after marriage and parenthood produce new relationships which replace the parents as the most important individuals in the young adult's life.

Psychological separation from the parents is followed by a second step— the synthesis of memories and images from the childhood past and the young adult present. For example, as their own children move from developmental phase to phase, young parents reengage memories of their own childhood and rework their childhood pasts by making constant conscious and unconscious comparisons with their children's present. They also gradually integrate a sense of themselves as parents by making comparisons between their parents' method of parenting and their own.

Friendships

In late adolescence and young adulthood, before the establishment of a committed relationship and parenthood, friends are often the primary source of emotional attachment and support. In the years between the family of origin and the family of procreation, the young adult finds him- or herself relatively unattached, missing the depth of commitment that was present in childhood and will be present in the future with spouse and children. I call this state the *loneliness of young adulthood* (Colarusso, 1990). Eventually the loneliness pushes the young adult toward committed relationships which hold the promise of more satisfying, secure connectedness. In the meantime roommates, apartment mates, sorority sisters and fraternity brothers, as indicated by the names used to describe them, are substitutes for family; temporary stand-ins until more permanent replacements are found and created.

As the twenties move into the thirties friendships become less important as spouse and children begin to dominate the real and intra-psychic world. The developmental shift from a single life to the family of procreation promotes a new form of friendship, namely couples friendships. These friendships often revolve around the children's activities and provide the young adult parent with the opportunity to make friends with others who are at the same stage developmentally and therefore able to understand and cushion the pressures of parenthood and young adult life. Couples' friendships tend to be more difficult to form and maintain because four individuals, not two (and often children as well) must be compatible.

Developing the Capacity for Intimacy: Becoming a Spouse

Erikson (1963) defined the major developmental dichotomy of young adulthood as intimacy versus stagnation. Offer and Offer (1975) observed in their study of adolescents that the capacity for intimacy in the sense used by Erikson was apparent in the highest functioning individuals by the fourth post-high school year.

The capacity for intimacy is related to the ability to experience someone else's needs, desires and concerns as equally important as one's own. It may be further defined as the ability to engage in a significant relationship with a partner that is elaborated over time and usually is associated with deep emotional commitment and shared parenthood. The degree to which one was treated with kindness and consideration as a child, the psychological separation from parents in adolescence, and the integration of a comfortable sexual identity during adolescence are the foundations on which the development of the capacity for intimacy in young adulthood is based. True intimacy can exist in adolescent relationships but for most individuals it does not become a sustainable capacity until the young adult years.

The shift from adolescent and young adult sexual experimentation to the desire for intimacy occurs gradually, for most in their late twenties and thirties, propelled by the lack of close relationships to others such as existed in childhood with parents and siblings. Brief sexual encounters in short-lived relationships no longer serve as significant boosts to self-esteem. Capable sexual performance has been mastered to one degree or another and mere repetition no longer provides emotional satisfaction. Increasingly the desire is for emotional connectedness in a sexual and non-sexual context.

The achievement of sexual and non-sexual intimacy produces significant mental and emotional change. Through the repeated fusion of sex and love, the self is increasingly identified with the partner. Feminine or masculine aspects of the self are projected onto and accepted and loved in the partner. The partner's aspirations for the future, particularly in regard to the major aspects of young adult life such as where to live, the desire for children and career ambitions become increasingly important and fused with one's own attitudes.

Another result of the development of the capacity for intimacy is the acceptance of the equal status and complementary nature of the male and female genitalia. Repeated experiences with foreplay, intercourse, conception, pregnancy, childbirth and psychological parenthood—all within the framework of intimacy—provide the optimal environment in which to abandon infantile notions and replace them with the recognition that female and male genitalia are equally important and interdependent for mature, adult sexual pleasure, intimacy and reproduction.

Based on the analysis of longitudinal date from the Grant Research Project, a study of college men that extended over five decades, George Vaillant (1977) noted that there was "probably no single longitudinal variable that predicted mental health as clearly as a man's capacity to remain happily married over time" (p. 320). Commenting on marriage, Emde (1985) said: "There is a recognition that in a marriage each partner has to work on a restructuring, where there is commitment, marriages are stable; where there is no such commitment . . . they are not stable, irrespective of troubles or turmoil" (p. 111).

Becoming a Biological and Psychological Parent

For both sexes the developmental task in young adulthood is to actualize the procreative purpose of the genitals, thus confirming the integrity of the body as a mature sexual instrument and solidifying masculine or feminine identity. This is not a simple or conflict-free process. Indeed it often creates tension within the developing young adult dyadic intimacy of marriage. Kestenberg commented (1976): "Entering her first adult developmental phase [Erickson, 1959] the young woman seeks intimacy with a new permanent object and is not ready for a new triangular relationship. Once the partners have become accustomed to the fact that they cannot be mother and father to each other, there is a partial disillusionment and a renewal of the search for ideal closeness. Planning a child, the young woman renews her position as a potential mother by consenting to have a child, the husband reclaims the role of a masculine protector . . . for him, the seed that perpetuates his father and himself is no longer wasted" (p. 227).

Hertzog (1982) related the ability to engage and master this powerful transition to the strength of the young couple's attachment to each other. In his case study of a twenty-three-year-old man, Gurwitt (1982) described the effects of his wife's pregnancy: "I propose that the period of impregnation and pregnancy constitutes an important developmental challenge for the prospective father, which like other developmental crises, brings about internal upheaval and change. . . . These psychological events occur in the context of the special tasks of young adulthood" (p. 244).

Biological parenthood begins the process of psychological parenthood, that mental state in which young adults become increasingly attached to their offspring. For both parents-to-be, pregnancy adds a new dimension to their sexual identity by confirming that their genitalia are capable of performing the primary function for which they were intended. After birth, each interaction with the infant enhances the new sense of sexual completeness and stimulates the desire to engage the baby who is so strongly identified with the self. When a young couple becomes parents for the first time, a family is created. The former child, now the parent, ministers to his or her own creation. As the child grows, the new parents undergo profound intra-psychic change, resulting from a reexamination of their own experiences as children and the growing sense of themselves as adults.

Becoming a parent also stimulates further individuation from one's own parents. Constant conscious and unconscious comparisons between child-rearing practices heighten the internal sense of difference between the generations while reinforcing connectedness and continuity.

Separating Psychologically from Parents while Facilitating Their Midlife Development

The ability to function relatively independently of the parents of child-hood—meaning without using them as a major source of comfort, security, and direction—comes to fruition during the young adult years. This process is greatly facilitated by a meaningful relationship with a significant other, usually leading to marriage; parenthood and achievement in the work place. As these adult experiences become the substance of everyday life they transform the real and intra-psychic relationship with parents from one of dependency and need to one of mutuality and equality. These transformations provide a powerful rationale for the young adult to remain invested in his or her parents because only parents and children place one in the center of a genetic continuity that spans three generations. As the young adult moves toward middle age and a growing preoccupation with time limitation and personal death, the importance of this genetic continuity grows.

By providing their parents with grandchildren young adults greatly enrich the lives of their progenitors and stimulate their middle and late adult development. The pleasure that grandparents express toward their grandchildren also provides the young adult parents with unconditional approval of their sexuality and new adult roles as parents. Throughout the young adult and middle years, living parents and grandparents provide examples of how the developmental tasks of these phases may be engaged. As the young adult parent and his or her children observe these examples, a foundation is laid for their own interaction in the years to come when their roles will be reversed.

The attainment of equality and mutuality with parents may continue for years or be short-lived, depending on the mental and physical well-being of the progenitors. At some point, the adult "child" will likely be confronted with the psychological and possibly physical task of caring for vulnerable, dependent parents who can no longer care for themselves. In the normal adult, the "child" reenters the parent-child dyad, now reversed, and assumes the role of caretaker.

Work

The establishment of a work identity is a central developmental task of young adulthood. When this developmental line is relatively conflict free, there is a smooth progression from high school to on-the-job training or from high school to college. The transition from learning and play to work may be gradual or abrupt, but at some point experience in the workplace leads to the recognition that work must become a central activity and result in the subordination of the pleasures of play and/or formal learning to the temporal and emotional demands of a job or career. Depending upon the work itself, and attitudes toward it, work may be experienced as a source of frustration, a necessary evil, or a source of pleasure and self-esteem that gradually leads to a shift in identity from child to adult and from player to worker.

CASE STUDY: KAREN

When Karen entered my office she was twenty-one years of age. Attractive and casually dressed, she appeared poised and calm. As she told her story her eyes wandered and I had the sense that she wished to be far away in a comfortable emotional place uncontaminated by what had happened to her and the need to tell me about it. My evaluation consisted of the diagnostic interview, psychological testing and a review of relevant records; and a follow-up interview two years later when she was twenty three years of age.

Initial Interview with Karen

At the time of our meeting Karen was in her third year of college. The relationship with her very concerned family had been significantly strained by the revelation of sexual abuse by her high school basketball coach, Coach P. They met when she was in junior high school when Karen tried out for the team. She was sixteen years old. Coach P was married and in his late thirties at the time.

Coach P began to pay special attention to Karen, sitting near her and asking if she wanted something to drink. He asked questions and told a few slightly off-color jokes. One day Coach P called Karen and asked what she was doing. When she mentioned that she was going to the mall he asked to meet her there. Not knowing what else to say, Karen agreed. It was "awkward" as they walked around. As they sat in his car in the parking lot Coach P said that he had been watching her. She was mature and he loved her. Shocked by his words, Karen didn't know what to say. "I wished I wasn't there."

Coach P asked to kiss her. Karen said no and he replied that someday he would. "I was shaking, flabbergasted. I didn't know what to do. I was scared about what people might think of me in that situation." Coach P called the next day and reiterated that he loved her. He began calling every day and asked her to a movie. Karen recalled having a mixture of thoughts and feelings. She was flattered by the attention. She loved sports and coaches were important people. It was hard to say no to a coach. At the same time Karen knew that going to the movies with Coach P probably wasn't a good idea. When Coach P met Karen at the movie theater he was dressed in shorts and a T-shirt. "He looked like a kid." At the movies he tried to hold her hand and rub her leg. Karen was anxious and worried that someone would see them. What would they think? After the movie Coach P invited Karen to stop by his home. His family was away for the weekend. Once inside the front door, Coach P pulled Karen toward him and French-kissed her.

During and after the kiss Karen felt that she was in "too deep. Why was I there? Why couldn't I say no? He was an authority figure. I have a lot of respect for them." Karen felt that Coach P was attractive. He dressed young, had tan skin, and bleached the tips of his hair. A few weeks later Coach P gave Karen a cell phone so they could communicate without her parents knowing. "After that, it's a blur. We talked every day. I must have been blind, I would have seen it if it was someone else."

Karen was invited by a friend to go to a concert in a nearby city and stay at the friend's home for the weekend. When Karen told Coach P about the concert, without asking, he bought two tickets so they could go together. Karen backed out of the plan to spend the weekend with her friend but didn't tell her parents of the change. "I was engrossed in the whole relationship. He called all the time. I wasn't spending any time with my friends."

Coach P rented a motel room for them. After checking in they watched TV as Coach P began kissing and touching Karen. After an hour at the concert he suggested that they leave. Karen didn't object because she was worried that someone she knew might see them together. They went right back to the motel. Coach P began kissing Karen and took her pants off. Then he undressed and penetrated her. He did not use a condom at first, then put one on for a bit and then removed it. He told Karen that she was beautiful. He loved her.

After the intercourse was completed Karen went into the shower for twenty minutes. "I was panicking." She couldn't believe that the relationship had gone that far. She was a virgin and hadn't expected to have intercourse. "How could I not have known what would happen!" The next morning they had sex again. "He didn't ask. He just started." After that Coach P would always perform oral sex on Karen. He didn't ask her to perform fellatio on him.

Karen began to go to Coach P's home whenever his wife and children were elsewhere. He began pushing Karen to consent to marry him when she turned eighteen. She had no desire to marry but played along, passively agreeing. It was the easiest thing to do and she couldn't say no. Coach P did not introduce pornography or try to involve anyone else in the relationship. The couple had sex approximately one hundred times. "I'm guessing. It was a lot."

Discovery

A student, who had observed the unusually close relationship between Karen and Coach P told a school counselor, who notified the police. When questioned Karen denied the relationship but eventually told a relative who told her parents. The police set up a recorded conversation between the two, which led to Coach P's arrest.

Karen read a letter at the trial expressing her anger. Coach P was convicted and sent to prison. Karen was sent to a therapist but she refused to continue. Looking back on her behavior at that time Karen felt that she was too humiliated to talk to anyone. After going to college Karen did see another therapist. She stopped for a while but began again because "I was a mess."

Symptoms

Migraine headaches began during the relationship with Coach P. Karen was seen by a physician who made the diagnosis and prescribed medication. At the time of my evaluation severe migraines were occurring once or twice a week. Karen did not have a prior history of headaches.

Karen began having sleeping problems after she found out that Coach P was out of prison. She became frightened that he would contact her. What if he showed up at college and tried to hurt her? Before going to bed Karen would plan an escape route in case Coach P appeared. Karen also began to have dreams about the coach. In the dreams Karen saw him somewhere and was frightened. "I don't remember the dreams. I just woke up with a headache." The dreams occurred approximately once a month throughout the freshman year. During the sophomore year when Coach P was out of prison they occurred on an every-other-week basis. Karen did not have frightening dreams or nightmares before the relationship with Coach P. Karen was preoccupied with thoughts about him during the day as well, particularly after he was released from prison. Concentration was difficult. Her grades dropped and she was unable to focus when involved with friends. Karen became depressed. During sophomore year, "I slept all day and gained twenty pounds.

I thought about suicide but I never tried. Who would miss me?" Karen had never been depressed before.

At the criminal trial "everyone backed him." That's why she feels responsible. "Some parents and kids blamed me. I was publically humiliated at school. I don't feel he has paid for anything he did to me. Sometimes crying feels so good. It hits me at night. My mind races."

Dating has been very difficult. Karen had a boyfriend during her freshman year at college. "I hid behind him and tried to study." In her sophomore year she began dating her present boyfriend. "Sex is a struggle. I hurry up and have sex and I'm not enjoying it at all." During her freshman year Karen would think about Coach P while having sex. "I tried so hard not to. I never told my boyfriend about him while we dated. "I couldn't stand oral sex." Karen told her current boyfriend about Coach P before they started dating. "Sex is better. I don't get as scared as I did in my freshman year. I just don't enjoy sex. I just don't like it. I can't explain it. I've never had a normal sexual relationship."

Mental Status Examination

Karen presented as a casually dressed, young adult female who was apprehensive but cooperative. She had a good vocabulary and spoke clearly. Affect or feeling tone was quiet and subdued at first. As we discussed the relationship with Coach P and the symptoms that resulted from the involvement with him she became agitated, openly tearful and clearly depressed. Thinking was logical and goal directed. There was no evidence of delusions or hallucinations. A strong tendency to repress thoughts and feelings about the relationship with Coach P was evident. There was no evidence of impairment of cognition.

Developmental History

Ages 0–12: Mother's pregnancy, labor and delivery with Karen were normal. Mother was the primary caretaker and there were no major separations from either parent. Karen had not had any major illnesses or operations in her life and did not have emotional problems or therapy prior to the experience with Coach P. Karen was a very good student in elementary school. She was well behaved and had lots of friends. The family was close and spent a lot of time together. Participation in sports was a major interest.

Ages 12–20: Puberty occurred at age 13. Karen was an honors student. She graduated from high school with an excellent GPA. Karen experimented with alcohol and marijuana in high school on a limited basis. She did not use either substance in college and has never been arrested or involved in illegal activities.

Psychological Testing Evaluation

An experienced forensic psychologist administered a battery of objective and subjective tests to Karen. The following excerpts convey the essence of his opinions.

"She meets the diagnostic criteria for PTSD . . . and her symptoms are considered as moderate to severe in comparison with other adults who have experienced a traumatic event. Her symptoms have caused significant impairment in her relationships and in social situations. . . . She does report having some suicidal thoughts. Karen is a tense, unhappy and pessimistic individual who is currently experiencing significant distress . . . she does demonstrate some risk of suicide, in that she likely experiences periodic, transient thoughts of self-harm."

"Karen has limited internal resources for coping with the demands of daily living. She often feels overwhelmed, and maintains stability in her life by keeping stress at a minimum and disturbing thoughts and feelings out of her awareness. She tends to be passive in relation to others, subjugating her needs and wishes to those of others, and seeking to avoid conflict whenever possible."

"There were certainly clear elements of sexual harassment involved, including the coach's abuse of the position of power to coerce and manipulate the plaintiff into having a sexual relationship with him. Because of her passivity and perfectionistic tendencies she was particularly vulnerable to his advances."

Review of Relevant Records

Karen was seen in individual psychotherapy by a social worker approximately twelve times during her freshman year at college. The therapist made a diagnosis of Adjustment Disorder with Depressed Mood. The therapy focused on the sexual abuse by Coach P and the symptoms that resulted from it. Karen ended the therapy because the therapist was stirring up memories and feelings that were painful and Karen wished to put the past behind her.

Approximately a year later Karen saw a psychologist. Although she initially made a diagnosis of Adjustment Disorder, as the treatment progressed the therapist changed her diagnosis to Major Depressive Disorder. Karen was described as an intelligent young woman who was passive and had difficulty putting thoughts into words. To some degree she was repulsed by Coach P but didn't know how to say no. She saw him as being very powerful and forceful. Karen was experiencing considerable guilt because she felt that she should have stopped the relationship. The patient knew that she needed to talk about the sexual abuse but felt worse when she did. These feelings caused Karen to interrupt the therapy for nearly a year. The therapist noted that the sexual abuse was particularly traumatic because it occurred during the formative years of adolescence. Karen had few friends and did little socially.

Second Diagnostic Interview with Karen

Karen was seen for a follow-up interview two years after the initial diagnostic evaluation. Since last seen twenty-six months ago Karen had graduated from college and returned to her home town where she found a job in an investment company. Her father was well but was "dealing with my Mom. I think he's aged ten years in the last one." Mother was depressed. "She's a mess, paranoid about everything." Mother continued to be preoccupied with the sexual abuse and repeatedly said, "I wish I could help my daughter."

Coach P "found God" in jail. After serving his sentence he returned to the town where he and Karen lived. Karen had not had any contact with Coach P but did see him walking while she was driving her car. She became acutely anxious but managed to control her anxiety, which subsided as she drove away. "I think about what he is doing now. He is moving on. He has a job and a life and I'm stuck in this rut."

Karen spends a lot of time thinking about the ongoing effects of the abuse. "I think of what my life and my mother's might have been like if not for him. I don't have a boyfriend. I used to get mad at my old boyfriend because of my thoughts about him [Coach P]." She continued, "I think I should have friends. I should have more self confidence. I wish I didn't get so angry."

At this point Karen began to cry and could not speak for several moments. "I get so angry at my mother for everything. She can't let it go. I get mad at everybody. I just want to be by myself. When I get mad I feel bad. I know I overreact."

Since returning home Karen has not made any good friends. "I don't confide in people. They don't know me. . . . I'm afraid people at home will know what happened or they may ask. I'm tired. I'd rather be in my room alone." With a depressed angry affect she said, "I'm not happy with who I am. I'm never comfortable with how I am. I think I feel worse than I did before. I'll be twenty-three soon and I should be better. I feel like my life is getting away from me. My boyfriend broke up with me because he felt I wasn't there for him. He was upset when I moved back home." Karen had not dated anyone in the past ten months.

Karen worked with a therapist throughout her senior year in college. When she graduated the therapist suggested that she continue in therapy upon returning home. "I just procrastinated." She hoped to get herself motivated enough to find a therapist. "Talking about what happened is so painful. I know it helps to talk but most of the time I just want to leave things as they are." As Karen talked about how unsatisfying her young adult life was she began to cry profusely.

Karen continues to experience many of the same symptoms that were present when I interviewed her two years ago. She still has migraine headaches. After a period of six months without the headaches they recently began to occur again, approximately two to three times per month. The recurrence is likely due to the very traumatic experience she had during her first deposition. Karen felt that the lawyer who took her deposition was mean and blamed her for the sexual abuse. A second deposition was planned for the near future.

Since returning home Karen has not been sleeping well. She has problems falling asleep as she ruminates about her unsatisfactory life but she is no longer having any dreams about Coach P. However, Karen is still occasionally fearful that Coach P will come after her. She doesn't think that he knows where she lives but feels safer when someone else is in the apartment with her. Karen fears that Coach P or an intruder will break in and kill her. Karen continues to be depressed and has occasional suicidal thoughts. "I have suicidal thoughts but I know I would never do it."

When involved with her boyfriend of two years Karen tried to enjoy their lovemaking but "I just didn't like it at all when he was at all aggressive. I would try so hard to enjoy it that it wasn't enjoyable . . . I still can't stand oral sex. I want to get married but I want my life to be in order first. I know that I'm not ready."

Mental Status Examination

Karen presented as a casually dressed young adult woman. Speech was slow and halting. A pervasive tone of depression was present throughout the interview. She was tearful on two occasions and unable to continue talking for a brief period. Thinking was logical and goal directed. There was no evidence of delusions or hallucinations.

Diagnosis

DSM-IV: Sexual Abuse of Child V61.21, Clinical Focus on Victim 905.53, and Major Depressive Disorder, Single Episode, Moderate, without Psychotic Features 296.22. A significant number of symptoms of Posttraumatic Stress

Disorder were noted during both clinical interviews and on psychological testing. Although Karen does not meet the criteria in DSM-IV for a character disorder, dependent features are becoming more prominent in her personality structure. Karen's migraine headaches began when the abuse started and are clearly related to it. Her mother's depression and family preoccupation with the abuse have been very difficult. Karen has a strong sense that her peers ostracized her and blamed her for the abuse, leading to marked social isolation. During the months of the abuse I rated Karen's symptoms in the 41–50, severe range. At the time of the first evaluation I rated them in the 51–60, moderate range. At the time of the follow-up evaluation two years later the severity remained in the 51–60, moderate range.

Treatment

An immediate course of individual psychotherapy, two to three times per week for two to three years, supplemented by the use of antidepressant medication likely throughout the course of the therapy, is strongly indicated. The therapist should be highly experienced and able to understand the long term, pervasive effects of chronic sexual abuse on children and adolescents and help Karen overcome her resistance to therapy and understand why the sexual abuse continues to have such a profound impact on her young adult development. At the time of marriage and childbearing an additional course of individual psychotherapy once per week for one to two years is indicated. Additional therapy may be needed during Karen's middle adulthood.

Prognosis

Because Karen's young adult development is severely arrested and many symptoms persist, even after the passage of several years since the abuse and a course of psychotherapy, the prognosis, assuming that the treatment plan outlined above is followed, is considered to be only fair.

Discussion

This teenage girl, who was subjected to months of relentless, aggressive sexual abuse by her coach, approximately twenty years her senior, has suffered profound psychological damage and an inability to engage the major developmental tasks of young adulthood. Like most child victims of sexual abuse, she was dealing with a person of authority who groomed her and then took advantage of her. Grooming behavior by Coach P included paying inordinate attention, telling Karen that she was pretty, saying he loved her and buying her a cell phone in order to maintain his psychological dominance on a daily basis.

In the midst of establishing an adolescent sexual identity Karen was vulnerable to this attention and flattery and because of her age and developmental level was totally unprepared for an intense sexual and emotional relationship with anyone, let alone an adult male. Further, she was totally unable to either consent or resist involvement in the relationship. Like many other teenage victims, she was sexually attracted to Coach P and was curious and fascinated by his attention.

All of the major developmental tasks of adolescence were seriously impacted. Karen became isolated from her peers. She developed a sense of disdain for her body and emerging sexuality and did not date peers in high school. When she did date in college the sexual experiences were not pleasurable and her thoughts were concentrated on Coach P rather than her sexual partner. Further, the abuse significantly interfered with her relationship with her family. Her mother became depressed and unable to come to terms with the abuse her daughter experienced.

Now in her early twenties, Karen is still suffering from the profound effects of the abuse. Her self-esteem is very low. She has not been able to establish normal dating and sexual relationships appropriate to her age, and her relationships with family members continue to be compromised. Karen returned home after college because she didn't feel safe living on her own away from home. Although able to hold a job, she finds concentrating on work difficult. Earlier plans for further education have been abandoned.

Although Karen would like to be married and have children, she doesn't see how these developmental steps will be possible because of her symptoms and inability to enjoy sexual and emotional intimacy. She worries that a prospective husband will reject her because of the shame associated with the sexual abuse and her inability to commit herself to a full, comfortable sexual relationship.

The effects of chronic sexual abuse such as Karen experienced will likely continue to be with her for the rest of her life—as will be demonstrated by the case histories later in this book of individuals in their fifties and sixties who were abused as children and still continue to be significantly impaired. Hopefully the harmful effects can be diminished by intensive therapy and medication and allow Karen to live a full life which would include productive work, close friendships, marriage, intimacy, children and comfortable relationships with her family. Without the benefit of prolonged treatment Karen's depression is likely to deepen and further compromise her present and future life.

CASE STUDY: BEN

The Diagnostic Interview

Ben was twenty-seven years old when he came for his evaluation. Casually dressed, hesitant but cooperative as the interview progressed, he seemed relieved to finally be able to tell someone "about my secret." Ben had a good vocabulary and was able to express his thoughts and feelings clearly. Throughout the interview he experienced intense shame, disgust, anger and depression as he told his story. A clerk in a large retail chain, Ben was single. Never married, and living alone, he was the father of a three-year-old girl whom he saw on a regular basis.

Ben was abused approximately one hundred times over a three-year period by a close friend of the family named Joe. He was about eight years old when the abuse started. The first episode took place at Joe's house while the two were watching television. Joe put his arm around Ben and then slid his other hand inside the boy's pants. Ben was confused but didn't resist. Joe told Ben that he was going to show him how to be a man. Joe had frequently talked to Ben about growing up and going out with girls prior to the first abuse. Ben hadn't the slightest interest in girls at the time but he did like listening to Joe's stories about having sex with girls and "jerking off."

The second episode occurred soon after. This time Joe moved his hands up and down on the boy's penis in a masturbatory motion. Ben had not masturbated on his own prior to this experience. Joe explained that "jerking off was fun." With considerable hesitation and shame Ben admitted getting an erection and enjoying the sensation in his penis. As he talked Ben volunteered that throughout the years he had tried not to blame himself for getting an erection and enjoying the feeling but he couldn't. He should have told someone or told Joe to stop but he was afraid that he would be blamed for what happened. Anyway, Joe had told him that it was their secret and Ben would know more about sex than the other boys.

Over the next three years Joe abused Ben nearly every time they were together. Ben slept over at Joe's house when his parents went away. Joe frequently drove Ben to school and to sporting events. Sometimes the abuse occurred in Ben's house while Ben's parents were there. Joe would just laugh if Ben worried that his parents might see them. So what if they did, Joe said, they wouldn't care. The abuse consisted of masturbation and oral sex. Sometimes Joe showed Ben pictures of naked girls or pornography. Joe never asked Ben to touch his penis although the boy did see him masturbate on numerous occasions. Ben never understood why the abuse stopped when he was about twelve. Joe just didn't abuse him anymore.

When he became an adolescent Ben wondered if he was gay. By then he knew that what had happened with Joe was wrong. He had learned in sex education class about inappropriate touching. Further, his mother and father were still good friends with Joe. They would never believe that Joe would do anything wrong. Joe was married and had kids of his own, he wasn't interested in boys.

Ben had many thoughts about the sexual abuse. "I don't trust any males, including the men in my family. I worry that one of them might abuse me. I don't want to hug any male. Keeping the secret was hard on me. I couldn't tell my mother or father, they wouldn't believe me. I couldn't tell my friends, they would laugh at me. When I heard stories about kids being sexually abused I was sure that people knew I was abused too. I learned to hate the word *faggot* or *gay*. I got very upset whenever anyone used those words. I got into a lot of fistfights." When Ben masturbated during adolescence he became very upset because thoughts about Joe would intrude into his consciousness. "It was always in the back of my mind. It played all the time. I had a mask on. I play sports. I tried to have a normal life." This attitude persisted despite the fact that no one ever directly accused Ben of being homosexual. "When I see or hear stuff about abuse it brings back all the memories, like a movie reel."

Ben is very worried that girlfriends will find out that he was abused and suspect him of being gay. He is particularly worried that his daughter's mother will find out. "I don't want my daughter to know. When I change her diaper I feel terrible. I'm not getting her clean. How much touching is too much?"

Developmental History

Ben didn't remember much about his early years but he did know that his parents were good to him and that his mother was home all the time. He had not had any major illnesses or operations in his life and had never been to see a mental health professional.

During the elementary school years Ben was more interested in playing than school. He had lots of friends and spent a lot of time with his father. Joe often went with Ben's father to watch Ben play Little League baseball. "Somehow I managed to do all these other things at the same time that Joe was playing with me."

Puberty occurred at approximately age thirteen. Ben had his first girlfriend and experience with sexual intercourse during the eleventh grade. He dated the same girl throughout high school. All of his adolescent and adult sexual experiences have been heterosexual. Ben barely made it through high school.

He was involved in numerous disciplinary actions due to fighting and tardiness. Ben used drugs a few times during adolescence. Presently he drinks alcohol, sometimes to excess but never when he has custody of his daughter. He doesn't have a police record. Ben has worked at his present job for several years. He attends junior college sporadically and hopes to get an AA degree some day.

Psychological Testing

On the WAIS-R Ben achieved a full-scale IQ in the average range. The psychologist felt that "it is possible that the observed results represent a mild underestimation of Ben's true intellectual and cognitive capacities. There were inconsistencies in his performance that . . . are frequently indicative of cognitive disruption associated with co-existing psychological difficulties such as anxiety or features of depression."

On the MMPI-2 "the level of psychopathology reported is indicative of very serious difficulties that include mood features, pronounced anxiety, unusual thought processes, and impaired reality testing operations." There was significant evidence of depressive processes. "He is quite concerned about the future and has found it impossible to psychologically 'bracket off' the molestation and relegate it to the past."

Based on the results of the Rotter Incomplete Sentences Blank the psychologist commented, "He is extremely distressed, ashamed, angry, resentful, and tense/anxious as a result of the molestation. He feels violated and exploited resulting in guardedness, feared persecution, distrust and hostility toward others, especially male authority figures." He feels . . . "permanently tarnished by the molestation."

Themes and projected material on the Thematic Apperception Test "are notable for expressed feelings of sadness, depression and isolation/aloneness as well as highly conflicted longings and struggles involving dependency, achievement, mastery and interpersonal relatedness."

Results from the Rorschach Inkblot Test demonstrated "evidence of significant cognitive and emotional disruption and disturbance . . . emotional stimulation tends to be avoided and minimized in most instances . . . findings are also indicative of pronounced concerns over physical functioning and body integrity, with a tendency to perceive oneself as physically compromised or damaged."

Using DSM-IV the psychologist made diagnoses of Major Depressive Disorder, Single Episode; Posttraumatic Stress Disorder, Chronic; and Sexual Abuse of Child. His symptoms were rated in the 50–60, moderate range.

The Memory Remains

Ben presented me with this personal statement of his feelings about the sexual abuse. I found it to be heart-wrenching and difficult to read but very illustrative of the ongoing mental torment suffered by an adult who was abused as a child.

"The memory remains with me. There is no cure for the pain and humiliation I have suffered through as a child. No matter how hard I try to forget the past, the pain will forever be in my mind and in my soul. I am now tattooed with this emotional pain forever. I will take this horrible memory with me until God decides to take me away from this earth. At times I question God. I ask him, 'If you love all your children, why did you let this happen to me? Was I a bad son?' Was God trying to teach me a lesson?

"I do not have the answers to any of the questions I have mentioned above but I do believe that God loves me. I believe that God will always be with me in my time in need. I hope that when God decides to take me, the pain will go away and never come back. It is not easy going through life knowing that you have been violated. I can try to forget, but the pain will forever be a part of my life. At times I feel hollow. It is as if my childhood memories have been erased, and replaced with horrible memories. I feel that someone came into my life and took something from me that I could never get back. I wish I could erase my past. I wish I could have lived a normal childhood with good memories like my friends did. I hate living a life that has been violated. He did not only violate me, he violated my family. He violated my trust. I feel that I can't trust anyone. It is horrible to go through life not trusting anybody. At times, I feel I could not trust my own family. The two adults that raised me, I did not trust. Three years of humiliation and violation will forever be in my life. Only three years, three years that have ruined my childhood as well as my adulthood.

"How come I did not ask for help? I was scared. I was scared that nobody would believe me. I was scared that somebody would try to hurt me if I told. I also did not tell anybody because I was embarrassed. Can you imagine if your friends found out that you have been violated? They would single you out or even make fun of you. I already felt alone on the inside. Why do I want to feel alone on the outside as well? Growing up in a small town is not always easy. People talk and things get around. Even if the rumors are false, people still tend to believe them.

"No matter what I try to fill that emptiness with, the past will always find a way to squeeze through to fill the empty spot. I will take this experience and try to leave it where it belongs in the past. It belongs in the past. I will take this whole experience and try to make something positive come out of it. Now that I am a father, I will use this experience as being a rebirth of my life. Let me tell you, changing your daughter's diaper is not always a fun job because I don't want to have her lose her trust in me. I don't want my daughter to think that I am violating her flesh when I am only trying to clean her up.

"I am tired of looking at my life through a kaleidoscope. It is a shattered past that went in circles. I can only wish that what I had experienced didn't happen to anybody else because the memories remain with you until you stop breathing. But in all reality it will happen, because there are monsters and predators feeding on the souls of the weak. These people take advantage of other people's flesh and at the same time destroy their minds. It makes me sick to think that there are human beings on this earth that are willing to take advantage of the weak. It makes me sick that in their minds they can justify this type of violation as being 'ok.' It makes me sick that people like this roam the earth.

"What scares me the most is that my daughter could become the next victim if I am not on my toes. I don't want my daughter or any other child to live a horrible childhood like I did. I don't want my daughter or any other child to go through life feeling insecure. I don't want my daughter or any other child to ever write a letter like this one. But most important, I don't want my daughter or another child to get molested. I must look into the future because my past is all behind me. No matter how hard I try to forget, the memory remains."

Diagnosis

DSM-IV: Sexual Abuse of Child V61.21, Clinical Focus on Victim 995.53, Posttraumatic Stress Disorder, Chronic 309.81, and Major Depressive Disorder, Single Episode 296.22. Ben was deeply concerned about acceptance by family and peers. He was intensely worried about being left out and considered to be a homosexual. On the Global Assessment Scale of Functioning I rated Ben's symptoms in the 51–60, moderate range.

Treatment

Individual psychotherapy two to three times per week for three to four years is indicated immediately. Antidepressant medication in conjunction with the psychotherapy is definitely indicated. In the decade of the forties or fifties, the timing to be determined by the treating mental health professional, an additional course of psychotherapy will likely be needed.

Prognosis

As indicated by Ben's statement in "The Memory Remains" he will be tormented by the memories of the abuse for the rest of his life but therapy may effectively reduce the level of depression and self-recrimination, bolster self-esteem, encourage more comfortable social interactions and reduce the level of intra-psychic torment.

Discussion

Ben's development was significantly compromised from the time of the abuse to the present. During latency his trust in his parents was undermined because they did not protect him from the family friend who was abusing him. He deeply resents his parents and other adults and authority figures who failed to protect him to this day. Ben felt estranged from his peers in latency and adolescence. They would never understand if they found out, would blame him and make fun of him. He remains isolated as an adult.

His sense of masculinity was and is seriously compromised. Ben was introduced to sexual involvement with another person, even worse, an adult male, at a time in life when he was unprepared mentally or physically for sexual activity. During adolescence normal masturbatory activity and beginning sexual experiences were contaminated with memories of the abuse. As a young adult he has been able to perform sexually but has not established an emotionally intimate relationship with a woman.

Ben's experience of parenthood is filled with anxiety any time he has physical contact with his daughter. He is both fearful of abusing her and is continually reminded of his own abusive experiences when in her presence. Instead of comfortably enjoying his daughter he is preoccupied with the need to protect her from the possibility of abuse by himself or others. As she reaches the ages when he was abused this overprotective attitude will likely intensify.

ARRESTED DEVELOPMENT IN YOUNG ADULTHOOD

Karen was twenty-three when I evaluated her. Ben was twenty-seven. Both were attempting, very unsuccessfully, to engage and master the developmental tasks of young adulthood. The fact that Ben was abused during latency and Karen during adolescence, one in a heterosexual relationship, the other in a homosexual one, made little difference in the symptom picture, diagnoses present or developmental interferences during young adulthood. What they did have in common was that both were abused multiple times over months and years. The abuse was chronic, the effects profound.

Both Karen and Ben were very depressed. I think a significant reason for the depth of the depression in both was the fact that being intelligent young adults they were able to understand the devastating effects of the chronic sexual abuse on their intra-psychic and real lives in a way that they could not as a latency-aged boy and an adolescent girl. As awful as the pain that Karen and Ben suffered then was, their comprehension of the incredible damage produced by the childhood sexual abuse on their lives as young adults caused even greater suffering and despair.

Neither Karen nor Ben had friends. Both felt isolated and unable to discuss the abuse with others. Neither was in a relationship. Although Ben had sexual relationships with women he was plagued by memories of his homosexual experiences with Joe. Karen had sexual relationships with boyfriends but was unable to comfortably enjoy the experience. Both were arrested along the developmental line of sexuality and intimacy at ages when healthy peers had integrated sex and intimacy into their adult lives. Neither was close to getting married. Ben had a child out of wedlock and longed to father his daughter but was plagued by his inability to comfortably touch her. Both are demonstrating character traits of avoidance and dependency which will result in Axis II diagnoses in the near future.

Ben's wrenching personal statement about his near-constant state of mental anguish as a result of the years of sexual abuse that he suffered at the hands of his perpetrator illustrates the basic message that I would hope readers will take away from this book in a most definitive manner. All my own words pale in comparison.

6

The Decade of the Thirties

IN CHAPTER 5 WE SAW HOW INDIVIDUALS in their twenties developed a more mature understanding of the effects of the sexual abuse on their young lives. In this chapter, which is about persons in young adulthood who are moving toward middle age, we see not only a similar type of in-depth understanding of the consequences of their sexual abuse but also a growing realization that there may not be time to undo the effects of symptomatic behaviors or actualize unrealized potentials.

In the case studies that follow, two young boys were sexually abused, alone and sometimes together, by a teacher at the school they attended. The boys never talked about the abuse that took place during and after sixth grade. After graduating from elementary school the boys went to different junior high schools and lost contact with each other. After sexual abuse cases began to appear in the media when he was an adult Louis decided to try to find Bill. Eventually the two men, now in their thirties, met and agreed to openly acknowledge what had happened to them and initiate lawsuits. My evaluations of Louis and Bill, who were seen separately, consisted of diagnostic interviews of approximately three hours in both cases. Psychological testing was scheduled but never completed because the lawsuits against the perpetrator were settled.

CASE STUDY: LOUIS

Louis was a small business owner who had recently married. He was determined to tell his story when he appeared in my office. Unlike other victims who were embarrassed and timid, Louis was anxious to talk. A grim-faced man, he described what had been done to him and how it affected his life. Obviously intelligent, Louis had a good command of the English language. His thinking was logical and goal directed and there was no evidence of delusions or hallucinations.

The Sexual Abuse

The perpetrator, Mr. D, was a single adult male in his forties. He was a teacher at a small private school. As previously mentioned, the abuse occurred during and after the sixth grade and ended when Louis went to a different school for junior high school. Bill was in the same class as Louis. The two boys were friends. They were close to Mr. D, who took a special interest in both of them and served as the coach of their basketball team.

Mr. D had been grooming the boys for some time by giving them special attention, making sexual references and telling dirty jokes. He began to inquire into the boys' sexual interests. On day Mr. D asked Louis if Bill jerked off. Louis replied that he didn't know (Louis didn't know that Bill was already being abused by Mr. D). Mr. D asked if Louis had ever had an orgasm. At the time Louis wasn't very surprised by the questions, although somewhat embarrassed. He had heard Mr. D make sexual references before, but never directly about Louis's sexuality. "I was in awe of him. He seemed to know everything. He was really a life mentor." Mr. D asked if the two boys ever jerked off together. Did they see which of them could shoot the farthest? Mr. D became a friend of Louis' family. He praised Louis to his parents and was often invited to dinner. "He got in with my family."

The first sexual abuse involving Louis took place at Mr. D's home. He had invited the two boys to stop by after basketball practice. Louis couldn't remember the details of how the boys' clothing came off but he vividly remembered that Mr. D encouraged the two boys to orally copulate each other. Louis was totally unprepared and surprised by Bill's willingness to suck on his penis but he went along with the activity because he didn't know what else to do. While the fellatio was occurring Mr. D asked if Louis had come. Was there any "pre-come"? He asked Bill what Louis's come tasted like. Louis thinks that Mr. D suggested anal sex but he doesn't remember if that actually occurred. While the boys were involved with each other Mr. D had removed his clothes and lay on the bed next to the boys, masturbating. Louis thought that there were other similar incidents in which he also performed fellatio on Bill but he couldn't be sure. I had the impression that some instances of the sexual abuse that Louis experienced were crystal clear but others had been partially or totally repressed.

A week or so later the boys were taking showers after basketball practice. Mr. D came into the shower with an erection. He told the boys that he would show them what "real come" was like and ejaculated in front of them. Louis was certain that a similar incident occurred at least several more times. On some of these occasions Mr. D would take Louis's hand and put it on his penis, moving the hand up and down. "I can see it in my mind like I was watching and then I don't remember." So in addition to the use of repression as a defense mechanism Louis also dissociated during some of the sexual experiences with Mr. D.

Louis described with embarrassment, disgust and anger how he began to initiate and suggest sexual activity to Mr. D. One day when they were in Mr. D's car Louis began to rub Mr. D's shoulders and asked if the teacher was going to let Bill suck his penis. On another occasion Louis was eager to masturbate in front of Mr. D to show him how far he could ejaculate. As Louis continued he appeared to be recovering memories of additional instances of abuse. He had never talked about his experiences in detail to anyone before.

Louis remembered the following incident. Mr. D took the boys and a third boy on an overnight trip to a nearby city. Louis remembers all of them being naked and had a vague memory of being in a bathtub with Mr. D. On this occasion the teacher showed the boys pornography and told them that they would all get in trouble if they told anyone what had happened. "I know there is other stuff but I can't pull it out of the memory bank."

Symptoms

After high school Louis was having sex with a girl when he had a flashback of Mr. D, Bill and him having sex. He vomited on the girl. After that every time Louis had sex he thought about Mr. D and lost his erection. This lasted for several months. During his twenties Louis would think about the "gay stuff" in an attempt to prevent premature ejaculation. Then he began to use various kinds of illegal drugs to try and blot out the memories. "I used a lot of drugs."

Louis began smoking marijuana in the eighth grade. He still does. "I smoked a lot the last two days. I feel it's the only thing that keeps me balanced. I think I'm addicted to painkillers. I'm not having pain but I take one or two every day. I've done everything you can imagine other than stick a needle in my arm. I'm looking for something to tranquilize me. If I don't take drugs I'm afraid I'll lose my mind.

"I don't trust anybody, only my family. I never let people get too close. I used to get good grades before junior high school. Then my grades went to hell." He continued, "I was pretty destructive as a kid. I made homemade bombs. I used to break into houses and destroy things. I love intense things. I like to do dangerous things. I drive my car way over the speed limit and take chances." Despite such behavior Louis did not have a police record.

"I used to have daydreams about the abuse." This preoccupation with the sexual abuse was present for years but has become particularly intense since revealing that he was abused. "In high school I was very worried that people would find out. I would see Bill occasionally and we would avoid each other." After pausing as if to refocus Louis said, "I think I could have done more with my life. I could have gone to college. I had disciplinary problems. I didn't use my potential. I should have made better choices.

"My parents never knew what happened. I used to battle with them all the time. When I should have been focusing on other things I was focused on sex and porn. I never told them because I thought it would break my mother's heart."

Developmental History

Louis was raised in an intact, loving family. His parents were happy and very involved in the lives of their children. Father was around much of the time and encouraged Louis to become involved in a variety of sports and other activities. Louis thinks his early years were good ones. He was healthy and never had any major illnesses or operations. Mother was his primary caretaker and there were no significant separations from either parent. Louis was toilet trained easily and did not become a bed-wetter.

During the elementary years Louis was an excellent student. He made the honor roll, was well behaved and got along well with his teachers. Everything was "great" until the sixth grade when the abuse began. Louis had a lot of friends and was very active in sports and the Cub Scouts. "In high school I blocked it out of my mind. Did that really happen? I barely graduated from high school. A couple of teachers kept me from dropping out. I got in a lot of trouble. I was always late. I got kicked out a few times. My GPA was one point something. They let me graduate. I was writing off school when everybody else was talking about college. I'm just coming to the point where I realize it would help me. I played sports for a while but I quit. No reason, I just quit." After high school Louis worked at various jobs. "For a long while I didn't stick to any of them. I was always pretty good at giving up."

In his twenties Louis worked for one company for several years. When that enterprise went under he decided to start a small business of his own. Over the past several years the business has made enough money for Louis to support himself and his wife. He has a good feeling about the future, business-wise. Throughout young adulthood to the present, Louis has continued to be troubled by the sexual relationships with Bill and Mr. D, hence the various symptoms described above and the strong sense that he was not living up to his potential and could not be happy. Louis has mixed feelings about telling others that he was abused. Most people have been supportive but Louis is continually worried that people will blame him and not understand why he couldn't say no.

Louis went through puberty in sixth grade while the abuse was happening. He had intercourse for the first time at sixteen with a girl his age. "I've had sex with about thirty women. I like the chase. I like going to bars looking for some stranger. I like oral sex and banging a girl pretty good. I like intense sex." Louis has not had any homosexual experience. "I'm not afraid of gay people. I know I'm not gay. I like chicks." Louis was involved in two serious relationships with women, one in his twenties and a second in his thirties. Each lasted about two years. "I broke them off. I wanted to have sex with other women." Eventually he married. He described the marriage as "OK." He feels some times that he has no right to be married because he is "damaged goods."

Diagnosis

Using DSM-IV I made the following diagnoses on Axis I: Sexual Abuse of Child V61.21, Clinical Focus on Victim 995.5, Posttraumatic Stress Disorder 309.81, Dissociative Amnesia 300.12, and Cannabis Dependence 304.30.

CASE STUDY: BILL

Bill was a neatly dressed, serious young adult in his mid-thirties when he presented himself in my office for the independent medical examination required for his lawsuit. Throughout the more than three hours that we spent together he was cooperative and thoughtful. His affect ranged from bland to extreme anxiety, embarrassment and puzzlement as he told me about the chronic sexual abuse he had endured as a child and the effects it had and continued to have on him. There was no evidence of a thinking disorder or of delusions or hallucinations. As will become evident as the clinical material is presented, Bill dissociated frequently during the episodes of sexual abuse. He was engaged to be married. Despite having a degree, he had been employed at a very low-paying job for several years.

The sexual abuse by Mr. D started when Bill was in sixth grade. Verbal and physical abuse preceded the sexual abuse. "If I didn't do my homework Mr. D would paddle me. I was terrorized. He threatened me and got red in the face. He was very angry. It was like looking into the eyes of a lion." Paddling took place on a regular basis in the classroom and a supply room nearby. As Bill spoke it was clear that he did not see that the verbal and physical abuse was Mr. D's way of preparing him for the sexual abuse that was to follow.

The first sexual abuse occurred in a room off of the classroom. Mr. D asked Bill to undress. Bill expected to be paddled again. Instead Mr. D had Bill sit on his lap. Bill asked why but Mr. D didn't answer. Instead, he began masturbating Bill, who got an erection and climaxed. He was not old enough to ejaculate. Mr. D asked Bill if it felt good and told him that the teacher was his friend and this was their secret. Then Mr. D pulled his pants down, masturbated and had Bill touch his penis as he climaxed.

The second incident of sexual abuse took place soon after at Mr. D's home. The teacher took Bill to his bedroom and told the boy to sit on the bed and watch TV. As Mr. D stripped to his shorts his erection was evident. He asked Bill to roll on his back. The teacher stripped Bill and masturbated him to a climax. Then he had Bill masturbate him to a climax. He repeated that this was fun and it was what friends did with each other.

Multiple similar experiences occurred, sometimes in a chair in the classroom, often after school, sometimes after basketball practice. Bill was uncertain how often the sexual abuse occurred but it was at least two to three times per week during his first year in sixth grade. Bill didn't tell anyone. "I was afraid to tell anyone. Mr. D was a friend of my parents. He was around all the time. He had a key to our house for god sakes." Mr. D had Bill repeat the sixth grade. Bill was not failing, but Mr. D explained to Bill's parents that another year under his guidance would help Bill mature

The sexual encounters escalated and began to include simulated anal sex and oral copulation. Mr. D would perform oral sex on Bill. After Bill was old enough to ejaculate—he had his first ejaculation as a result of stimulation by Mr. D—the man would swallow his semen. These experiences occurred once or twice a week throughout the spring and summer of Bill's second year in sixth grade. As if the realization of what he had just revealed was too much to bear, Bill confessed, "I knew that guys and girls were supposed to be together. I knew that what Mr. D was doing to me was wrong." The sexual abuse was most frequent and intensive during the summer after Bill's second year in sixth grade. By then Mr. D made Bill fellate him. He was not sure if Mr. D ever ejaculated in his mouth. Mr. D would also have Bill put one or two fingers in Mr. D's anus while masturbating him.

Mr. D gradually involved Louis in the sexual activity that had been occurring for some time with Bill. Mr. D "had us do things to each other. We never talked about it."

"When Mr. D would do things to Louis I would go into a *black hole.* I'd close my eyes, go into darkness and hear nothing." This happened many times. Bill remembered "drifting right into the scene" when Mr. D would come into the shower with the boys and tell Louis to touch his penis. He often had a memory gap of minutes or hours after such an experience. The same thing happened when Mr. D abused Bill, particularly with simulated anal sex or fellatio. "I have a lot of blanks. I can't remember a lot of what happened."

Bill's recollection of his first sexual experience with Louis was similar to that reported by Louis. They were at Mr. D's house. He told both boys to undress (Bill sighed and had difficulty continuing) and told them to masturbate each other and perform oral sex on each other. "I closed my eyes. I don't remember if there was ejaculation or not. I have another dark memory of something happening in the shower but I can't remember what it was." Bill thinks he and Louis were forced to be sexually involved with each other at least two times. There are distinct gaps in his memory due to the dissociation that occurred during the sexual abuse. The abuse ended when Bill called Mr. D after his second year in sixth grade. "I told him I didn't want to do that anymore. I was shaking on the phone. He pleaded with me. It never happened again."

Symptoms

"I began drinking when I was fourteen to take my mind off it. In my senior year I drank more than you can imagine. Today on weekends I get drunk 95 percent of the time. I haven't had any DUIs but I've driven drunk." Bill also used marijuana, LSD, mushrooms, cocaine and heroin during his teenage years and throughout his twenties. He tried heroin once. Bill stopped using drugs about five years ago when he became a Christian. "Mr. D made me a Christian."

"I'm thirty-five years old and I barely make enough to live on. I have a degree. I should be making a lot more. I've never been able to save any money. My fiancée pushes me every day. She makes four times as much as I do. I've never had any drive to do more."

Bill is depressed and has occasional suicidal thoughts. Suicidal urges occurred when he was high on drugs in the past and now when he is totally sober. When the thoughts occur Bill asks God to help him. He has never acted on these thoughts.

Bill is struggling sexually. His fiancée wants to have sex but he doesn't feel like it. She wonders if she is the problem. Bill tries hard not to think about the sexual abuse both before and during sex. If he thinks about it he will either avoid having sex entirely or attempt to finish as quickly as possible. Bill has been approached by homosexuals but has no interest. "I laugh it off." He had intercourse for the first time in his early twenties and was sexually involved with three or four women before meeting his fiancée. Bill watched pornography compulsively during adolescence and in his twenties. He watched all varieties of heterosexual porn and avoided any form of homosexual porn. While masturbating when watching pornography Bill concentrated on thinking about women.

"I feel bad that I never told anyone. I didn't help the boys who were molested after I was."

Developmental History

Bill's parents divorced when he was young. Both parents remained involved in his life on an ongoing basis and he spent time in both homes throughout his childhood. Both parents were totally surprised when Bill told them what had happened.

Pregnancy, labor and delivery were normal. Developmental milestones such as walking and talking occurred at expectable times. Mother was the primary caretaker and there were no significant separations from either parent. Bill was toilet trained easily by age three and has not had any regressions. He has been healthy throughout his life and has not had any serious illnesses or surgeries. Bill was a "decent" student before the sexual abuse began in sixth grade. He had friends and was well behaved. Sports were a major interest. Both parents fostered various activities both before and after their divorce.

Bill was an average to below average student during junior and senior high school. He tried out for various sports teams but was not very successful. Bill had friends, and as previously described, became heavily involved in drug and alcohol use. He dated occasionally but never felt comfortable approaching women due to marked concerns about the intrusion of thoughts about the abuse. After high school Bill worked as a clerk for several years and obtained an A.A. degree from a community college. He did not have a juvenile record despite his extensive drug use.

Bill worked at various low-paying jobs through his twenties. As he approached thirty he went to school on a part-time basis and eventually was awarded a B.A. degree. He became an active Christian during his twenties and began a relationship with his fiancée in his early thirties. Bill would like to become involved in law enforcement.

Diagnosis

Using DSM-IV I made the following diagnoses: Sexual Abuse of Child V61.21, Clinical Focus on Victim 995.55, Posttraumatic Stress Disorder 309.81, Dissociative Amnesia 300.12, and Polysubstance Dependence, Sustained Full Remission 304.80.

THE EFFECT OF THE ABUSE ON
ADOLESCENT AND YOUNG ADULT DEVELOPMENT

Chronic sexual abuse tends to affect all major developmental tasks in subsequent phases of development. This is certainly true of both Louis and Bill. Both boys experienced their first ejaculations with Mr. D in the midst of an abusive relationship. The first ejaculation normally occurs through masturbation or a wet dream. For a year or more after puberty much of their sexual arousal, and all of their sexual activity, occurred in a homosexual context, thus undermining the consolidation of a heterosexual orientation.

Both boys were repeatedly stimulated and sexually aroused. Sexual impulses, attitudes and experiences became associated with another person who dominated and controlled the sensations coming from the maturing body. In normal development early sexual experience consists primarily of masturbation, which is controlled by the adolescent himself, allowing over time for the slow integration of sexual arousal and physical sensation prior to the engagement of others.

The rapid physical and sexual maturation of the body requires alteration in psychic structure to manage the new physical and sexual capabilities that are emerging. As the mind experiences this destabilizing transformation mood swings and inconsistent behavior become the norm. Both Louis and Bill were unable to manage the emotional changes of early adolescence due to the tremendous overload of stimuli that resulted from the chronic abuse. They resorted to extensive drug and alcohol abuse and to depression and destructive behavior in attempts to manage their feelings.

All adolescents psychologically separate from their parents as they individuate and develop the mental and emotional capabilities needed to eventually become self-sufficient adults. Self esteem is enhanced as parents remain involved, provide love and appropriate limits and support the movement toward independence. A comfortable relationship with parents allows adolescents to gradually emancipate themselves while knowing that they have a stable support system available at home to fall back on if needed. Louis and Bill, and every other victim in this book, were not able to tell their parents what was happening to them. Because of a sense of shame and the belief that they would not be believed, or would be blamed, for what was occurring, they suffered in silence. Both boys experienced a sense of parental abandonment and went through adolescence without a sense of parental support or protection. The adolescent/parent relationship was completely undermined.

The adolescent peer group plays a vital role in the adolescent transition by providing relationships in which thoughts, feelings and new relationships can be explored and compared. For males, acceptance by the same-sex peer group solidifies sexual identity. Both Louis and Bill withdrew from peers, afraid that their secret would be discovered and they would be teased, considered gay and ostracized.

During adolescence teens prepare for careers beyond high school. Grades and attitudes toward learning and work become more focused and serious. Both boys were not able to utilize their academic potential in high school. As a result of low self-esteem and preoccupation with the abuse they were not able to fully concentrate on academics or plan for a future that would be consistent with their potential.

Treatment Recommendations for Louis and Bill

Louis and Bill are in need of intensive, individual psychotherapy to attempt to minimize the effects of the sexual abuse on their emotional stability, self-esteem and present and future development. Both of these men utilized dissociative defense mechanisms to an extreme degree in an attempt to cope with the sexual experiences while they were happening and used other defenses such as repression and isolation of affect to repress and modify memories after the abuse ended. The presence of dissociative defense mechanisms indicates severe psychopathology that would require exquisite sensitivity on the part of the therapist in order to slowly help Louis and Bill tolerate in consciousness the recovery of repressed experiences and the powerful, disruptive affects connected with them. Although both were chronically abused, Bill's abuse appears to be more severe because it occurred over a period of approximately two years, twice as long as Louis's, and was initiated by threats and intimidation.

Both men are intelligent, suffering and very determined to live a full life. These characteristics and attitudes will be major assets in the treatment process. A beginning course of psychotherapy two to three times per week for two to four years is indicated for both of them. A second course of psychotherapy of one to two times per week for two to four years in the decade following the completion of the first course of therapy will likely be needed, particularly for Bill. Anti-anxiety and/or anti-depressant medication should be utilized, particularly if the therapeutic process leads to the recovery of repressed memories and experiences.

During young adulthood all significant aspects of normal development were compromised. Sexual arousal continued to be associated with the sexual abuse, undermining the emergence of a solid, integrated heterosexual identity and the capacity for intimacy. Young adulthood is the phase of development in which most individuals in Western culture marry and establish a family.

Both Louis and Bill have moved in that direction but are struggling with issues of intimacy, openness and honesty with their partners. Should they have children, male children in particular, their ability to enjoy parenthood without undue concerns for the safety of their children will be significantly undermined. This is a recurrent theme in the case histories throughout this book. Adults who were abused as children either refuse to have children, particularly of the same sex, or are extremely preoccupied and worried that their offspring may be abused as they were.

The establishment of a career is a central developmental task of young adulthood. Over the course of the decades of the twenties and thirties young adults pursue higher education, gain knowledge and experience in the work place, advance professionally and earn a living sufficient to support themselves and their families. Both Louis and Bill obtained education beyond high school but both feel that they have not been able to fully utilize their knowledge or intelligence to live up to their potential in the workplace. Louis considers himself to be a late starter but is now making progress toward becoming self-sufficient and Bill feels that his progress in the workplace has been severely impeded.

Prognosis

The prognosis for both men, assuming that the treatment regime just outlined is followed, is fair to good. Fair because the twenty-five years of compromised development during adolescence and young adulthood and the lost opportunities for academic and social advancement and emotional stability and maturity cannot be recaptured; but good, particularly in Louis's case, because both men are intelligent, aware of the tremendous effect of the sexual abuse on all aspects of their development and eager to engage life in a full, healthy manner in the long future ahead of them.

CASE STUDY: DALE

When Dale walked into my office shortly before his fortieth birthday to begin the psychiatric evaluation needed for his lawsuit his furrowed brow, piercing eyes and rapid movements immediately conveyed a sense of a man in great inner turmoil. With pressure of speech and affect that ranged from agitation to depression, unlike many sexual abuse victims who were very hesitant to talk about their experiences, Dale plunged into a discussion of the sexual abuse that tormented him in the past and the present. He had been married for nearly fifteen years and had a seven-year-old son. Currently unemployed,

Dale had recently "been fired for I don't know how many times." The family scraped by financially from month to month, relying primarily on his wife's income.

Dale had a need to tell me his story and did so without prompting. His abuser was a relative who was about fifteen years older than Dale. This man abused Dale hundreds of times when he was between the ages of approximately ten and twenty. The perpetrator, who was married, lived in the same city and visited Dale and his parents frequently.

Dale was abused for the first time at age ten when he was at home alone. The perpetrator, whom we will call Joe, came in, told Dale to sit down, opened the boy's pants and masturbated both of them. Dale, who was not close to puberty, refused to touch Joe's penis. The boy was completely surprised by what happened. He had never been abused before, and was even more surprised when Joe gave him money and left without a word of explanation.

The second and third instances, which were very similar to the first, happened several days apart. Since Joe knew the family well he was able to choose times when Dale's parents were not at home. Dale reached a dry climax as Joe masturbated him and was amazed when the abuser ejaculated. On the fourth occasion Joe performed fellatio on Dale. He also told Dale that if he told anyone no one would believe him and he would be sent away to a jail for children. Joe always gave Dale money, sums ranging from $5 to $75. Dale was aware of liking the physical sensations that Joe produced in him and began to covet the money.

As the abuse continued Joe would suck Dale's penis and testicles and rub his nipples and his butt. Joe had been telling Dale that he would ejaculate soon. When Dale began to ejaculate at about age thirteen Joe became very excited and increased the frequency of the abuse, swallowing Dale's semen each time. He seemed to have an endless supply of money which the boy could not resist taking. Joe would occasionally repeat that if Dale told anyone he would be sent away. "I had a family, I couldn't lose them."

The abuse continued unabated throughout the teen years. Although he resisted for several years, Dale finally let Joe undress him but refused anal intercourse. Looking back on the years of abuse during adolescence Dale shamefully wondered why he didn't stop Joe when he was big enough to resist. "It was the money, I think. I had enough to do whatever I wanted. None of my friends did. I never told anyone and no one ever suspected. I finally stopped him when I was about twenty-one."

Dale got "horny" after the abuse began. He became "obsessed with sex" and after beginning to date had intercourse frequently. "I put him and what happened far away." Dale never used condoms and got one girl pregnant. His masturbatory fantasies during adolescence were sometimes about girls, sometimes about Joe. "I had two different sex lives, the one with Joe, for money; and the one I had with girls. I always had sex on my mind."

When asked to tell me how the sexual abuse had affected him Dale immediately poured out his thoughts and feelings with the same pressure of speech and anxiety that he had demonstrated when discussing the abuse. He began using drugs at thirteen, particularly marijuana which he used every day into his late twenties. Dale also tried crystal meth, coke and acid. "My friends liked it that I always had drugs. If I ran out of money I'd call Joe and let him use me. Sometimes I'd get almost $500 in a month."

"I have thoughts about the sex every day. I'm horny, I can't control it. I have one-night stands all the time. I can't stop. A couple of guys wanted me but I never had sex with another man. I masturbate two to three times a day. I always have. I can't be around girls. It stirs me up. Why can't I just be with my wife and be happy?" The sexual thoughts and urges are strongest when Dale uses drugs or alcohol. Dale began drinking at age fourteen. He drank excessively until his early thirties. Now he drinks two or three beers a day, mostly on weekends. "I had a DUI. I spent three months in jail after a bar fight when I was twenty five."

"I dropped out of school in the ninth grade. I had money from Joe, why did I need to go to school? I can read a bit but I can't spell or do math. I began to have thoughts about killing myself after Joe would leave. They got bad when I got older. I tried to kill myself when I was twenty-three. I took a whole lot of pills but I vomited them up. I still get thoughts about killing myself because I cheat on my wife all the time." With tearful anguish Dale said, "I can't touch my son. I'm afraid I'll do something to him. I can't give the kid a bath. I can't even kiss or hug him."

There was an interval of two weeks between our first and second diagnostic sessions. With concern and mild agitation Dale remarked that the last session had "opened a door." Thoughts about the abuse came back to mind causing him to drink heavily and smoke pot. "I went back to how I was. I can't close it off. I just left work. I fought with my wife. She's about to leave me. I shaved my head and my pubic hair to be young again. When I masturbated I was a kid again being sucked off by Joe. My wife wants to know what's going on."

Dale described classic symptoms of Posttraumatic Stress Disorder. Throughout the abusive years Dale's mind was flooded with thoughts about the abuse. "I felt like a prostitute." He had vivid, arousing sexual dreams about the relationship with Joe several times per week. During the two-week interval between our first and second diagnostic interviews they occurred on a daily basis. Flashbacks occur regularly to the present. "I can hear his voice and feel him on my penis. It always causes me to masturbate."

Developmental History

Dale's parents separated when he was five. He spent his childhood alternating between the homes of both parents, often surrounded by various aunts and uncles. As far as he knew mother's pregnancy, labor and delivery were uneventful. She was the primary caretaker. Dale was physically healthy throughout his childhood, indeed, throughout his life. All the early developmental milestones such as walking and talking occurred on time. He was toilet trained easily and did not remember wetting the bed or soiling himself.

The elementary school years were difficult. The moves back and forth between the parent's homes were disruptive. Dale was not a good student but was well liked and had lots of friends. He played sports and was a very good athlete. The abuse began during the elementary school years and quickly began to dominate his mental and emotional life. Dale's hyper-sexuality during adolescence has already been described. He estimated that over the course of his adolescent and young adult years he had sexual relations, always in the absence of an ongoing, caring relationship, with more than seventy-five women. During adolescence he had minimal adult supervision and a steady supply of money given to him by the perpetrator.

Indiscriminate hyper-sexuality became a central feature of Dale's work experience. Because of his lack of education all of his jobs were low-level, entry positions. On several occasions he left, or was fired, because of sexual involvement with other employees or bosses. Long periods of unemployment, sometimes for a year or more, occurred between jobs. At one workplace Dale initiated involvement with another employee. He felt bad afterwards and worried that they might be discovered and she would lose her job, so he quit. On two occasions in his twenties he became sexually involved for months at a time with female bosses. In one instance the woman approached him. In the other he initiated the contact. Dale was fired by these women because he bragged about his "conquest" of them to others.

Psychological Testing

Dale told the psychologist that he never told others about the molestation. This left him feeling very isolated and markedly different from other kids. Dale felt sexually confused, ashamed and embarrassed over "having lost my manhood." "I should have stopped it a lot sooner than I did." He described himself as very driven sexually. "I'm very sexual all the time . . . very obsessed. If I meet a girl, I always want oral sex." He regularly watched pornography and masturbated compulsively. Dale's marriage was described as difficult. "My wife sees me as near crazy and says I need help." Despite his intense sexual preoccupations sexual relationships with his wife are infrequent.

Dale's IQ was in the low average range. Significant defensive rigidity was evident, a pattern often observed in individuals who have experienced significant trauma. Specific responses were indicative of profound defensiveness and distortion regarding perceptions about himself, relationships and the environment.

Stories about sadness, helplessness and passive resignation were evident on projective tests. Passive and dependent longing resulted in frustration, pain and disappointment. "Of particular importance, Dale endorsed items indicating feelings of hopelessness and suicidal ideation. These findings, along with his reported history of a recent suicide attempt and ongoing suicidal fantasies, warrant immediate evaluation and psychotherapeutic intervention . . . The overall level of observed avoidance, emotional disruption/instability, impaired cognitive operations and reality testing, and limited coping abilities are consistent with the effects of sustained psychological trauma."

Utilizing DSM-IV the psychologist made diagnoses on Axis I of Major Depressive Disorder, Sexual Abuse of a Child, ruled out Posttraumatic Stress Disorder, Chronic and ruled out Alcohol Abuse or Dependence. Avoidant and dependent personality features were noted on Axis II. Dale's symptoms were rated in the serious range.

Diagnosis

Using DSM-IV I made the following diagnoses on Axis I: Sexual Abuse of Child V61.21, Clinical Focus on Victim 995.54, Posttraumatic Stress Disorder, Chronic 296.23, Major Depressive Disorder, Single Episode, Chronic 296.23, and Alcohol Dependence 303.90. Avoidant and dependent personality features were noted on psychological testing.

Dale was experiencing major problems in family and marital relationships. In addition to significant social withdrawal, the lack of a high school education, inadequate finances and an inability to hold a job made life difficult indeed. I rated Dale's symptoms in the 41–50 range.

Treatment

Individual psychotherapy three times per week for four to five years is indicated in the immediate present. Antidepressant medication should be prescribed for the foreseeable future. In the decade of the fifties, a second course of individual psychotherapy, two times per week for three to four years, will be needed. Psychiatric hospitalization is likely on one or more occasions. Vocational rehabilitation is strongly indicated. This should include earning a GED certificate.

Prognosis

The prognosis, even with intensive treatment, is very guarded due to the extremely limited ability to maintain intra-psychic stability and function in the real world.

Discussion

The chronicity of the sexual abuse and the extreme psychopathology that resulted from it may seem to the reader as an exaggerated caricature rather than an actual history. Unfortunately, it is not. Histories such as this one are more common than anyone would want to believe. As difficult as it is to read, this story provides mental health professionals, educators, parents and other interested adults with insight into the abusive methods used by this perpetrator and the profound developmental effects that resulted from the decade of abuse during adolescence.

Dale's first sexual experiences, which occurred before he was physically and sexually mature, were at the instigation of a known and trusted relative. Intense sexual arousal and exposure to adult genitalia and sexual functioning were forced upon this young boy before his mind and body were ready for such experience. Dale entered puberty in the midst of an ongoing abusive relationship. Unable to slowly adjust to his maturing body through masturbation and eventual sexual relationships with peers, he was flooded with repeated experiences of sexual arousal that his immature mind could not integrate. The result throughout adolescence, and the entire phase of young adulthood, to the present (age thirty-nine) was and continues to be indiscriminate sexual behavior in the absence of a caring and loving relationship. Dale feels that his body and mind are sexually driven and out of control. He is totally unable to experience the hallmarks of mature sexual functioning in young adulthood—namely love, intimacy, mutuality and respect.

During adolescence peer relationships suffered significantly. They quickly became organized around drug and alcohol use, fueled by the endless supply of money from the perpetrator. Drug and alcohol use became habitual in an attempt to master the chronic, traumatic stimulation. The lack of a high school education severely limited Dale's ability to earn a living. Throughout young adulthood Dale has been unable to keep a job for any length of time because of his emotional instability and a compulsive need to become sexually involved in the workplace. Low self-esteem, depression and limited opportunities led to months, even years, of unemployment.

In his marriage Dale has relied on his wife for stability and support. It is questionable whether the marriage will last because of Dale's instability and very limited ability to be faithful and loving. Almost unbearably poignant and difficult to listen to was Dale's tortured description of his inability to touch his son's body without experiencing intense anxiety and conflict because of the constant intrusion into consciousness of memories of the sexual abuse he experienced as a child.

Dale enters midlife completely ill-equipped to engage the developmental challenges of the forties and fifties. Even with therapy and medication, which he may be unable to utilize and maintain for any length of time, the future is bleak. This is a ruined life, an all too common result of chronic childhood and adolescent sexual abuse.

COMMENTS ON THE THREE CASES

Bill and Louis are the first individuals looking upon the effects of the sexual abuse on their adult development who express the idea that they do not have the time to make up for what has been lost, particularly in regard to success in the workplace and a comfortable integration of an adult sexual identity. Now in their thirties, they look back at a shattered youth with dismay. In the previous chapter, Ben and Karen were aware of the degree to which the sexual abuse had complicated their young adult development but were still optimistic that they had time to work through the trauma and live more normal lives. By the time individuals reach their thirties they are just beginning to be aware of time limitation, a theme which will be a central developmental issue in midlife. Dale, at age thirty-nine and severely damaged, is almost too traumatized to recognize what he has lost.

All three failed to realize their academic potential and had not established stable careers in their thirties, a time when successful individuals are often beginning to assume positions of power and considerable financial success. Dale failed to graduate from high school and had only been able to be employed in low-paying jobs. But he was unable to keep those for any length of time due to his inability to control his hyper-sexuality in the workplace. Thus, because of the painful recognition of a relatively limited future and failure to master the developmental tasks of young adulthood such as marriage and career the decade of the thirties became a painful watershed for these men. Twenty to thirty years have elapsed since the sexual abuse ended and all three are now looking back on their lives from an adult perspective surveying the havoc that the sexual abuse produced in the past—and continues to produce in the future. It is a sobering picture, indeed.

I can't think of anything more damaging to an emerging sense of adolescent sexuality than having your first ejaculation occur in the context of an ongoing sexual abuse relationship. Each of these three men not only experienced his first ejaculation as a result of masturbation and fellatio by the perpetrator, but all of their subsequent early adolescent sexual experiences occurred in the same manner. The contrast between these abusive experiences and normal adolescent sexual development has already been addressed.

Further, Louis and Dale were able to acknowledge that they enjoyed the sexual sensations produced by the perpetrators. This is the natural physiological response to manual and oral stimulation of the genitals. As they grew into manhood and became sexually active with women their compliant responses to the perpetrators become more conflicted, causing great pain and concerns about their heterosexual orientation and sexual identity. None of the male victims in this book became homosexuals due to the chronic child sexual abuse. I choose not to speculate as to why because I feel that the answer, likely different in each case, would only be possible after a long-term, intensive psycho-dynamically focused treatment experience.

Both Louis and Bill have severe dissociative symptoms. We will also see the use of dissociative mechanisms in a number of the cases of older individuals that will be presented in later chapters. The continuation of dissociative defense mechanisms decades after the childhood sexual abuse ended speaks to the severity of the trauma and its lifelong effects. I wonder if the use of dissociative defenses in Bill, expressed as going into a "black hole," was partially in response to seeing Louis being abused. Bill described that as particularly difficult and painful. In the final chapter in the book we will see a similar response by a young girl as she watched her sisters being abused in her presence.

Both Dale and Ben, in chapter 5, described the torment experienced in not being able to comfortably bathe, diaper and lovingly touch their children. In later chapters we will see similar behaviors and, indeed, a refusal to have children at all on the part of several women.

7

Middle Adulthood:
Ages Forty to Sixty-Five

DEVELOPMENTAL THEMES

FOR MANY, POSSIBLY MOST, MIDDLE ADULTHOOD is the best time in life. Often referred to as the golden age of adulthood, the years between forty and sixty-five are usually an extended interval of relative stability characterized by physical health, emotional maturity, an established sense of self, competence and power in the workplace and involved relationships with spouse, children, grandchildren, parents, friends and colleagues. There is no sharp physical or psychological demarcation between young and middle adulthood. The process of aging, which was beginning to become evident in young adulthood, accelerates. Due to obvious signs of aging, an increase in major illnesses, and the death of parents and contemporaries, thoughts and feelings about the aging body become a major influence on mental life.

Stevens-Long (1990) described the transition as follows: "Development in young adulthood seems to be embedded in close relationships, intimacy, love, commitment, and the analysis of relationships within a finite system—all seem related to the mastery of those relationships most immediate to personal experience. The transition from young adulthood to middle age implies a widening of concern to the larger social system. The emergence of intro-systemic thinking implies the differentiation of one's own social, political, and historical system from others, appreciation of its strengths and weaknesses, and an ability to identify with, and hence feel compassion for, another human system. In young adulthood we learn to comprehend and identify with another human system (p. 154). Erikson (1963) described middle adulthood in terms of generative, Maslow (1968) spoke of self-actualization and Jung (1933) the emergence of wisdom.

Physical decline begins to have an effect on psychological development in young adulthood. However, by midlife because of the obvious, universal evidence of aging and the marked increase in major illnesses and the death of contemporaries, thoughts and feelings about the aging body become a major, sometimes dominant influence, on mental life. Marcia Goin (1990) described the effect as follows: "The appearance of one's body in midlife takes on a different significance. Efforts to remain trim and fit are not made to develop a sense of identity or to separate and individuate, but to maintain health and youthfulness and to deter the effects of aging. The struggle is to retain body integrity in the face of anxieties about aging, the vulnerabilities of failing health, and the potential loss of independence" (p. 524).

In addition to the obvious changes in vision, hair color, reflexes and skin tone, there are equally important changes in the more private aspects of physical functioning. These include cessation of menstruation, increase in urinary frequency and diminished force of the urinary stream and alterations in sexual functioning.

Each midlife individual must mourn for the lost body of youth. In healthy men and women acceptance of the aging process in the body leads to a major change in body image which gradually results in a more realistic appraisal of the midlife body and the ability to enjoy the pleasures which the midlife body can continue to provide, particularly if it is cared for properly (Colarusso and Nemiroff, 1981). Pathological attempts to deny aging include inappropriate plastic surgeries, attempts at fusion with younger bodies, refusal to accept appropriate levels of participation in sports and other physical pursuits, excessive preoccupation with cars, clothing and castles which become narcissistically gratifying substitutes for the body, and failure to care for the body through regular checkups, exercise and a healthy diet.

Thoughts and feelings about having a limited time left to live increase in frequency and intensity and force a significant reexamination of all aspects of how life has been lived and how it may be approached in the present and the future, particularly in regard to marriage, family and work. Stimulated by the aging process, the death of parents and contemporaries, the growth of children into adulthood and the approach of retirement direct the midlife individual to thoughts of his or her mortality with the painful but unavoidable recognition that the future is limited and that he or she will die.

Jung (1933) called the midlife preoccupation with aging and time limitation "midlife introversion," and Neugarten (1979) called it "interiority." The assessment of personal successes and failures, the intense scrutiny of interpersonal relationships are part of what Butler and Lewis (1977) called the life review. This evaluation of one's existence continues into late adulthood. For some the mental work is performed primarily at an unconscious level. These individuals usually deny that time limitation and personal death occupy an important place in their mental life but they demonstrate the same changes, normal and pathological, as their more aware counterparts.

The acceptance of personal time limitation may greatly enhance the quality of life by stimulating a reexamination of goals, a reordering of priorities, and a greater appreciation of significant relationships and the true value of time. For others who struggle emotionally or are dissatisfied with their lives, the increased awareness of a personal end and time limitation may precipitate various forms of symptomatology, including the stereotypical—but very real—midlife crisis.

Whereas the young adult is involved in developing the capacity for intimacy, the midlife individual is focused on maintaining intimacy in the face of powerful physical, psychological and environmental pressures. In longstanding relationships inhibitors of sustained physical and emotional closeness include changes in attitudes about sex and sexual functioning and the realistic demands of work, caring for children and elderly parents, financial pressures and planning for retirement.

Maintaining sexual involvement depends on the ability to accept the appearance of the partner's middle-aged body, to continue to find it sexually stimulating, and the capacity to accept the age-related changes in the ability of the body to perform sexually. For instance, men have more difficulty achieving and sustaining erections and experience a longer refractory period after ejaculation while women, due to diminished estrogen production, experience a thinning of the vaginal mucosa and decreased lubrication (Masters and Johnson, 1966).

Environmental interferences with midlife intimacy include the demands of raising children and adolescents, lack of time and energy due to the pressures of work and the multiplicity of social obligations. If physical changes and environmental interferences significantly interfere with sexual relationships one or both partners may experience intense feelings of nostalgia for former lovers, mourn for missed opportunities, and struggle with the question of whether to settle for the status quo, divorce or seek out other sexual partners in a search for greater satisfaction.

During middle adulthood children become adolescents and young adults. Their inevitable progression through the phases of childhood, adolescence and young adulthood affects every facet of parents' lives. Young adult parental vigor and unchallenged control of young children go hand in hand; but so do the middle-age awareness of physical decline and time limitation and the inevitable loss of control of adolescent and young adult offspring. The manner in which the once all powerful progenitors let go and work to achieve a new relationship with their offspring and their spouses and children which is based on equality and mutuality makes the difference between a life full of richness and love and one rampant with rancor, bitterness and emptiness.

Gerald Pearson (1958) was the first developmentalist to describe the conflict. "By the time an individual is in his late thirties or early forties—usually when his children are becoming adolescents—he begins to realize that he will never fulfill some of his postponed ideals. He perceives that he has already started on the down grade toward old age and death, and this realization invigorates his fantasy of the reversal of generations" (p. 177). Also, "he observes that his adolescent child is growing rapidly into a vigorous young adult with all his success ahead of him. He contrasts his lessening opportunities for success and his now rather static capacities with the budding development of his child, and unconsciously he feels envy" (p. 21).

As the parent moves into the later stages of middle adulthood and the son or daughter into the second half of young adulthood, all vestiges of the "child" disappear. Further he or she is likely self-sufficient and living away from home, significantly involved with others sexually and emotionally and raising a family. The presence of these adult relationships and capabilities pushes the parent-child dyad toward equality. The healthy parent not only accepts the "child's" autonomy and independence but promotes it whenever possible. Such behavior is not entirely altruistic; it is a reflection of the recognition of the central importance of the newly constituted family to the parent's mid- and late life development.

As elderly parents become less able to care for themselves the roles of parent and child reverse. The "child" becomes the "parent" of the parent, increasingly performing the roles of physical and mental caretaker. Caring for aging parents is one of the most difficult and most frequently avoided developmental tasks of midlife. In addition to presenting difficult realistic issues concerning daily care; the reversal of roles forces a reworking of childhood issues with the parents, further focus on the midlife developmental task of coming to terms with time limitation and personal death, and anticipation of the inevitable role reversal which will occur with one's own children in the future. Avoidance of this poignant and painful relationship has considerable psychological consequences, particularly guilt and depression. Upon the death of an elderly parent, no matter how expected or anticipated, a mourning process ensues. Long after the acute phase of mourning is over the intra-psychic relationship with the dead parent continues to be dynamic and emotionally charged.

In addition to stimulating thoughts about personal death, the demise of parents also, almost paradoxically, focuses thoughts and feelings on succeeding generations. The relationship with children and grandchildren facilitates the acceptance of personal death by ensuring a form of psychological and genetic immortality, for they are the recipients of the elders' genes and will remember them when others forget.

For the majority of adults in Western society, work is a psychic organizer of major importance, regulating identity and self-esteem, providing meaning and purpose to life, organizing the use of time and providing significant relationships and income. Midlife in the workplace is a time of achievement and the exercise of power. Overinvestment in work may indicate an inability to recognize and plan for the eventual loss of work as a central organizing function; in other words, to plan for retirement and replacement by the next generation. The recognition of the juxtaposition of maximum achievement and power in the workplace and the acceptance of loss and displacement is a significant challenge for midlife workers.

The essence of that challenge is the need to pass on knowledge and power to the next generation while recognizing that the act of mentorship is the means of one's displacement. Healthy individuals do not act on their anger and envy of subordinates to any great degree. They process these feelings at a mental level and sublimate them into generativity.

Play is a lifelong human activity, reflecting over the life cycle physical abilities and limitations and mental capabilities and preoccupations. The unique features of play at midlife are, not surprisingly, a reflection of the aging process in the body and major psychological preoccupations. The forms of play do not change much beyond childhood and adolescence. Adults and children alike prefer games such as baseball, football, golf and tennis; chess, cards and board games, which were learned before adulthood began. Normal aging processes force the abandonment of most contact sports and the modification of others. Those who do not mourn for the lost body of youth and alter their physical activities often end up in emergency rooms. The psychological meaning of sports and exercise also changes in midlife. Instead of being used as a joyous expression of physical and mental competence physical forms of play in midlife are increasingly associated with maintenance of physical integrity and enhancement of the aging body.

Further, both physical and mental forms of play are increasingly used to deal with the developmental task of accepting time limitation and personal death. For example, golf is a game full of beginnings and endings; in other words, opportunities to conquer time and imperfection by beginning over and over again, something that is not possible in real life. There is always another shot, another hole, another nine; unlike life, which has one beginning and end. Mental games such as cards and chess eliminate the need to involve the increasingly imperfect body in play. They, too, have rhythmic beginnings and endings and the ability to begin anew as often as one desires (Colarusso, 1993).

CASE STUDY: BERNARD

First Diagnostic Interview

Bernard got lost attempting to find my office and was late for our first interview. As I began to gather identifying information he cried, stating that he didn't want to talk about the abuse. He had seen another doctor a few days before our interview and was afraid that discussing the abuse would make him feel victimized. For this reason I chose not to address the abuse directly during the first interview. The information gathered during the two diagnostic interviews with Bernard is presented in the order that it was collected.

Bernard was a forty-seven-year-old unemployed retail clerk who lived with his wife and three teenage children. The couple met when he was in his twenties but did not marry for several years because of Bernard's hesitation about becoming involved sexually and emotionally.

Bernard's parents divorced when he was a child. Contact with father had been sporadic to the present but their relationship was cordial. Bernard was close to his mother and saw her frequently. "My mother was my father," he said. Mother was Bernard's primary caretaker. When he was about two years of age she began to work and Bernard was cared for by his grandmother. Early development was uneventful. Bernard was physically healthy and developmental tasks such as weaning and toilet training were mastered without difficulty. During the elementary school years Bernard had friends and was well behaved. He was not a great student, preferring to spend his time playing sports. Uncles and teachers served as role models in father's absence.

Puberty occurred at age thirteen. Bernard began to date when he was sixteen. School records indicated that he graduated at the bottom of his class. Bernard volunteered that he had been an altar boy. The priest/perpetrator, whose name he could not speak at first, gave the altar boys wine, beer and cigarettes when Bernard was thirteen. "My first drink came out of the church." He was drunk for the first time shortly afterwards. I took his volunteering this information to mean that Bernard was feeling less anxious than he was at the beginning of the interview. I continued to let him set the pace of the interview, asking only the most general questions in an effort to establish a good rapport. Soon after being given alcohol by the abuser Bernard began to use other drugs. Drug use continued, unabated, until approximately age forty. Bernard used coke, marijuana, and pills and sniffed glue. He stopped the use of all illegal drugs and alcohol at the same time after his wife "got on my case."

After repeatedly being given alcohol by the priest Bernard began to get into trouble with the authorities. For instance, he was taken to juvenile hall after crashing a party and vandalizing the scene. His mother was very upset. After high school Bernard worked at a number of different jobs before being hired by a large retail chain.

During his twenties Bernard worked, did very little dating, and was heavily involved with alcohol and drug use. He didn't have a good memory for details or dates but did remember one or two DUIs. I had the sense that in many ways his twenties were a lost decade. His extended family was very concerned about his drinking and tried, unsuccessfully, to get him to stop.

After marrying in his late twenties Bernard attempted to be a good husband. However, within a few years he began to stay away from home for weeks at a time, always after heavy drug and alcohol use. With considerable shame he described cheating on his wife during these periods away from home. Bernard lost his job as a result of his unreliability and would have gone heavily into debt if not for his wife's salary. He became involved with other women. Bernard experienced great guilt about these relationships.

Feeling more comfortable as the interview progressed Bernard volunteered, "I stay to myself. I don't have any friends. I don't want to see alcohol. I have to stay sober on my own." He did not attend AA after he stopped drinking, nor does he now. Bernard added that he was not pursuing a lawsuit for the money. Sobbing, he said that he was hurt and never wanted that to happen to another kid.

Bernard began to spontaneously to talk about his relationship with his wife. She tries to hug him and be close but he doesn't cuddle or show love. "I guess I don't have the sex I'm supposed to have. I put all this behind me and I had to bring it all out. That's probably why." When his wife touches his "part" (penis) it confuses him. "I'm so confused," he said, again beginning to cry.

Near the end of the first interview Bernard spontaneously verbalized the following. "I did go back to church but it was never the same. I became a different person. I never told my mother. You couldn't talk about the church bad. I didn't want to break my family's heart. The altar boys never talked about it, never!" After a painful pause he continued, "When I saw on TV those preachers do this, my kids were going to church. I was worried about them. I read in the newspaper that a priest abused a fourteen-year-old girl. I had to talk to someone or go crazy."

Mental Status Examination

Bernard presented as a somewhat overweight adult male. After settling down he sat calmly, spoke in a soft voice and cried frequently. A strong sense of depression was present throughout the interview. Affect ranged from flatness and depression through sobbing sadness, anxiety and expressions of guilt over past behavior. Suicidal ideation had been present periodically for many years but never acted on. Bernard was extremely ashamed as he discussed the sexual abuse. Thinking was logical and goal directed. There was no evidence of delusions or hallucinations. Bernard was oriented as to time, person and place.

Second Diagnostic Interview

Bernard arrived on time. He was calmer and able to talk, volunteering that he had recently begun to see a therapist because his wife wanted him to because of what he had done to her and her family. Sometimes she attends the sessions. They talked about what he did to his family when he was drinking and on drugs. Everyone he loved had been very caring. He was tired of hurting people.

Feeling that I could now approach the matter of the abuse, but without directly asking for details of what was done to him, I asked Bernard to describe the ways in which the sexual abuse had affected him. He volunteered the following: "I don't like men or friends touching me. It feels dirty. It seems gay." He had avoided being touched every since the molestation began. "When I get haircuts I always get a woman. I don't want a man going through my hair."

"I keep everything inside, my feelings. I don't tell my wife what happens at work. I didn't tell my mother. I didn't want to upset her. I should have told her so someone would have stopped it. All the altar boys never talked about it, even now. I hid it away in the back of my mind for a long time. I thought I would take it to my grave but I began to hear stories about priests abusing kids. I had kids." These feelings caused Bernard to go to a lawyer. "I was looking for justice." Describing himself as ashamed, guilty and disgusted, he began to cry.

Bernard said he was usually pretty quiet and didn't get angry easily. When anger did build up he often got in fights or broke windows. Such behavior led to drinking and drug use. "Being abused made me an alcoholic. All the drugs I abused. I don't want to think about it. When I talk about it, it's like it's all happening over again." The anticipation of talking about the abuse to me or the therapist disturbs his sleep. "I can't sleep at night when I have to talk about it." Bernard has nightmares. "Someone is dragging me off a bed, like the devil, and I can feel his hand on my legs and arms." He wakes up screaming, sweating and afraid. Bernard was uncertain when the nightmares began but they occur at least once per week to the present.

"I feel ashamed, guilty and disgusted. I shouldn't have been there. I should have known better. I saw [the perpetrator] come out of prison. I wondered where the monster was."

At this point I asked Bernard to tell me about the actual abuse. Haltingly, and between sobs, he revealed the following: "I was touched by his hand inside my pants, jerking me off." The priest would masturbate himself in front of the boys while watching pornography. The perpetrator always wanted to wrestle. When he did he put his hand on Bernard's crotch. He would only have to touch the boy briefly and he would ejaculate. Bernard tried to hide the fact that he was wet. The masturbation happened "many, many times." Bernard was unable to say how many with any certainty.

The most difficult abusive experience for Bernard occurred in the back of the priest's van. It was getting dark and some of the altar boys in the van were drinking and smoking. Bernard was sitting down. The perpetrator was lying across several boys' legs. "It was quick. Everyone was laughing and there was a lotta smoke." With enormous shame Bernard reported that he thinks the priest unzipped his pants and "sucked on me." Bernard bolted out of the truck. Wet when he got home and took a shower, Bernard threw away his underwear.

The abuser would show the boys pornography, men and women having sex. The priest would play with his penis in front of the boys. Sometimes the boys laughed at him. The priest always grabbed their rear ends. Bernard thinks someone put a spoon in his anus. He and the other boys must have been so drunk on occasion that neither he nor they know exactly what happened to them.

Bernard did not have a very clear sense of when the abuse started or ended. He thinks it started when he was approximately twelve or thirteen years of age and ended when the priest was reassigned three or four years later. At the time of the abuse Bernard had not had any sexual experience. He did not remember if he masturbated before he was abused.

After the abuse ended, when he was having sex, Bernard didn't think about the priest. "I locked this stuff so far away I never thought I would speak of it. It's like it's all new to me. And I used the drugs to really put it behind me." Bernard was never abused by anyone else. He has little interest in pornography.

Psychological Testing

Bernard's IQ was in the low normal range. There was no evidence of significant neuropsychological impairment. He was in moderate to severe current emotional distress and did not exaggerate. On the Minnesota Multiphasic Personality Inventory there was evidence of significant distress, symptoms of Posttraumatic Stress Disorder and chronic depression and low self-esteem. There was extensive use of denial and repression. Bernard was seen as introverted and extremely shy.

Using the DSM-IV the psychologist made the following diagnoses: Posttraumatic Stress Disorder, Chronic 309.81 and Dysthymic Disorder 300.4. Alcohol Dependence 303.90 was considered to be in early sustained remission. On Axis IV the psychologist noted sexual abuse and on Axis V categorized Bernard's symptoms at 45, in the severe range.

In his discussion the psychologist described the negative effects of the molestation on Bernard. In addition to very low self-esteem and inability to trust others, which was noted earlier, he mentioned Bernard's strong need to isolate himself by staying away from work and social situations. Bernard was in need of individual therapy, which would likely make him very uncomfortable. He could be a suicide risk and might require hospitalization. Psychotherapy was indicated periodically throughout life. Group therapy centered on male victims of child sexual abuse would be helpful, as would AA and couples therapy. Medication was indicated.

Information Obtained from the Depositions of the Perpetrator, a Psychiatrist, and the Altar Boys

During many hours of deposition the perpetrator acknowledged abusing boys at every pastoral assignment. He estimated the number at between one hundred and two hundred, but did not recall the names of some when their names were suggested to him. He did not remember Bernard but did acknowledge sexual involvement with various boys in the back of his truck. Bernard described the van as the place where the priest performed fellatio on him.

A psychiatrist saw Bernard on two occasions several years before my evaluation. He made diagnoses of Posttraumatic Stress Disorder and Major Depressive Disorder and prescribed antidepressant medication. Bernard did not show up for subsequent appointments.

Altar Boy Depositions

Altar boy number 1: This man did not know Bernard. He met the perpetrator when he was ten years old. The perpetrator touched him inappropriately and fondled him on the first day that they met. He had vague memories of the abuser being involved in fondling, oral copulation and self-masturbation with him and other boys.

Altar boy number 2: The perpetrator abused this man when he was eight or nine. The abuse consisted of touching in a swimming pool and oral sex in the priest's apartment. He did not know Bernard.

Altar boy number 3: The perpetrator abused this man between the ages of ten and twelve. He spent nights with the priest and went on field trips. The abuser showed the boy his penis a few times and asked him to touch it, which he refused to do, and masturbated in front of him. This man witnessed sexual activity between the abuser and other boys.

Altar boy number 4: Abused between the ages ten to twelve, he ejaculated for the first time when the perpetrator masturbated him. He saw the abuser on top of a boy, apparently having anal intercourse. This man also saw Bernard being abused by the perpetrator. Recently Bernard had called him to discuss the sexual abuse.

Altar boy number 5: At age eight the priest performed oral sex on this man. On another occasion he woke up with his underwear around his ankles, his rear end wet, and the priest behind him, naked.

Altar boy number 6: Multiple experiences of oral sex occurred when this man was eleven and twelve years old.

Altar boy number 7: The perpetrator touched him inappropriately twenty to thirty times, including masturbation to ejaculation. After observing the priest in bed with another boy, this man refused to be involved with the perpetrator, who slapped him across the face when he refused to comply.

Altar boy number 8: This man described numerous experiences of sexual abuse by the perpetrator, including masturbation and oral sex. He also observed sexual activity between the priest and other boys, including one experience in which he and another boy spent an overnight with the priest. He began to use drugs and alcohol shortly after the sexual abuse began.

In the deposition of a relative of Bernard the boy was described as an "excellent kid." He changed radically during adolescence and became withdrawn and difficult. A few years ago Bernard described the sexual abuse by the perpetrator.

Diagnosis

Using DSM-IV, I made the following diagnoses: Sexual Abuse of Child V61.21, Focus on Victim 995.53, Posttraumatic Stress Disorder, Chronic 309.81, Dysthymic Disorder 300.4, and Alcohol Dependence, Sustained Full Remission—No Use for twelve months or longer. Bernard had not used alcohol in four years. Although Bernard's psychopathology is best understood within the context of the diagnoses described on Axis I, in the past he did demonstrate characteristics of Antisocial Personality Disorder. In the present he has signs of Avoidant Personality Disorder.

In regard to psychosocial and environmental factors Bernard disrupted his family by separating from his wife and children in the past. He was very isolated from peers and the community at large. Low academic achievement and discipline problems in school led to periodic unemployment and financial problems. Bernard had DUIs in the past, was a victim of crime and was in the midst of a lawsuit. At the time of my evaluation I rated his symptoms in the 41–50, serious range.

Treatment

Bernard was in need of intensive individual psychotherapy, three times per week for three to five years. Antidepressant medication was indicated in conjunction with the psychotherapy, likely for the entire course of the psychotherapy. The use of antidepressants may be indicated for the indefinite future. At some point during the decade after the completion of the first course of psychotherapy a second course of psychotherapy, one to two times per week for one to two years, is likely to be indicated.

Attendance at AA is strongly recommended for the foreseeable future. Couples or family therapy, once per week for two to three years, would be helpful. As noted by the psychologist, participation in a group composed of adult males who were sexually abused as children would be useful after Bernard worked through enough of his feelings in individual therapy to tolerate sharing his experience with others.

Prognosis

The prognosis, if the extensive treatment plan outlined above is implemented, is fair. No amount of treatment will completely erase the trauma and developmental interferences caused by the chronic sexual abuse. Without treatment, Bernard may become a serious suicide risk.

Discussion

The chronic sexual abuse of Bernard by the perpetrator had a profound and ongoing effect on all aspects of his life. Occurring as it did, just as he was becoming physically and sexually mature (a familiar story by now to the reader), it severely altered the course of adolescent development. In addition to un-

dermining his sexual development, the abuse affected other critical aspects of
the teen years such as academic performance, peer relationships, contact with
and use of alcohol and drugs, and control of aggression and social behavior.
Bernard and the other altar boys were introduced to alcohol by the priest to
make them more available for sexual seduction. As Bernard expressed it, he
got his first drink through the Church.

In young adulthood the abuse significantly impacted relationships with
spouse and family and was a critical factor in the continued abuse of alcohol and drugs, which contributed to ongoing irresponsible and antisocial
behavior. Instead of developing into a confident, responsible man, father
and husband, Bernard struggled throughout these decades. Mentally and
emotionally he was, and is, a tormented man, uncertain of his masculinity,
depressed and struggling with guilt over his antisocial past and abandonment
of his family. Sadly, his story is similar to those of many other older victims
of childhood sexual abuse. More than four decades after the end of the abuse,
after attempting to repress the experience through various psychological
mechanisms and actions, including the use of illegal drugs and alcohol;
Bernard deals with his thoughts and feelings about the abuse as though it
happened yesterday. Struggling to comply with the need to discuss his experiences in detail—for the first time after so many decades—to professionals
who are strangers to him, Bernard finds it extremely difficult and shameful
since the homosexual experiences involved run so counter to his sense of
himself as a man. The inconsistencies in his recall of what happened and how
often he was abused are, in my experience, the usual and expected response
from someone who was abused in the distant past and has just begun to
discuss what happened to him. During the course of treatment, after much
of the shame and other painful emotions associated with the sexual abuse
have been worked through, a clearer picture of the episodes of abuse will
likely emerge. Further, in this case we have volumes of deposition from the
perpetrator and numerous victims who describe multiple episodes of sexual
abuse similar to those reported by Bernard. Such confirming evidence adds
great validity to the substance, if not the details, of Bernard's memory of the
abuse by the perpetrator.

CASE STUDY: ANDREW

Diagnostic Evaluation

When Andrew appeared in my office for the diagnostic evaluation in connection with his lawsuit he was so nervous that he could barely talk. In his
forty-eight years of life he had never told anyone other than his lawyer that he

had been molested and had never talked of the details of the molestation with anyone. Casually dressed and small in stature, Andrew frowned constantly and cried frequently during the interview. Married and the father of a child, he worked in a warehouse.

With great reluctance and intense shame Andrew slowly told the story of the nearly ten years of molestation by a close friend of his family. When Andrew was four years of age the abuser would grab his buttocks and fondle his penis. Eventually the touching became prolonged masturbation which "became routine."

At approximately age five the abuser began to have Andrew masturbate him. As the molestation progressed the perpetrator wanted the relationship to become more personal and began to kiss the boy. Andrew tried, unsuccessfully, to resist. The abuser began to fellate Andrew when he was about eight years of age. Soon after the perpetrator taught Andrew to perform fellatio on him. When the boy began to ejaculate a few years later the perpetrator's interest in oral sex increased. At about the same time the abuser began to anally penetrate his victim. As he approached puberty Andrew began to resist the perpetrator's advances but despite his efforts the abuse continued until he was in junior high school and able to physically resist his oppressor. The abuser told Andrew that if he told anyone he and his family would become homeless. Andrew estimated that the total number of sexual molestations was well over 100.

Nearly thirty years after the chronic sexual abuse ended, Andrew's mental and emotional life continued to be dominated by its effects. Intrusive thoughts about the molestation haunt Andrew on a nearly daily basis. He continues to have nightmares about the abuser pursuing and anally penetrating him. Other nightmares focus on the perpetrator's attempts to pursue Andrew's child. In addition he frequently wakes up at night expecting the abuser to be in the room ready to rape him. Premature ejaculation began during adolescence and continues, unabated, to the present. Andrew has problems maintaining an erection and frequently becomes flaccid during sex. When he was involved with the abuser his erections were firm. In his early twenties Andrew had two homosexual experiences in which he allowed men to perform oral sex on him.

In ninth grade Andrew began to use drugs and alcohol. Within a year he was using cocaine, marijuana and acid. Extensive drug use, which Andrew related to his attempts to control intense feelings of depression and blot out memories of the abuse, continued into his thirties. Andrew had a DUI in his twenties. He has been sober for the past several years.

Andrew has intense feelings of shame and revulsion and has not been able to enter a church since the abuse ended. When the abuse became known to his family within the past ten years it caused a serious disruption in family relationships which continues to the present. "We're strangers to each other. I haven't been talking to my family at all. I get angry being around them. They act like this is all my problem." Soon after the revelation Andrew made a serious suicide attempt.

Psychological Testing

Andrew's IQ was in the high average range. The MMPI-2 results described depression, distress, anger, resentment, insecurity, suspiciousness and dependency fears. Symptoms of Posttraumatic Stress Disorder were also noted on both the MMPI-2 and the TSI.

The testing indicated that Andrew had many risk factors indicating the likelihood of a poor adult outcome. The sexual abuse was by far the most severe stressor that Andrew faced as a child and had a great negative impact. The substance abuse was the direct result of the childhood sexual abuse. The psychologist made a diagnosis of Posttraumatic Stress Disorder.

Diagnosis

Using DSM-IV I made diagnoses of Sexual Abuse of Child, Focus on the Victim 995.53, Posttraumatic Stress Disorder, Chronic, with Depression 309.81, Premature Ejaculation 302.75, Alcohol Abuse, in Remission 305.00, and Polysubstance Dependence, in Remission 304.80. Psychosocial and environmental factors included severely damaged family relationships, social isolation, victim of crime and litigation. On Axis V I rated Andrew in the 51–60, moderate range. In the childhood, adolescent and young adult past, the severity of his symptoms was likely in the 31–40, very severe range.

Treatment Recommendations and Prognosis

As with many of the other severely impaired individuals in this book, no amount of therapeutic intervention will restore Andrew to complete health. However, he has made strides on his own in the past decade and is receptive to the idea of therapy. A course of Individual psychotherapy, two to three times per week for three to four years, has a reasonable chance of diminishing the ongoing effects of the severe childhood sexual abuse. During the decades of the fifties and sixties, one to two additional courses of individual psychotherapy should be helpful. Antidepressant medication is strongly indicated and may be required indefinitely. The prognosis is guarded to fair.

Developmental Discussion

Every phase of development from early childhood to the midlife present was profoundly impacted by the chronic sexual abuse which began at about age four and continued until the early teen years. Interference with sleep began at the time that the abuse commenced and continues to the present in the form of nightmares, dreams, and frequent awakening in anticipation of having to ward off the perpetrator. Toilet training was not mastered at an appropriate age (three to four) and bed-wetting continued into the elementary school years.

The process of integrating a comfortable male sexual identity, which normally takes place during the years before puberty within an immature body and mind, in the absence of sexually activity with others, certainly without involvement with an adult, was totally undermined. Andrew was introduced to sexual behavior by an adult male at a time when neither his body nor his mental development would allow him to understand or integrate the sexual arousal associated with masturbation and fellatio or the pain associated with anal intercourse. Further, he was encouraged to hug and kiss the abuser and feel affection for him.

As with so many other male victims in this book his first ejaculation, which is usually experienced through a nocturnal emission or masturbation, was produced by stimulation by the perpetrator. The fact that the abuse occurred over a period of approximately ten years, including the early adolescent years, completely corrupted the normal adolescent developmental process, which involves a gradual period of acceptance of the physically and sexually mature body through masturbation and later beginning sexual involvement with chronological peers. Andrew entered adulthood with a deeply compromised sexual identity, intense shame and difficulty in sexual performance.

Despite possessing an average to above average IQ Andrew performed poorly in school and barely graduated from high school. The continuation of the abuse throughout the elementary school years and the use of alcohol and drugs during junior and senior high school prevented Andrew from experiencing the self-esteem and pleasure that accompany successful academic performance.

During the young adult years (20–40) Andrew struggled to integrate a sense of himself as a stable, productive adult. The lack of higher education and the pervasive use of drugs and alcohol throughout his twenties and into his thirties prevented the establishment of a satisfying work identity and financial achievement. Relationships with the opposite sex were continually problematic because of intrusive memories of sex with the perpetrator. Intimacy, the young adult ability to care for the sexual partner with tenderness and love, was and is compromised by a deep sense of insecurity about his masculine identity and concerns about sexual performance. Andrew was eventually able to marry and father a child but his experience of parenthood is filled with fear, as evidenced by nightmares in which the perpetrator abuses his child.

Further, the young adult and middle adulthood task of achieving a sense of mutuality and adult equality with parents and siblings has not occurred due to the disruption of familial relationships which followed the inability of his family to acknowledge and understand the reality of the abuse and its consequences for Andrew. The fact that the perpetrator was welcomed into the family as a respected and admired friend appears to have complicated the ability of the family to accept the painful reality of his effect on Andrew. One of the most painful, and incomprehensible experiences of child sexual abuse victims, both in childhood and adulthood, is the fact that very often they are not believed and/or are blamed for the sexual interactions. Now well into midlife Andrew is faced with the daunting task of looking back and accepting a life of unrealized potential, drug and alcohol abuse, and compromised relationships with self, family and friends.

CONCLUDING THOUGHTS

There is little that needs to be added to the discussions following each of these cases. The major point to be made is that both of these men, in their late forties, continue to be effected both intra-psychically and in the real world on a daily basis by the childhood sexual abuse that occurred more than three decades ago. In the last two chapters of this book we will see that the effects of chronic child sexual abuse continue, unabated, after half a century. There is little reason to think that if Andrew and Bernard were followed to the end of their lives, with or without treatment, the effects of the childhood sexual abuse would not continue to be obvious and interfering with late life development.

Bernard's and Andrew's stories are, not surprisingly, very similar. Both were abused as children, both began to act out in adolescence, becoming involved with alcohol and drugs. Both had DUIs. Neither man wants to be touched. Both continue to have struggles with their masculinity and sexual activity despite being married and having children. Neither has accomplished very much in terms of work and career and both continue to be plagued with feelings of doubt, embarrassment and shame. Both men withdrew from close relationships with family and friends and suffered in silence, never discussing what had happened to them so long ago. The reluctance to seek help because of shame, embarrassment and feelings of responsibility for the sexual abuse is one of the most consistent findings not only in these two men but in most of the men and women in this book, particularly the older ones who were abused at a time when there was little public discussion or understanding of the phenomenon.

8

The Sexual Abuse of
Six Girls by a Clergyman

C HAPTERS 8 AND 9 DETAIL THE CASE HISTORIES of ten women who are nearing or are at the end of middle adulthood. In all ten instances the devastation begun in childhood continues decade by decade, culminating in the forties and fifties in bitter realizations of how the abuse that took place so long ago continues to dominate their lives. Most of these women had never discussed the childhood sexual abuse until recently. The intense affects and suffering that accompany their attempts to begin to deal with what happened to them half a century ago graphically demonstrate the undiminished, lifelong power of childhood sexual abuse.

The case studies in this chapter concern six girls between the ages of eight and twelve, all members of a church choir, who were among others who were repeatedly abused by a priest from the parish they attended with their families. At the time of my evaluations they ranged in age from fifty-nine to sixty-four. None had come forward over the half a century since the abuse occurred until the widespread abuse within the Catholic Church was reported in the press and on television. All pursued legal action at that time and were part of the settlement that resulted from the legal process against a large diocese.

The material in this chapter will focus primarily on their very similar descriptions of the chronic sexual abuse, their symptoms and psychopathology and a general description of the various applicable diagnoses and treatment recommendations. Psychological testing was not a part of any of these evaluations.

JULIE

Julie was sixty-four years of age at the time of the evaluation. Mildly agitated and rambling as she talked, Julie later revealed that she had to take medication before coming to our interview to contain her anxiety. "I have to work to get it out." One day when Julie was twelve Father T invited her to gather hymnals with him. As they were working Father T reached over and touched her breast. "This can't be happening!" At that point things became vague in her mind. She is not sure what else happened. "I wondered where the nuns were. Why didn't they help me? I'm very angry at the nuns." Julie thinks she bolted and ran. The next thing she remembered was walking home not knowing what to think. Julie had gone through puberty before Father T touched her breast. Trying to make sense of her experience Julie said, "So strange, very, very weird, I can remember classmates back to third grade but I don't remember any of the girls in the choir." Julie remembered the pews in the choir loft. The girls faced forward. Father T stood behind them. The nuns were in front, clearly in a position to see what Father T was doing.

Julie didn't tell anyone. She was ashamed. Later when her mother read in the paper that Father T had been transferred she asked Julie if he had ever done anything to her. Julie said no. She had not read the stories of the other girls. "I don't want to know. It's abominable. I came face to face with pure evil. After my deposition I was afraid I would fragment into five people, I mean pieces. When I got back home I couldn't function. I guess I like my world rose colored. I had a beautiful world until then . . . the anxiety I went through after my deposition was horrible. I couldn't go out of the house. I lost twenty pounds in a few weeks. I had diarrhea. I went on medication to stop the panic attacks I was having." She became involved in the lawsuit after reading an article in the paper about others accusing Father T of sexual abuse. "I always thought he probably abused others. You only hear about priests molesting boys. I didn't think anyone would believe me."

Julie described the following symptoms. "I can't go into a church. I wouldn't go to my mother's funeral if it was held in church so my sister planned it at a mortuary. I began to be careful about men. They are on the prowl. I don't want to see or hear priests . . . After the abuse I was very ashamed of my breasts. I tried to hide them. I spent a lot of time outside. You can trust nature."

In the decades after the abuse "I would see him in my mind, like a vanguard. He was there. I couldn't see him clearly but I could describe him. When I got depressed it was as though he was there. At the deposition it was like he was there, right next to me on my left side, a presence. I knew it wasn't real." Racing from thought to thought she continued, "I used to think there was something about me that attracted him to me. He would pick little losers. I still see myself that way. I had nightmares about him all the time until I was about thirty. I don't know why they stopped. I remember very little of what happened. I didn't want to remember. I would have lost myself, fallen apart and not existed anymore." Clearly, Julie used dissociative defense mechanisms to manage her response to the abuse.

Julie went into therapy after her deposition and took medication for her enormous anxiety. She was still seeing the therapist at the time of our evaluation. She had not had any treatment prior to the deposition.

Julie was raised in an intact family. Mother was the primary caretaker and early development proceeded normally. Julie was never physically or sexually abused other than by Father T. She was an excellent student in elementary school and had friends and hobbies. Julie did well academically during high school and was involved in many activities. She was not involved with drugs, alcohol or the police during adolescence. Dating began during high school and Julie married in her twenties. The marriage was and is very good. "My husband is my refuge." After the birth of one of her children Julie developed a postpartum depression and was on medication for several years. Most of the young adult years were spent in raising her family. After they left home Julie obtained a college degree and worked until recently.

KAREN

Karen was sixty-three at the time of the evaluation. Like the other women, she had great difficulty telling her story. She first met Father T when she was eleven years of age. After Karen joined the choir Father T was very friendly. After practice one day she was alone in the church building. "He was stalking me. He came up behind me and gave me a French kiss. I felt disgusted." The priest had tobacco breath and a strong body odor. Karen felt his hard penis against her body. "I have no memory past that point." Her father was always very modest. "I didn't know about a penis." Sex was never talked about in their home. "He always had his hands on us, before, during and after choir."

A second incident occurred soon after in Karen's home. Karen was ill. Her mother was in the house but not in her room. "We hold a trust in our priests and nuns. Our parents taught us that." Father T sat on the bed. Karen said that she was feeling better. "That is the end of the memory right there." After this encounter Karen had great anxiety and felt like she was suffocating if anyone came to stay at their home. "I think there must have been something that happened with Father T and my conscious mind won't let me remember." Karen was never abused by anyone else.

On other occasions Karen remembered the priest's hand on her back and buttocks. She does not "distinctly" recall his putting her hand on his penis. With deep sighs and sadness Karen reported seeing Father T with his arms around other girls who were crying. On another occasion a girl was crying hysterically in the back seat of his car. "We couldn't help her. We didn't know what happened." Karen never told anyone about the abuse. "A girl, Nancy, said that Father T molested her. I never said a word. Then Nancy disappeared from school."

Karen has been married for over thirty years. She also withheld information about the abuse from her husband. He learned of the abuse when Karen became part of the clergy lawsuit and encouraged her to join the litigation. "I just had to bring the suit for justice."

Karen reported a number of symptoms. She did little dating during adolescence and became very upset when her friends talked about sex. "I don't like movies about nudity. As a kid I didn't like dirty jokes. I don't know how I got married. I didn't like sex, the closeness, touching, nudity. This caused difficulty in my marriage. I felt my husband would divorce me. I cooperated but I didn't enjoy it." Her husband told Karen that he couldn't go on like this. Things had to change. She encouraged him to leave if he had to. He chose to stay. "I don't fully trust men. I fear they might do something. I won't be with a man alone." Workmen are not allowed in the house unless her husband is there.

"I stopped being a Catholic. After graduating from high school that was the end. I never went to a Catholic church again." Karen attends a church of another denomination and has faith in God. She added, "I have insomnia every night. I'm awake for two hours every night. I think, why am I so wide awake?" During the years of the abuse Karen had "daymares." She would think of Father T following and French kissing her. These "daymares" went on for years. After a long pause and a sigh she continued, "There's a deep sadness inside of me and not knowing why, for as long as I can remember. It comes and goes."

Throughout the interview it was clear that Karen used the defense mechanism of repression to an extreme degree. She had great difficulty remembering details. "The abuse seemed to follow me along in my life. The marital situation was as bad as Father T following me around in school. It was always there." She continued, "No oral sex. I didn't like that at all. Period. None of that. And I didn't like French kissing either. And I don't undress in front of my husband to this day. I could have passed my entire life without sex. If my husband dies I will never remarry. For my husband's sake I never should have married to begin with. When I was dating I didn't want to sit near the boy. I went to the proms. One double date caused me great fear. We parked and made out. I swore if I got home safely I would never go out with him again.

I had such terrible anxiety." A depressive tone permeated Karen's thoughts. She obviously felt great anger and guilt about her lack of sexual desire for her husband.

Karen was raised in an intact family. Developmental milestones occurred on time. Mother was the primary caretaker. There were no significant separations from either parent during the first six years of life. Karen was quiet in school and did not cause problems. She had a few friends and enjoyed reading and roller skating. The sexual abuse occurred during the elementary school years. Puberty occurred at age twelve. There was no discussion of sex at home or at school. In junior and senior high school Karen was an average student. During adolescence she didn't use drugs or alcohol and did not have any problems with the police. Karen did little dating and avoided sexual discussions with peers.

After high school Karen attended college where she met her husband. They married soon after. "I tried to please him as a newlywed. Father T would be in the back of my mind." A child was born early in the marriage. "I was an at-home Mom. The marriage was good outside of the sexual area. I would clam up rather than talk about my feelings. After my husband gave me the ultimatum about responding to him sexually I tried."

MONICA

Monica was sixty-two when I evaluated her. She was married and had a child. Monica was watching television coverage of the Boston sexual abuse revelations with a relative who commented, "We took care of that," and ended the conversation. Monica volunteered that Father T had been "mean" to her but said nothing more. She had never told anyone about being abused. Monica thought she was the only one and was embarrassed and uncomfortable talking about what had happened. She has clear memories of two occasions of abuse and likely rape at her home. Monica was almost certain that there were more instances of abuse at her home. In addition, she has memories of abuse in a car and at choir practice.

The first abuse occurred at Monica's home when she was ten years old. Both parents were working and since it was summer Monica was home alone. Father T knew that because he was a friend of the family. He came by one morning when Monica was in her pajamas. "He put his arms around me. He was hot and sweaty and his genitals were throbbing. He moved back and forth when I was on his lap. He French kissed me. I did nothing. I thought I would be sick when his tongue was in my mouth. I was really naïve. He was one mass of sweat. I knew nothing about sex. My parents never talked about it. I had no knowledge of what was going on." Monica was upset about not doing anything to stop the priest. "I'm trying to look at it from an adult perspective."

The second time occurred soon after, during the same summer. "He came to the door and said he wanted to talk to me. I refused to sit near him but he pulled me to him. He was standing, rubbing around me, sweating and kissing me. I couldn't get away. His hands were all over my back and buttocks. After he left I took a bath. I'm not really sure what happened. I can't remember." Monica's memory stops at the point where he is holding her and rubbing his erection against her. "Such a complete blank, it upsets me."

A third incident occurred the same summer. Father T knocked on the door and asked to be let in. Monica crawled on her hands and knees into her bedroom in the hope that he would think she wasn't home. The door wasn't locked. Monica remembers sitting in the corner of her bedroom with Father T knocking on the door. She has no memory after that. "It's the same kind of complete blank that occurred during the first time he came to the house." These are the memories that are clear. Monica is unsure if there were other episodes. She was intensely perplexed and angered at her inability to remember more.

During choir practice Father T sat next to Monica. "I thought he was holding my hand. I can't remember anything else. He was in his cassock." As an adult she came to believe that he was moving her hand on his penis. "I have such a clear memory of other things. Why didn't I say anything? Why didn't I tell my parents? I hated the choir. I have memories of being in the choir and then of leaving and not knowing what happened in between. I know he sat next to other girls. I remember him comforting one girl who was crying. The nun director would look at him. She knew he was there. He sat wherever he wanted. He was there all the time. It was like he was part of the choir."

Monica went to confession with Father T. She had to. She remembers the nuns telling her to go to Father T. "I was a very compliant child." She did as she was told. Now she believes that Father T told the nuns which children he wanted to hear in confession. This occurred several times. "He would say, 'Hi Monica' and laugh. He wanted me to know he knew who I was."

Symptoms: "I've been uncomfortable all of my life with men. I drank a lot and then I could date." Monica did very little dating in high school and college. She was a virgin when she married. "I don't like sex. The only time I could have sex was after I drank a lot. After divorcing, "I had a lot of one-nighters after drinking. When I would drink when I was younger everything was a blur. I don't like French kissing. I never had a good handle on my sex life. . . . I don't like sex with my current husband who is a great guy. We are loving to each other but no sex. I feel guilty all the time about my single days, having sex, using birth control. I've separated my faith from the church. I'm angry at the people who say we should let bygones be bygones. I believe in God but I don't believe in organized religion and I don't go to church."

Monica was raised in an intact, loving family. Her early years were uneventful. Mother was at home caring for her children on a full-time basis. The elementary school years were good ones from an academic standpoint. Monica was a fine student. She had lots of friends and was well behaved. The sexual abuse occurred during these years.

Monica graduated from a Catholic high school with a GPA of 3.8. She spent time with friends but did very little dating. Monica did not use drugs other than alcohol, and little of that substance before college. Her relationship with her parents was comfortable. Monica graduated from college four years later. She drank heavily during these years. Monica has never been to AA and does not consider herself to be an alcoholic. During college she didn't have a serious boyfriend. Petting occurred, but no intercourse.

Monica married at age twenty-five and divorced several years later. After the divorce, which was initiated by her husband, Monica worked and raised her children. She met her second husband when she was in her early forties. They married soon after and remained married at the time of the evaluation. Monica described the relationship as loving but essentially asexual.

NOREEN

Noreen was a sixty-two-year-old married woman when we met. She was more direct than several of the other women in this chapter and was clearly extremely angry at what had happened to her. Like the others, she was a member of the girls' choir and in sixth grade when the sexual abuse by Father T began. One day at choir practice Father T sat next to Noreen and put his hand under her dress. He then put her on his lap and placed her hand on his penis. When Noreen tried to get him to stop Father T said that he would abuse her younger sister if she didn't obey him. He placed his fingers in her vagina and forced her to rub his penis until he ejaculated.

After choir practice he took her into the church and put his penis in her mouth, forcing her to suck on it until he ejaculated. Noreen gagged, cried and begged but it made no difference because Father T held her down. Her sister waited on the front steps of the church, crying because Noreen was not there. Mother was angry at Noreen because she left her sister alone. This same pattern took place every Saturday and Sunday. "It was never ending." There were times during the school week when Father T would ask the nuns if Noreen could help him with something. He always abused her on these occasions.

The children went to confession on a regular basis. Noreen told another priest that she had committed adultery. The priest laughed. When Noreen told him what Father T had done to her the confessor called her a liar and said that her sins would not be forgiven until she recanted her lies. Sobbing, Noreen said that the story was true and ran out of the confessional. There were times when Noreen would have to confess to Father T. There was no confessional booth, only a kneeler and a screen on the altar. "Those experiences were torture."

Noreen told her mother that she didn't want to go to choir practice but mother, who was very religious, insisted. When Noreen told her mother what Father T was doing to her, her mother hit her and punished her for lying. Noreen estimated that she was sexually abused more than 100 times during the sixth and seventh grades. She was raped on a number of those occasions. Noreen remembered being forced to go places with Father T despite screaming to her mother that she didn't want to go. In the car Noreen was forced to rub the priest's penis. Then he drove to a secluded place and raped her. Noreen remembered screaming from the pain. "I never, ever forgot that," she said. After that Father T raped Noreen on several more occasions in church buildings. All of the sexual abuse occurred before Noreen went though puberty at about age fourteen. During choir practice Noreen saw Father T sit next to other girls but she never looked at him. She always kept her eyes closed, hoping that he would not sit next to her. The abuse ended abruptly when Father T was transferred.

Noreen was very distressed by her symptoms. "I can't go into churches with choir lofts. I can't go to the places were he raped me. I hate to speak to adults and for the most part I'm withdrawn. I have dreams and nightmares which are terrible. I sleep with something in my right hand all the time because if I don't to this day I can feel his penis in my hand. I hold a teddy bear most of the time." She continued, "Sexually life with my husband is hell. He describes me as a dead body." Noreen rarely climaxes. She has to work up her courage to perform oral sex on her husband and gags when she does. "My husband has been very supportive. I told him I was abused when we dated but I didn't tell him about the rape until five or six years ago."

"I have to control everything. I'm extremely careful of my grandchildren. I don't want to let them out of my sight. My daughter thinks I'm crazy because I'm always telling her to watch her children. She doesn't know what happened to me."

"My weight got up to over 300 pounds. Then I forced myself to lose some but I'm on the way back up. I dig at my arms. I bite my nails all the time. I always had a very low opinion of myself. I feel fat and unattractive. To this day I wonder what my husband sees in me . . . I think I've been depressed for years. I would go someplace in my mind to avoid painful thoughts." Noreen had and has many suicidal thoughts but has never made an actual attempt.

She began having nightmares shortly after Father T left. They continue to the present on a two- to three-times-per-week basis. In the nightmares Noreen is in a pit, trying to get out. Something big is holding her down. "There are penises everywhere." Other dreams are about rape or being pushed into choir lofts in churches. "There is always a power struggle."

Mother died without ever believing her daughter. After mother's death Noreen tried to help herself. She saw a psychologist and wrote letters to her priest, the district attorney and the bishop. The district attorney never replied. The pastor told her to call the bishop's office. The office offered counseling if they could receive reports. Noreen refused. She contacted an attorney when the newspapers and TV began to describe abuse in other parts of the country. "Every decision I made in my life was a response to being abused, even for something as simple as asking directions."

Like most of the girls, Noreen grew up in an intact family. She was physically healthy. Mother was a full-time at home caretaker. There were no significant separations from either parent. Noreen was well behaved during elementary school, the years in which the sexual abuse occurred. Puberty occurred at age thirteen. Noreen did some dating during high school. She graduated in the upper third of her class and did not have problems with drugs, alcohol or the police during adolescence. She married in her early twenties to the first man that she dated and spent her young adult years raising children and working. Noreen never let her children out of her sight. At the time of the evaluation she continued to work. The marriage was intact despite the near-total absence of sexual relations.

OPHELIA

Ophelia, who was divorced twenty years prior to the evaluation, worked and lived alone. She had frequent contact with her children. Ophelia believes that the sexual abuse by Father T began when she was in the fourth or fifth grade. On Saturday mornings her father would drop her off at the church for choir practice. Father T invited Ophelia to come into the church with him. When they were alone he put her hand under his cassock. He was not wearing any other clothes. Ophelia was confused as she was forced to close her fingers around his penis and masturbate him. Afterwards he gave her a Kleenex tissue to wipe the ejaculate off of her hands. She didn't know what the fluid was at the time.

This form of abuse occurred at least twenty times. "I see it from above. Sometimes I'm watching myself go through it." This dissociative reaction occurred while the abuse was actually taking place. "I was watching myself and thinking this was a weird feeling but I didn't want to stop the distance." Ophelia doesn't remember if she actually saw Father T's penis or was asked to suck it. He would rub her chest as he held her. Ophelia had not yet gone through puberty. "I wanted someone to help but no one came." Father T would constantly watch to see if anyone was approaching. Ophelia never talked to anyone about the abuse until she confided in her attorney several years ago.

Ophelia also remembered being held against a wall in a classroom and being forced to masturbate Father T. This form of abuse likely occurred twenty or thirty times. Ophelia does not remember dissociating during these occasions and does not know why she would dissociate when the abuse occurred in other places. "I remember his body odor." The smell is still strongly associated with her memories. The smell of strong, male body odor makes her sick. "In my teens and twenties it [the memories] was always there. When I was a senior in high school and people were writing nice things about me [crying] it surprised me and made me feel like a fake. They wouldn't write that if they knew I was ugly, evil and horrible. I blamed myself. It was my fault."

When the Boston cases became public, "it had nothing to do with me. It was different and no one would believe me anyway." Later Ophelia saw victims speaking on local TV. Father T's picture was there. "I went into a tailspin, like I was having a heart attack. My heart was pounding, my stomach was upset and I couldn't breathe. I wanted to tell those women that I believed them. I blamed myself because I never really thought about it. I didn't study it. It was just natural to blame myself. I always thought I was the only one."

Headaches began during the years of the abuse and continued through high school and into the young adult years before abating. They returned after Ophelia saw Father T's picture on television. Presently, if she focuses too hard on the sexual abuse, the headaches return. Vomiting occurred every Saturday morning before going to church. Ophelia did not feel safe until she returned home in the afternoon. Then the vomiting became associated with every new experience, such as going to the first day of school. The family doctor could not find an organic cause for the emesis, which continued until Ophelia was in her twenties.

"I just ate and ate." The overeating began during the abuse and continued into high school. "I thought I was fat and ugly." Ophelia was nearly seventy-five pounds overweight when she went on a diet in her forties. When under stress Ophelia still overeats. "I was afraid to be seen outside. I didn't wear shorts in the summer. I hated to go to the beach and I never learned how to swim. I still don't want to be seen. It's a daily battle I have with myself. I wait until dark to take the trash out."

Flashbacks have always been present but Ophelia tried to ignore them. However, in the past year, "I've focused on this so much, it's just there constantly. In most of the flashbacks I'm on the church steps masturbating him. . . . As a child I was afraid something would happen to my parents. I couldn't sleep when they were away. I was afraid to sleep alone. I slept against the wall because I didn't want someone to grab me." Ophelia was aware of being depressed as a teenager but she is much more aware of her depressed feelings in the present. "As a child I was tired all the time. I couldn't see how other kids could play all day."

Ophelia was raised in a happy, intact home (as were all of the women in this chapter). Grandmother and mother raised Ophelia. She was a healthy young child who did not have major illnesses or surgeries during childhood. The repeated sexual abuse by Father T began when Ophelia was nine or ten. She was a very quiet, good girl who did not cause trouble and made decent grades in school. During adolescence Ophelia was shy and inhibited. She did not participate in extracurricular activities and spent most of her time studying. Ophelia did not date until she went to college. There she met her future husband. Like a number of the women in this book who were abused as children, she married the first man she dated and has never had a relationship with anyone else. Ophelia was "surprised and grateful" when her husband pursued her. She had no idea how to respond when he made sexual advances. "I wanted desperately to like sex but nothing happened for me." Ophelia was "repulsed" by her husband's penis because seeing or touching it reminded her of how Father T's penis felt in her hand. "Sex was never enjoyable. I tried very hard. It just wasn't." When her husband began to go outside the marriage for sexual satisfaction, "I tolerated it. I thought it was the best I could do." Eventually the marriage ended in divorce. Ophelia has no desire to remarry and spends her time working and enjoying her grandchildren. Recently Ophelia began to deal with the sexual abuse. She began to see a therapist approximately two years before this evaluation.

PAULETTE

Paulette was the youngest of the six women in this chapter. She was fifty-nine at the time of the evaluation. Like most of the other women she was ashamed and embarrassed during the interview, crying and sobbing frequently. Paulette said that she was abused approximately seven or eight times, possibly more, when she was seven or eight. The first abuse occurred in the church when Father T accused Paulette of stealing. She was unsure of what happened but knows the priest gave her a gift to take home with her at the end of their interaction.

Father T frequently came to choir practice and sat next to Paulette. He put his arm around Paulette's shoulder and said nice things. Father T took Paulette's hand and put it in his cassock, on his penis, flesh to flesh. "He moved my hand around on his penis." When he ejaculated Father T held Paulette's hand on his penis so that her hand would become wet. Paulette didn't know what a penis was or what Father T was doing. She was confused and embarrassed when her hand got wet. The priest had a white cloth which he used to wipe his ejaculate off of Paulette's hand. After practice Paulette washed her hands and went home. She didn't tell anyone. She didn't know what to say.

The second episode during choir practice was similar to the first. As Father T approached Paulette she thought "he will do it again and make my hand all sticky." This time she resisted but he was too strong. The masturbation was more forceful and faster paced. Paulette looked intently at the nun who was leading the choir. The nun definitely saw Paulette's wet hand and did nothing.

The third through the sixth episodes during choir practice were all about the same. Paulette tried to resist each time but without success. She knows that Father T talked to her during the abuse but didn't remember what he said. There may have been additional incidents of abuse in a car. On one occasion Father T had Paulette sit next to him. She didn't have a clear memory of what happened but thinks she was forced to masturbate the priest.

Paulette had a vivid memory of being raped. After paying attention to several girls on the church school playground, Father T asked Paulette to go for a walk with him. She had on a school uniform and a special sweater that she had begged her mother to let her wear to school that day. In a secluded area Father T took off Paulette's sweater and had her lie on her back. Paulette has a memory of looking up at the sweater and "being poked with a stick." She has no memory of the priest being naked or penetrating her with his penis. Paulette remembers looking frantically for her sweater. "I never found it. I got into trouble with my mom because I lost it." Paulette doesn't remember how she got home. She discovered blood on her underwear and legs and a cut on her labia. Urination was painful for some time afterwards. Paulette showed her underwear to her father and said that her privates hurt. Father told mother, who said she was becoming a woman. Mother gave her a vaginal pad and told her to go to bed. Paulette thinks there was s second rape but she has no clear memory of the event.

Paulette lamented, "It took my soul. It took my trust in god, my self-worth, and my ability to love and be loved. I can't feel loved and I don't trust anybody, no one at all." Paulette described a strong dislike of anything sexual. "I don't have sex. I didn't like sex. I didn't want anyone, including my husband, to touch me. I don't like to be hugged. I never even hugged my children when they were growing up."

Paulette doesn't have friends. "I want friends but I'm afraid to trust anyone. I don't feel anyone wants to be my friend. This was a priest who did this to me. He was from God. I never thought God would do anything like this to me. My life is to go to work, make dinner, and go to bed. I don't talk to anyone and I don't do anything else." With pressure of speech and associations she described the loss of her faith. She doesn't go to church and feels alone and isolated from God.

"I struggle with alcohol. I've been battling it all of my adult life. I'm on antabuse and I've tried everything but I can't seem to stop." Since becoming aware of how widespread the sexual abuse was across the country and becoming involved in a lawsuit herself Paulette has gained nearly fifty pounds. Although she was slightly overweight prior to that time, her weight had been stable for many years.

The early years proceeded uneventfully until the time of the abuse during the latency years. During adolescence Paulette had intercourse for the first time when she was fifteen, with an eighteen-year-old man. He said they had to get married because she was used and no one would want her. They were married soon after Paulette turned eighteen. Paulette never dated anyone else. Her first child was born when she was nineteen. During high school Paulette didn't participate in extracurricular activities. She had a boyfriend she didn't want and was unable to get out of the relationship. "I didn't want to marry him, I didn't even like him. I tried. I didn't know how to get away from him. The divorce took twenty-seven years."

During the decade of the twenties Paulette was home raising her children. She felt trapped in a very unhappy marriage. At that point in her life Paulette did not relate the early sexual experience during adolescence and the emotionally imposed relationship and marriage to the sexual abuse by Father T. Heavy drinking began during these years. As her children grew Paulette decided to work outside the home. She managed to avoid thinking about the abuse. "I stuck it away real good. My husband continued to be a jerk." In her mid-forties Paulette tried to leave her husband but returned home after a brief separation. After several months she left for a second time, this time for good.

Paulette became very upset when the media began to report about the Boston sex scandals. The publicity brought her own abuse back into focus and Paulette tried to find out what happened to Father T. She began to have problems at work because of her preoccupation with the abuse and eventually learned that Father T was dead. Paulette always believed that she was the only one who had been abused. She heard of a survivors' organization and eventually spoke to other abuse victims. These conversations led to her involvement in the lawsuit in her diocese. Paulette had been seeing a psychotherapist for five years. The frequency varied from once to twice a week. Paulette describes the therapy "as helpful at times." Antidepressant and anti-anxiety medication and antabuse were prescribed.

DISCUSSION

Julie, the first of the six women, used repression and dissociative defense mechanisms to deal with the sexual abuse. She expressed a fear of fragmentation, of losing herself, as she put it, if she tried to deal with the abuse directly. Dissociation is a strong response to trauma, leading in the extreme to multiple personalities. This fear of losing one's self or fragmenting is one of the major reasons that Julie, and others like her, find talking about the abuse so difficult and why such victims avoid therapy. Therapy with these individuals requires exquisite sensitivity to the level of tolerance at any particular therapeutic moment for discussion of details of the abuse.

Karen, the second woman in this series, was raped. Rape is horrific enough for adolescent and adult women, but even more difficult and painful for latency-aged girls whose vaginas are not able to lubricate or big enough to contain an adult's penis. The pain described by Karen and other rape victims in this series of cases and the case material to follow in the next chapter was excruciating. The absence of any understanding of the concept of intercourse also added to the sense of being brutalized. Despite the clear evidence of repeated forced brutalization, in some cases more than one hundred times, many of the women in this chapter tended to minimize the extent of the abuse and its effects. In part, this limited intellectual and affective response can be understood as a defensive attempt to maintain some semblance of conscious comfort. Isolation of affect and repression are two of the main defense mechanisms utilized by these victims.

Not one of these six women became involved in a comfortable, secure marriage. Most had extreme revulsion and avoidance of sex with their husbands. In particular, they were disgusted by the penis and particularly by anything having to do with oral sex. One of the six, Monica, could allow some sexual expression and enjoyment, but only after heavy drinking. Unlike some of the younger victims described earlier in the book, most of the older victims did not resort to drug or alcohol abuse. They were good children, brought up in religious families. Any form of illegal behavior was severely frowned upon. During adolescence most were good girls who were quiet, on the fringe of the peer group, and relatively uninvolved in extracurricular activities.

Monica and Noreen also typify the experience of having no refuge, no safe place in which to avoid the perpetrator. Because of the relationship between the clergyman and their parents, the perpetrator was welcomed into the home, even into the children's bedrooms. Like the home, the church buildings themselves are places of safety and protection for many; but for these women the church grounds were places to be victimized. All of these women lost their religion and fifty years later still react emotionally when passing by a church. This sense of no place to hide and no one to go to for understanding is vividly evident in Noreen's history. During choir practice she tried her best to avoid Father T. When she did he threatened to abuse her little sister. When she told another priest what had happened he told her to recant or go to hell. Noreen turned to her mother for help and was slapped in the face for her efforts. Later in life she developed an extreme eating disorder. Her body continued to be a source of revulsion.

Several of the women, including Ophelia, married early to the first man who expressed a serious interest in them. Not having any prior experience in dating, and having been subjected to forced victimization, they lacked the ability to slowly integrate sexuality and dating as healthy adolescents do. They never learned to say no in dating situations to men who were not of their choosing. Because marriage was highly valued in their families and religion, and they wanted to live normal lives, they agreed to marry despite fearing sex and being wholly unprepared for married life. Having no sense of equality with males and feeling inadequate as women, they were surprised and grateful that any man showed an interest in them.

Paulette is the clearest example of pathological development in regard to sexuality, intimacy and marriage. She had intercourse for the first time at age fourteen, victimized and abused by an eighteen-year-old man. Her "boyfriend" controlled her throughout the high school years and consequently Paulette had little involvement with friends and school activities and no involvement with other boys. When she reached eighteen Paulette entered into a marriage that she didn't want. She was unhappy in the relationship from the beginning and, as she put it, "the divorce took twenty-seven years." Even then, Paulette was unable to be assertive in her own best interests and ended the relationship, passively, by having sex with another man. Like many of the other women in this and the next chapter, Paulette took refuge in work. The workplace provided a place of stability and predictability and allowed the women to avoid thinking about the abuse. Paulette "stuck it away real good."

Paulette and Ophelia became involved in therapy after the clergy abuse became public knowledge. Neither felt that she benefited much from the experience. From the little information that they provided the therapy was superficial and limited in frequency. Clearly our ability to help such victims is limited at best. The half century since the abuse took place, and the decades of compromised development, make the therapeutic task daunting. Therapy for victims of chronic abuse, particularly older victims, should be thought of in terms of multiple times per week and for years.

After half a century all six women have DSM-IV diagnoses which are related to the childhood sexual abuse. All six meet the criteria for Sexual Abuse of Child V61.21, Focus on Victim 995.545; Posttraumatic Stress Disorder, Chronic 309.81, and Religious Problem V62.89. All six also manifested Hypoactive Sexual Desire Disorder 302.71 and, as previously discussed, none of the six ever developed a comfortable sexual relationship in or out of marriage. Four of the six meet the criteria for Dissociative Amnesia 300.12. This is a striking finding, likely related to the victims' ages, multiple abusive experiences and the use of force and violence. Three meet the criteria for Major Depressive Disorder 296.33 and one for Dysthymic Disorder 300.4. Diagnoses of Panic Disorder with Agoraphobia 300.21, Eating Disorder NOS 307.50, and Depersonalization Disorder 300.6 were each indicated in one of the six.

9

Four Sisters: The Effect of Chronic Childhood Sexual Abuse on Fifty Years of Adolescent and Adult Development

---

FOUR SISTERS, IN THEIR LATE FIFTIES AND EARLY SIXTIES at the time of my evaluation of them, were sexually abused during childhood over a four-year span by the same priest. Until shortly before the evaluations they had told no one about their experience and never received any psychological diagnostic evaluations or treatment. As with all the other case histories in this book I evaluated the sisters in connection with their lawsuits, in this instance, against the Catholic Church.

The case histories in this book have demonstrated the effects of child sexual abuse on children and adults from the preschool years through latency, adolescence, to young and middle adulthood. This chapter, and the one immediately preceding it, provide a rare opportunity to describe and understand the ongoing, pervasive effects of untreated, chronic child sexual abuse on developmental processes over half a century. In each instance the women were describing the details of the abuse and the effects on their development for the first time. Not only did these four women not tell their parents or others about the abuse, but until the initiation of their lawsuits a few years ago, they never talked to each other about what had happened, despite the fact that they were abused in one another's presence.

Each evaluation consisted of a detailed diagnostic interview, conducted by me, lasting approximately three hours; a psychological testing evaluation conducted by an experienced forensic psychologist; and a review of relevant records.

Chapter 9

The four sisters, listed according to age from the oldest to the youngest, will be referred to as Anna, Beth, Casey and Dana. All direct quotes refer to the words of the four women spoken during their diagnostic interviews.

ANNA

Anna was sixty-one years old at the time of our interview. Retired from a business career, she was married to her third husband for approximately ten years. Anna did not have any children because she did not want to bring children into a world where they could be abused as she was. The sisters were raised in an intact family. Both parents were hardworking, strict and religious.

The sexual abuse began when Anna was ten years old and ended when she was fourteen. As soon as she began to develop breasts Father C lost interest in her. Anna estimated that the abuse occurred at least 200 times over the course of the four years. The children were abused at home, on the beach, in Father C's car, at church and at a drive-in movie. Almost all of the abuse that Anna experienced occurred in the presence of her sisters. The abuse began when Father C put his hand under Anna's blouse and touched her chest. Then the touching progressed to rubbing Anna's genitals over her underpants and eventually to digital penetration of her vagina. Father C placed Anna's hand on his phallus. He would spread Anna's legs and stare at her vagina, rub his penis over her vagina and stick the tip inside. He ejaculated many times. Father C did not perform oral or anal sex or introduce pornography or drugs; nor did he involve other adults in the abuse. His sexual interaction with each sister differed. The priest would threaten the children, indicating that if they told anyone they would go to hell.

The sisters had to watch while their siblings were being abused. For example, at the drive-in movie the sisters would be told to change seats in the car. Usually two of them would be in the front seat with Father C. At the beach, under a blanket that covered them all, the children would watch one another being abused. "I knew my turn was coming." With great sadness and guilt Anna told of being glad when her sisters were being abused instead of her. "This was almost worse than being molested myself. My baby sister was six when I was ten." The abuse stopped when Father C went away. The children did not know why he left. They assumed that Father C, who had also abused other children in their community, was moved to another parish.

The parents of the sisters were very religious people who went to church regularly and frequently invited Father C to Sunday dinner. They were honored to have a priest in their home. "There was no place safe from him. Not even home." Anna was distressed and tearful as she related this information with great difficulty.

When asked to describe any physical and/or psychological symptoms that she related to the abuse Anna listed insomnia, nightmares, flashbacks, problems with intimacy, a loss of faith, difficulty in trusting anyone and a strong desire not to have children.

Insomnia began shortly after the first molestation. Anna would force herself to stay awake because she was afraid that she would die while asleep and go to hell. The insomnia continued to the present, particularly during periods of stress or when she is afraid. On the average Anna sleeps three to four hours per night. Nightmares wake her up. She worked for many years feeling tired and fatigued. The insomnia had been particularly severe during the past four years because of the need to talk about the abuse in connection with the lawsuit.

Nightmares began to occur once or twice a week soon after the abuse began. Anna mentioned that all of her sisters also had nightmares. During the adult years from ages twenty to the present, the nightmares occurred less frequently, averaging two or more times per month. Father C appears in the nightmares some of the time. On other occasions there is a sense that he is present. Anna tries to scream but cannot. Her sisters and later her husband told her that sometimes she screams in her sleep. Her husband tries to awaken her and although she appears to be talking to him she doesn't remember these interactions in the morning. Flashbacks have occurred approximately ten times since the abuse ended. They occurred frequently during the years of abuse. The last one occurred recently when Anna was filling out a form for the lawsuit. "I could actually see C's face and smell him."

Anna doesn't believe that there is another human being who knows who she really is other than her sisters and her husband. She doesn't make close friends or rely on others. Husband and wife do have couple friendships but "there is no one to call or talk to in any depth . . . I couldn't tell anyone what happened. Father C would hurt us or we would go to hell. You couldn't slip and talk. If you can't trust a priest, who can you trust? I don't take friendships to that deeper level."

Anna does have sex with her husband but never really shares herself. "Underneath it all I think sex is dirty." She is relieved when her husband doesn't request sexual relations. "Penises are not beautiful things to me." Anna used birth control to keep from having children. "The sad thing is I really love children." Years ago she had an abortion. "I just couldn't have children." Further, Anna stopped going to church in her twenties because she felt deeply betrayed by the church. She went until that time because of parental insistence.

Anna never sought treatment for her symptoms. The abuse was never discussed with anyone until stories about the widespread nature of the sexual abuse of children by priests began to appear in newspapers.

Anna presented as a well-dressed adult woman who had a fine vocabulary. She was angry about having to discuss the abuse with me because she found any focus on the abuse difficult and very painful. Feelings of anger, sadness, guilt and low self-esteem were evident throughout the interview. Thinking was logical and goal directed. There was no evidence of delusions or hallucinations.

Anna has little memory of her early life. She knows that Mother was her primary caretaker and that she had no significant problems during these years. Anna went to a parochial school where she was an excellent student. Her parents were strict but caring and very involved with the clergy. When the couple went out for social evenings Father C would watch the girls in their home. Anna had friends and activities but her closest friends were her sisters. The sexual abuse began at age ten.

Menarche occurred at age fourteen. Anna attended a Catholic high school where she did well academically. Due to her parents' restrictions Anna's social life during high school was very limited. She did not begin to date until her sophomore year in college. Like many other abused women Anna married her first boyfriend. After college she began to work for a company that remained her employer until she retired in her fifties. The marriage lasted seven years and ended when her husband had extra-marital relationships, in part because of his dissatisfaction with Anna's sexual responses and inhibitions. Anna met her second husband and became a stepmother to his children. She enjoyed caring for them but remained adamant that she did not want to bring children of her own into the world. Her continuing difficulties with intimacy led to a separation and eventual end of the marriage. During these years Anna continued to work and receive frequent promotions. Despite this success, she always worried that she was not acceptable.

Anna married her third husband when she was in her mid-forties. Sometime during these years she began to hear about sexual abuse in the church from newspapers and TV shows and recognized that she and her sisters were not the only ones who had been injured. Feeling a responsibility to others, Anna called her sisters and discussed the matter. They discovered that Father C was dead. When a law was passed that allowed older victims of childhood sexual abuse to sue the church all four siblings agreed to begin legal proceedings. Recent years were painful as the legal process unfolded, exacting a great emotional toll on Anna. Despite her pain, Anna is determined to see justice done.

Psychological Testing

The following is a summary of the findings of the psychologist who tested Anna.

"Data from the MMPI-2 reflect significant mood and neuro-vegetative symptoms of Major Depression . . . Additional findings from the MMPI-2 indicate disruptive levels of worry, tension and anxiety . . . It is likely that [Anna] experiences perceptions of social alienation and interpersonal detachment . . . Analysis of the Critical Scale Items indicates pronounced features of acute anxiety, mental confusion, and depressed/suicidal ideation."

On the Incomplete Sentences Blank Test "[Anna] is quite angry and resentful about the molestation . . . She tends to generally avoid closeness and keep most relationships at a non-threatening distance. She is fearful of the Catholic Church and believes she is continuing to be attacked, abused and damaged by that institution and its representatives during the litigation process . . . She reports severe and ongoing sleep disruption, nervousness and agitation."

Findings from the Thematic Apperception Test "are notable for projections and material associated with the devastating impact of traumatic events and painful losses."

"Structural data, indices and content from the Rorschach Inkblot Test are consistent with an individual who is chronically completely overwhelmed, experiencing pronounced features of Major Depression, and lacking in basic psychological resources and coping abilities . . . Interpersonal relationships tend to be very limited or completely avoided based on expectations of rejection, betrayal, persecution or exploitation. None of [Anna's] responses indicated a normative capacity for mutual, pleasurable and satisfying relationships." Using the DSM-IV, the psychologist suggested diagnoses on Axis I of Major Depressive Disorder and Posttraumatic Stress Disorder, Chronic. He rated Anna's symptoms in the moderate to serious range of impairment.

BETH

Beth was sixty years old at the time of the evaluation. She had been married for more than thirty years and had two grown sons. Beth was molested by Father C between the ages of eight and twelve.

When Father C came to dinner he would appear to be playing with Beth and her sisters but would actually begin to fondle them while mother was preparing dinner. Sometimes at the drive-in theater Father C would abuse the sisters, one at a time. While her sisters were being abused in the front seat of the car Beth "was there but I didn't watch." In the summer and fall he would take them to the beach and molest them on a blanket and in deep water where they were unable to stand. Beth was also abused while saying prayers at night before getting into bed and on a vacation that Father C took with the family. Beth cried as she described the abuse. Father C would stick his finger in her vagina. He made her massage his penis. "Once he made me suck it. He put his penis in my anus when we went to the beach. If I cried he would drop me in the water where I couldn't stand. And I couldn't swim." Beth did not know if Father C anally penetrated her sisters. They never talked about it.

Beth was forced to suck Father C's penis about three times. She was not sure if he ejaculated but remembered "messy, smelly stuff." Father C penetrated Beth vaginally when he came to the house. This occurred about once or twice a month during the first two years of the abuse when Father C lived nearby and about six to ten times during the last two years when he would return to visit the family. The priest told her not to say a word because no one would believe her. "He would force me, take my hand by the wrist and put it on his penis." The abuse also occurred on church property. Father C would suggest they go off on some errand and would abuse Beth when they were alone.

Beth tearfully described how she confessed the abuse to another priest. When the confessor asked why she didn't go to confession with Father C Beth replied that she didn't like what he was doing to her. The confessor told her to stop lying about Father C. If she lied she would go to hell. Beth felt that the sisters didn't talk to each other about the abuse because they were so ashamed. "I lived in my own little world. It was hard for me to tell anybody anything."

In addition to physical pain from anal and vaginal penetration Beth described the following symptoms, at times crying or sobbing. "I always wanted to be by myself. I felt safer. I used to run away from school. They got used to it. A policeman would bring me back. . . . I wanted to get away from him. . . . These things haven't been out for a long time. I'm so embarrassed." Avoidance of others continues to the present. "I'm alone. I don't have close friends. It's hard to let anyone know me. My greatest pleasure is my kids. I lie before I'd tell the truth so I don't have to talk to people."

Beth reported the following nightmares. "I'm lying on a couch asleep. I'm watching this [in the dream]. Father C is coming and I can't wake up. I'm watching myself." In another dream "I'm at the beach with Father C. A big wave is coming. It will wash me away and I'm happy." The nightmares occur about six times per year to the present. During the years of abuse Beth frequently had the following dream. "A big black dog is under the bed. It would come up to get me. I would wake up frightened. Mother would come in and try to reassure me. When she got tired of my screaming she would say the devil would come and take me to hell, so I couldn't get out of bed. I would wet my pants."

"I could never touch my husband's penis." Beth told her husband about the abuse when the lawsuit was filed. "Sex is not enjoyable." Beth never initiates sexual relations with her husband. "When I do have it sometimes I feel kind of sick. It's not pleasurable." Her first sexual involvement was with her husband. For years she could not eat sausage because it reminded her of Father C's penis. Further, Beth can't undress in front of her husband. She feels ashamed. "I don't like my body. I'd be ashamed if it was perfect. I never wanted girls. If I knew I would have a girl I would have had an abortion. My husband wanted children when we got married. I didn't. We waited five years. I'm glad I have them now." Beth was extremely protective of her sons at all times.

Over the years Beth tried to shut out thoughts of the abuse but would find herself crying for no apparent reason or she would become very sad. "You know it's there, but you don't let it surface." The nightmares would bring the abuse back to consciousness. So would insensitivity to children. "Once I took care of a baby [sobbing with rage]. The father of the baby was abusive. I hid a knife. I thought I would stab him if he was going to abuse the baby. That's terrible. I'm not that kind of person. I've never told anyone that. I'm not that kind of person. I feel so bad about thinking that."

Beth described her tendency to lie rather than face a difficult reality. Once she took money out of the couple's joint account. When her husband asked about the money she said that she didn't take it, yet it was obvious that she had. Such deceptions have caused problems in the relationship. "I haven't done anything wrong but it feels that way. I can't tell the truth, I can't." Lying began during the abuse. One day Father C took Beth's underpants. She told him that she would get into trouble. When mother asked where they were, rather than describe what actually happened Beth said they must be in the laundry.

Beth presented as a well-dressed middle-aged woman. There were no unusual mannerisms and she had a very good vocabulary and normal speech production. Affect ranged from quiet and composure to sobs when talking about the abuse. There was considerable embarrassment at times and feelings of anger and rage. Beth was amazed at the powerful feelings aroused by telling me about the abuse and her symptoms because she had never talked about the abuse in such detail in a protected setting before. Thinking was logical and goal directed. There was no evidence of delusions or hallucinations. She was oriented as to time, person, and place and interpreted proverbs abstractly.

Like her sisters, Beth had few memories of her early years. She thinks she developed normally and was toilet trained early. As previously described Beth would run away from school during the years of the abuse. She was not a good student and did not like school. Puberty occurred at age fourteen. Beth was not prepared by her mother who never talked about sex. During adolescence Beth did not have problems with drugs, alcohol or the police. She never dated during high school and worked part-time during these years.

Beth married at age twenty-six. She dated one other person for a short period of time before meeting her husband. When he expressed a serious interest in her she didn't know what to do. As the relationship progressed Beth found his sexual attention very upsetting but didn't want him to lose interest in her. She frequently wonders why her husband has stayed with her, considering her lying and dislike of sex. Beth's sons were born when she was in her thirties. After their births she stopped working outside of the home for several years. During these years the marital relationship was good and Beth remained in close contact with her sisters. From her early twenties to the present Beth has worked for a business in a clerical position.

Psychological Testing

On the Detailed Assessment of Posttraumatic Stress Test "Beth reports having experienced a significant amount of emotional and cognitive distress at the time of the traumatic event. The distress she experienced included significant feelings of fear, helplessness, horror, being upset and fearing she may be killed. She also reports experiencing a significant amount of dissociation during the trauma. It should be noted that having significant peritraumatic distress and experiencing peritraumatic dissociation has been associated with increased severity of posttraumatic stress . . . She makes conscious attempts to avoid people, places, conversations and situations that might trigger intrusive re-experiencing symptoms and also avoids her feelings. She also demonstrates sustained hyper-activation of the sympathetic nervous system . . . Her symptoms have caused significant impairment in her relationships and in social situations. At the present time, she reports having severe dissociative symptoms as well as mild suicidal ideation."

On the Trauma Symptom Inventory Test "Beth demonstrated significant elevations on scales related to depression, intrusive experiences, defensive avoidance, dissociation and sexual concerns. She reports having upsetting memories of her victimization and repetitive, unpleasant thoughts that intrude into awareness . . . she reports having significant dissociative symptoms." On the TSI Beth responded "as a complex trauma victim, someone who is chronically distressed, overwhelmed by intrusive symptoms and potentially likely to act out painful internal states because of a lack of internal resources."

On the Beck Depression Inventory Test Beth scored in the mild range of depression. Her most significant symptom is feeling worthless. On the Adult Manifest Anxiety Scale Beth reported mild levels of anxiety. "Although generally appropriate, she is a high-strung individual who tends to do well despite her insecurities. Her tendency to worry may interfere with some of her relationships. She is overly sensitive to criticism and may be compulsive about some specific matters."

On the Personality Assessment Inventory Beth's profile "is consistent with an impression of extreme social isolation. She has few relationships that could be described as warm or close . . . Her social isolation and detachment serves to decrease the distress and discomfort that is fostered by interpersonal contact . . . She is more troubled by self-doubt and feelings of inadequacy than is apparent to others."

Using DSM-IV, the psychologist suggested diagnoses of Posttraumatic Stress Disorder, Chronic, and Dysthymic Disorder. He rated Beth's symptoms in the moderate range of severity.

CASEY

Casey was fifty-eight years of age at the time of the evaluation. She lived with her husband of more than twenty years. They have no children. Casey hesitated to tell me about the abuse. After a long pause she commented that talking was difficult and she did not know me. As the interview progressed she became more comfortable and related the following story. As best she could recall the abuse occurred between the ages of seven and eleven. Her first instance of being abused occurred at her first Holy Communion. As she sat on his lap in her white dress Father C inserted his finger in her vagina. It hurt badly. Casey wet herself after the abuse. This scared her. From then on, if an adult sounded stern "I would pee my pants." The loss of bladder control began a few years after she had been fully toilet trained. Casey recalled experiencing very painful urination during the years of the abuse, possibly from continued digital penetration. She did not know if she mentioned this symptom to her parents or went to a physician because of it. Casey also began to wet the bed at some point during the years of abuse. Wetting during the day continued until she was eighteen years of age. This made dating during adolescence very difficult since Casey lived in great fear that she would wet herself and be unable to hide the urine on her clothing from her date. At age eighteen Casey told herself that she must regain control of her bladder and the daytime wetting never occurred again. The enuresis stopped by the time she was an adolescent.

When Father C began to abuse her, "I would go into this black box and hide in the back of it. I would disappear. I would go way inside myself. It was like I was outside watching and I would say, 'who is this little girl and what is happening to her?' There was this white space where I could peer out. Then I would know when to come out." Casey's memories were vague and she was uncertain of dates. After the first experience of abuse, the digital penetration, which she did remember, Casey had no detailed memories of the subsequent experiences of abuse. "I don't want to go there." However, she does have memories of events leading up to the various instances of abuse. For example, she remembers going to the drive-in movie with Father C. He would have the sisters change seats so that each of them would sit next to him for a while. "He would put his arm around me and I would go away."

Casey also remembered going to the beach. It was always so lonely there. No one would be around. Father C would take the children, one by one, into the ocean. Waves would crash around them. Casey was petrified. Father C would laugh. "He always had a blanket. He would start rubbing us and then I would disappear." Casey had a vague memory of rubbing Father C's penis. She thought this was odd. "These things float in." She had no memory of abuse while driving in the car or during the occasions that Father C babysat the sisters.

As she reflected on the various instances of abuse she returned to the digital penetration on the day of her first Holy Communion. "He did it in front of everybody. How could he do this to this little girl in this dress? I didn't like dresses after that. They gave access." Referring to later instances of vaginal penetration she said, "I remember my legs being spread apart, then being hurt. Then I would go away." Casey associated to confessing to Father C. "He would talk about impure thoughts. He would go through a list. It was yucky."

Casey has no fully conscious memory of touching Father C's penis or of him ejaculating. However, after I asked this question she made a sound with her mouth as though she were spitting something out. "I do that to try and get it out of my body." Casey also had no memories of anal stimulation but she did remember painful defecation during the years of abuse. "The intestinal problems lasted forever."

Father C would catch her in church, in the stairwell. He was always "lurking" but she doesn't know what happened there. "I remember looking at his face. I don't remember the rest of his body. I could draw his face. Whenever I think of talking about this I'm afraid I'll walk over the edge and not come back!" Casey didn't think that her parents knew about the abuse. "They loved the priests. Priests were God." In regard to being aware that her sisters were also being abused Casey commented, "We were such a unit. I knew but I didn't know. I never discussed it with my sisters." Recently Casey had some psychotherapy. She told the therapist that she had been abused but was unable to discuss the abuse in the therapy sessions. "I was so ashamed. I was damaged and ugly. I didn't even realize I was carrying this around. It was something to hide."

Casey described dreams in which she would step off of a curb and be hit by a car. In others she was at the beach and a wave was coming to wash over her. She couldn't recall when these dreams began. They had always been there. In her sleep Casey yells "Help me! Help me!" Her husband wakes her up at that point. Casey does not recall any dreams in which Father C actually appeared. These nightmares occur approximately two times per month to the present. Approximately twenty times per month Casey will wake up in a panic. "My heart is racing so bad I have to catch my breath." She had no memory of a specific dream associated with these panic attacks. "This was happening ten, twenty, thirty years ago. As a child I had eight or nine bears. I would line them up and get in the middle. My bears would protect me. I still have a teddy bear at the bottom of the bed."

Casey had a dream both before and after her deposition, which occurred three days before our interview. She wrote down her memories of the dreams and referred to a sheet as she told me about them. In the first dream, just before the deposition, "I started peeing the bathtub. It got so full it overflowed. It started to go under the door. I was afraid someone would see it. I tried to push it under the door. Then I woke up." Casey never had a dream like that before. "I think I was letting go of the shame. It's flowing out whether I want it to or not. It's a release." The second dream involved being trapped in a moving car that was about to hit people.

Casey recalled being unable to control her urine until she was eighteen. "It affected all parts of my life. What if I peed my pants in school? I'd be so ashamed it would be horrible."

Casey told about her first sexual experience with intercourse. "It was scary. I screamed." The first few times that she made love Casey urinated in the bed. "I stopped going to church at about the same time as I stopped peeing. I was sitting in church thinking what right does he [the priest] have to talk to me. I stopped going that day. We kept being told that we would go to hell."

Casey met her husband in her early twenties. He loved her and was a good person. He didn't pressure her sexually. "I don't have to make love if I don't want to." After they had been together for four years he wanted to get married but Casey did not. "I knew I wouldn't be a good wife. I got married knowing no one would control me sexually." Occasionally while having sex with her husband there were times "when I went into the black box." (She stopped talking for a while.) "I feel really bad about this. If I separated things out I could enjoy sex. But if I put it together with my husband it's too much." Casey seemed to gain insight as she spoke, saying that she had not related her sexual problems to the abuse. "I just split. I split sex and a husband." She related that she never liked adults. "I didn't want to become one of those people."

Casey related her refusal to have children to the sexual abuse. "I'm such a child myself. I couldn't protect a child. When I was thirty-eight I had a dream I would leave the baby on top of a car and forget it." Casey was capable of having children but chose not to. "If I had a child and someone hurt it I would kill that person. I was very active in making sure I never got pregnant."

She developed a serious gambling problem. "It was a way to get away. I would stare at that machine. During the last four years it got real bad. Whenever I'm in a lot of pain, now, I say, it's OK to feel. Don't go away, don't go gambling. Cry if you want to. Get angry if you want to. It's OK." Casey estimated her gambling losses at approximately $40,000 over the last four years while dealing with the lawsuit. "I tie the gambling with the trip to Las Vegas that my family took with Father C. It's weird talking to you and putting things together."

Casey presented as a well-dressed adult woman. Noticeably apprehensive at first, she participated fully in the interview and as we discussed the abuse began to make connections between her symptoms and the abuse for the first time. Affect varied from cautious anxiety to anger, sadness and depression. There was very frequent mention of "disappearing" or going into her black box during the actual abuse, indicating the use of the defense mechanisms of isolation of affect, repression and dissociation. Thinking was logical and goal directed and there was no evidence of delusions or hallucinations.

Casey made the following comment about her mother. "I have a sense of darkness and sadness." This was related to not having been protected from Father C. During the elementary years, when the sexual abuse occurred, Casey was a well behaved, good student. Very shy, she had few friends. She relied heavily on her sisters for support. Puberty occurred in mid-adolescence. During high school Casey was a poor student. "I couldn't focus. I was a ditz. I knew I would disappear a lot. I would appear happy. I was becoming the person who always wanted to have a good time and laugh a lot." Dating began at age sixteen. After graduating from high school Casey worked as a secretary and took college courses.

Casey married at age twenty-five. The young couple moved frequently. Casey remained in close contact with her sisters. She felt that her symptoms seriously interfered with her enjoyment of life and marriage. Casey worked throughout her young and middle adult years. In her early fifties she became ill and had surgery but was able to deal with this trauma consciously. "I didn't have to reject it and go into my black box. I wasn't ashamed."

Casey went into therapy after her illness. The abuse was mentioned but Casey was unable to bring herself to discuss it despite seeing the therapist once per week for nearly two years. Two years ago, after starting to gamble heavily, Casey again went into therapy. Once again the abuse was mentioned but not discussed.

Psychological Testing

The Mini-Mental Status Examination did not reveal evidence of cognitive impairment.

When discussing the Detailed Assessment of Posttraumatic Stress Test the psychologist said: "She reports having experienced a significant amount of emotional and cognitive distress at the time of the traumatic event. The distress she experienced included significant feelings of fear, helplessness, horror, guilt, shame, humiliation and disgust. She also reports experiencing a significant amount of dissociation during the trauma.

She meets the diagnostic criteria for PTSD according to this instrument, and her symptoms are considered as severe in comparison to other adults who have experienced a traumatic event. Her symptoms have caused significant impairment in her relationships and in social situations. At the present time, she reports having severe dissociative symptoms as well as some suicidal ideation."

On the Beck Depression Inventory Casey scored in the moderate range of depression. "Her most significant reported symptoms include those of self-loathing, agitation, lack of interest in anything, indecisiveness, worthlessness and a lack of interest in sex." On the Adult Manifest Anxiety Scale Casey presented as someone with clinically significant levels of anxiety, a fearful individual who is prone to excessive worry and unproductive ruminations.

On the Personality Assessment Inventory Casey presented as "overly self-critical, she tends to focus on past failures and lost opportunities . . . She avoids experiencing and expressing her emotions as much as possible. This emotional constriction, while serving a self-protective function, causes her to have difficulty relaxing, being spontaneous, showing her feelings and relating to others in a casual, informal manner."

Using DSM-IV the psychologist suggested the following diagnostic possibilities: Posttraumatic Stress Disorder, Chronic; Major Depressive Disorder, Recurrent, Moderate; and Generalized Anxiety Disorder. Relating the diagnoses on Axis I to the molestation in childhood he rated Casey's symptoms at 51 on the GAF.

DANA

Dana, the youngest of the four sisters, was fifty-seven at the time of the diagnostic evaluation. She was divorced and has a close relationship with her only child. She continued to work full-time. Dana presented as an anxious, cooperative woman. Her affect was clearly depressed. Anxiety and great shame were evident as she discussed the abuse. There was no evidence of a thinking disorder or cognitive impairment.

Dana began to be abused by Father C when she was six years old. She remembers sitting on his lap and feeling his erect penis through her clothing. Not knowing what was occurring, the experience was "shocking." As the incidents of abuse continued the priest put his hands under her dress, on her vagina. Eventually he began to penetrate her with his finger. Father C made Dana rub his penis. If she took her hand away, he forcefully put it back on his phallus. He also rubbed his penis against her vagina. At the beach, in the water, Father C would fondle her. While undressing her after swimming, he would rub her vagina before putting her clothes on. The molestation also occurred in their home when Father C babysat. Dana estimates that she was abused approximately one hundred times.

Dana watched her sisters being abused on many occasions. When he abused them "I felt helpless and scared. I never looked at his face." Dana never confessed the abuse or told anyone. "I guess because my older sisters were there." At age eight or nine she noticed spots of blood on her vagina. Dana told her mother who took her to a physician. He said her hymen was broken. Mother never asked how this might have occurred and never discussed any bodily functions with Dana or her sisters. The sisters tried to protect each other. None of the four ever told their parents. Mother was very religious and "priests came from God. Mother would not have believed us. She would have said that we lied."

For the past twenty years Dana has experienced itching on her hands and arms. She relates this to the abuse because the itching occurs when she thinks about the abuse. Dana also had strong feelings about having children. "I did not want a baby girl! I felt very strongly about this. I didn't want a girl to go through what I went through and not be able to protect her." Once she had a son, she didn't want any more children.

Dana described a series of depressed and self-critical thoughts. "All my life I always felt down, that something was keeping me from being happy. I'm always afraid. All my life I've destroyed things. I ruin it before someone ruins it for me. I don't have many friends. I'm afraid to get close to anyone. Also, I don't have any self-worth. I'm always saying I'm sorry for no reason.

It sounds pretty messed up." Later Dana mentioned that she wished she could trust her husband. The relationship was a very good one but she felt guilty about their sexual relationship and worried that he or she would ruin a good thing.

"In high school I wrote a journal about the abuse. After high school things were going bad so I burned the journal hoping it would release me. Then I let it go, I had to go on with life." After seeing Cardinal Law of Boston on television Dana wished she still had the journal and could use it to do something that would keep other children from being abused. Long before seeing the cardinal on television Dana had stopped going to church.

"I pray to God on my own. I'd feel like a hypocrite if I went to a Catholic church. How could God do this to children? I did baptize my son because my parents wanted me to. I was so naïve. I never thought that little boys would be abused."

Dana has no memory of the first five or six years of her life. The abuse started at the end of this period. The absence of early memories was striking in all four sisters. Like her sisters, Dana attended parochial schools throughout the elementary school years. These were the years of the abuse. She was well behaved, had a few friends and made slightly above average grades. The sisters played together and the family went on driving vacations and visited relatives. Puberty occurred at age thirteen. Dana was not prepared by her mother. She asked her sisters about maturing but "we never talked about our bodies."

At age fourteen she had her first kiss and told her sisters that she thought she was pregnant. Dating began at age sixteen and her first boyfriend eventually became her husband. She never dated anyone else. Dana graduated from a Catholic high school with above-average grades. She did not participate in any organized clubs or sports.

Her relationship with her parents was not difficult. She had the fewest problems of any of the sisters and was the one who cared for their parents when they became ill and eventually died. Dana married at age twenty-one. Her son was born four years later. She had a tubal ligation after her son's birth to preclude the possibility of having a girl. Dana worked throughout these years and described the marriage as fairly happy. Sex was always difficult for her. When Dana was thirty-one years of age her husband left her for another woman, likely due to the lack of sexual responsiveness. After the separation Dana raised her son and continued to work. Both of her parents died during this decade. At age forty Dana began a new relationship, which continues to the present. The couple has never lived together nor made a formal commitment, despite the fact that they have been together for nearly twenty years, because Dana is fearful that the relationship will fail.

Psychological Testing

Dana scored in the average to above average range on the Wechsler Adult Intelligence Scale-R. "It is also very likely that existing psychological symptoms and difficulties are producing inconsistent intellectual performance and some degree of cognitive impairment." On the Rotter Incomplete Sentences Blank, Dana "demonstrated significant difficulty, concerns, symptoms and perceptions indicative of pronounced features of depression and anxiety. She feels victimized, attacked and traumatized by both the past molestation, as well as perceived current attacks by church representatives.

She views herself as weak, compromised, unsuccessful and unaccomplished in her life's endeavors and pursuits. She lacks a positive sense of competency and mastery stating, 'I have let life get away from me.'" Dana tends to escape from painful and difficult reality through the use of fantasy and avoidance. She described the wish to be a child again in another world, there having the opportunity for a better and more fulfilling past and current existence.

Findings from the Thematic Apperception Test reveal marked indications of traumatic and pathological relationships with powerful and malevolent male authority figures. "Stories included experiences of great despair, helplessness, abuse, coercion, rejection, and abandonment at the hands of significant, powerful males." On the Minnesota Multiphasic Personality Inventory-2 "clinical scale elevations are consistent with significant features of depression and anxiety, and the likely use of avoidance or some possible somatization to minimize conscious awareness of existing emotional and psychological difficulties."

On the Rorschach Inkblot Test "her defenses, however, were completely unable to ward off or regulate powerful, depressive, and disruptive emotional stimulation and processing. Findings are indicative of a person with a significant underlying depressive disorder, with the mood and neuron-vegetative symptoms with such a diagnosis. Dana attempts to minimize and avoid emotional stimulation because she experiences such feelings as negative, painful, overwhelming and disorganizing."

Using DSM-IV, the psychologist suggested diagnoses of Major Depressive Disorder and Posttraumatic Stress Disorder, Chronic. He rated her symptoms in the 55–60, moderate range.

DEVELOPMENTAL AND DIAGNOSTIC CONSIDERATIONS

It is a basic tenet of adult developmental theory that all adult experience, normal and pathological, cannot be reduced to, or entirely explained by, experience during the first five or six years of life. Similarly, all of the pathology found in these women cannot be attributed solely to the sexual abuse. Pathology, at any point in the life cycle, is always the result of experience from the past and the engagement of phase-specific developmental tasks of the present as interpreted by the mind as it exists in the present.

The various forms of abuse that these four girls experienced included fondling, masturbation of the perpetrator to ejaculation, digital vaginal penetration, fellatio and vaginal and anal intercourse. Physical force was used and verbal threats were made. All major developmental tasks from adolescence through midlife were compromised by the sexual abuse.

During adolescence the following developmental tasks were compromised: comfortable integration of the physical and sexual changes of puberty, emergence of a healthy body image, beginning relationships with the opposite sex, peer relationships, academic achievement, integration of religious belief, individuation from parents and trust in mentors and other significant adults. Indeed, the total rejection of the few attempts that the girls made to report the abuse while it was occurring led to a perceived alliance among parents, church and priest against them. There was nowhere to turn, no one to help. There was no safe place, not even home. The eventual result was distant relations with their parents during adolescence and adulthood and a total rejection of Catholicism and to a lesser degree a belief in God.

Throughout the young and middle adult phases normal development was compromised by interference with the developmental tasks of the achievement of mature sexuality, the development of the capacity for marriage and intimacy, the desire for children, the establishment of adult friendships, the reasonable use of money and involvement in society.

All four women are certain that their parents had no awareness of the ongoing sexual abuse. They considered their parents to be highly religious people who thought of priests as holy men, close to God, who had dedicated their lives to the service of others. Unlike today, at the time of the abuse there was very little public awareness that sexual abuse by clergy was possible or likely. Having children spend time with the parish priest was thought to be a way of instilling highly valued moral and religious values.

All aspects of sexuality were considered to be highly private matters which were not discussed in public. Mother, in particular, was extremely modest and unable or unwilling to discuss sexual matters, including the onset of menstruation, with her daughters. Although they saw little signs of outward affection between the parents, father and mother were clearly close to each other and a stabilizing constant in the children's lives.

The women's adult problems with intimacy and parenthood appear to be primarily related to the ongoing, untreated effects of the chronic sexual abuse— sexual experience was nearly always associated consciously and unconsciously with their encounters with Father C. However, their adult realization that their parents were unable to protect them from abuse led to an emotional withdrawal from both parents that continued until their deaths. A further consequence of the parents' failure to protect their children led to the conclusion on the part of all four that despite their heightened sense of awareness of the potential danger of predators, it was better to avoid having children at all, and girls, in particular, at all costs.

DIAGNOSTIC CONSIDERATIONS

Utilizing DSM-IV, which although limited in usefulness for understanding pathology within a psychodynamic framework is the most widely used diagnostic nomenclature in the field, the following diagnoses are applicable to the sisters: Sexual Abuse of Child—all four; Posttraumatic Stress Disorder, Chronic—all four; Major Depressive Disorder—two of the four; Dysthymic Disorder—two of the four; Dissociative Amnesia—one of the four; Pathological Gambling—one of the four; Religious or Spiritual Problem—all four. On Axis V, at the time of the evaluations, three of the four were rated in the 51–60, moderate range and one in the 41–50, serious range.

SUMMARY OF DIFFERING EFFECTS ON
EACH OF THE FOUR SISTERS

The severity of the damage caused by childhood sexual abuse varies from person to person and circumstance to circumstance. The sexual abuse experienced by Anna and her sisters was particularly devastating because it occurred repeatedly, likely more than 100 times over an extended period of four years when they were young, very vulnerable children. As the oldest of the sisters Anna felt responsible for, and unable to protect, her siblings.

Beth described more severe kinds of abuse than her sisters', namely multiple episodes of vaginal and anal penetration and fellatio. The effect of the abuse on her life has been profound, affecting self-esteem, relationships and enjoyment of life. She has been chronically depressed and somewhat isolated. Her relationships with her husband, two sons and sisters have sustained her and allowed Beth to achieve a limited level of integration and involvement in life.

Casey had great difficulty with bladder control throughout her adolescence. This affected all aspects of adolescent functioning, particularly the consolidation of a mature body image and dating and sexuality. As an adult she developed major problems with sexual and emotional intimacy, did not have children and developed a significant gambling problem. Further, like her sisters, she lost her faith.

Dana was the youngest of the four. The effect of the abuse on such a young child, approximately age six at the time it began, was extreme. Dana had difficulties in relationships with men, friendships, self-esteem and self-worth, attitudes toward having children and career advancement. She is a functioning individual who has limped through life with a sense of depression, restriction and failure. In her mind the only success in her life is her son.

COMMENTS ON PSYCHOPATHOLOGY AND TREATMENT

Psychopathic Sadism: Some readers may have wondered, as I did, why none of these sisters, or the six women in the preceding chapter, became perpetrators themselves. Victims of child sexual abuse, in the midst of a working therapeutic relationship, are sometimes able to acknowledge that pleasurable sexual feelings were part of the experience. Victims who become perpetrators can sometimes be helped to see that their sexual attacks on children are attempts to master their own experience as victims. Will such feelings be expressed during the treatment of these women? I doubt it, although a definitive answer will only be available at the end of the treatment process, not before one has begun. I think it unlikely that these children (or any of the girls in earlier chapters who were also forcibly raped) experienced much physical pleasure from their experiences with Father C and Father T due to the violent nature of much of the abuse—for example, the forceful digital and penile penetration of the immature vagina and anus—and the repeated threat of physical danger (drowning) and psychological damnation. These men made little effort to groom their victims. They used their position and physical force to attack the children sexually. The intent appeared to be to produce pain in their victims, not sexual arousal.

Attributing motives to an individual who has not been evaluated is obviously limited, but Fathers C and T appear to be sadistic psychopaths. Their sexual sadism, a variant of sadism in general, pleasure through the domination and suffering of another, was extreme. Meloy (2002) describes psychopaths as "aggressively narcissistic." This aspect of their character pathology "is often expressed behaviorally by the repetitive devaluation of others, not predominantly in fantasy, as we see in narcissistic personality disorder, but in reality." Further, "another psychodynamic that contributes to the psychopath's propensity to commit evil acts is chronic emotional detachment from others. For the psychopath, relationships are defined by power gradients, not affectional ties" (p. 631). Psychopathy and sadism are particularly indicated by anal penetration. "The anal assault of a child always raises the strong possibility of both psychopathy and sexual sadism because at best, the callous attitude of the perpetrator has overcome the plaintive wail of the child, or, at worst, the child's suffering enhances the perpetrator's sexual arousal" (Meloy, 1997, p. 278).

Further, Meloy (1986) has addressed the issue of narcissistic psychopathology in the clergy. He suggests that narcissistic character disorders are prevalent among members of the clergy because the profession provides strong reinforcement for such pathology. The identification as an agent of God provides the clergyman with both the omnipotence and rationalization for his behavior. This tends to make psychopathy among priests particularly nefarious because they may use their special link to God, as they experience it, as a way to threaten and dominate their victims. Based on these ideas we may characterize Father C and Father T as particularly cruel and sadistic sexual psychopaths.

TREATMENT CONSIDERATIONS

Although treatment recommendations based on a diagnostic evaluation conducted for forensic purposes must be necessarily tentative, it is clear that all ten of the women in these two chapters are in need of intensive therapeutic intervention and that anti-anxiety and antidepressant medication should be considered in conjunction with the dynamic treatment. Treatment should be provided by experienced therapists who understand the pervasive nature of the psychopathology, recognize the fragility of the women, and are able to proceed sensitively and slowly without undermining vital defense mechanisms prematurely. I have not specifically recommended psychoanalysis because I think these women will need, particularly during the beginning stages of treatment, an empathetic, real relationship with the therapist. Typical analytic reticence, relative silence and lack of face-to-face contact could be too depriving and increase anxiety and feelings of being judged and rejected. As the therapy progresses consideration could be given to a more classical analytic approach. However, the entire theoretical basis of the therapeutic intervention would be psychodynamic, both theoretically and technically. In particular, transference would be a major focus of the interaction between patient and therapist.

Transference

Transference themes will play a vital role in the treatment of these women. The raw anger, shame, embarrassment and pain which were abundantly evident during the diagnostic evaluations would eventually be expressed through the transference in an intensive, dynamically oriented therapy. It can be anticipated that the support and comfort that each woman felt during the diagnostic interview because of my attitude of non-judgmental acceptance and empathy would be followed by ambivalence toward the therapist as various aspects of the abuse were focused on and brought into consciousness.

The transference would be a particularly important vehicle for the eventual expression of dissociated and repressed aspects of the abuse. Further, the therapist would be the recipient of significant negative transference due to the therapeutic attitude of being willing to listen to such "disgusting" material and ask for further elaboration. To some degree this will be experienced by these women as abusive behavior on the part of the therapist who, like the priest, is another figure of prominence and trust seemingly pursuing his own interests as he addresses the re-creation of aspects of the original trauma and its associated painful effects. Thus the transference can be conceptualized as the major therapeutic vehicle facilitating a re-creation of the trauma leading to clarification, interpretation and whatever degree of resolution is possible.

Countertransference

Although I've learned over the years to neutralize my disgust and anger at perpetrators of child sexual abuse—particularly after I treated some and gained a better understanding of the individuals' dynamics involved—I found myself reacting to the systematic, relentless cruelty of several of the men in this book with a sense of amazement, revulsion and fear. The nature of psychopathic sadism, as described above, provided an intellectual basis for understanding but did not protect me from my emotional response. I have treated many victims of sexual abuse in the past but none by perpetrators with such extreme psychopathic sadism. As previously stated, I have not treated any of these women nor do I expect to, but past experience has taught me that any therapist involved with them would need to be constantly aware of the effect on his or her current sexual functioning and past sexual experience on attitudes and interactions with the patient. As previously mentioned, strict analytic neutrality may be inappropriate with patients who have been so victimized, particularly at the beginning of treatment; but excessively supportive interventions or expressions of anger at the perpetrator, brought on by the therapist's reaction to the extreme cruelty and identification with the victim, may compromise the treater's ability to help the patient with the daunting tasks of allowing repressed memories into consciousness and recognizing and accepting the devastating effect that the sexual abuse had on their lives over half a century.

We have no effective treatment for psychopathic perpetrators, and our ability to help victims of sexual abuse is limited at best. The research challenges that face those of us who seek to understand both perpetrators and victims are many and daunting. Hopefully the clinical material in this book will contribute to our knowledge, particularly of the effect of child sexual abuse on developmental progression throughout the life cycle, and on our ability to help.

References

Anda, R. F., V. J. Felitti, J. D. Bremner, J. D. Walker, C. Whitfield, and B. D. Perry. 2006. The enduring effects of abuse and related adverse experiences in childhood: A convergence of evidence from neurobiology and epidemiology. *European Archives of Psychiatry and Clinical Neuroscience* 256: 174–86.

Bergen, H. A., G. Martin, A. S. Richardson, S. Allison, and L. Roeger. 2003. Sexual abuse and suicidal behavior: A model constructed from a large community sample of adolescents. *Journal of the American Academy of Child and Adolescent Psychiatry* 42: 1301–9.

Besser, A., N. Vliegen, P. Luyten, and S. J. Blatt. 2008. Vulnerability to postpartum depression from a psychodynamic perspective: Extensive systematic empirical base. *Psychoanalytic Psychology* 25: 392–410.

Blos, P. 1979. *The Adolescent Passage.* New York: International Universities Press.

———. 1967. The second individuation process of adolescence. *Psychoanalytic Study of the Child* 22: 162–86.

———. 1962. *On Adolescence: A Psychoanalytic Interpretation.* New York: Free Press.

Brent, D. A., M. Oquenda, and B. Birmaher. 2002. Familial pathways to early-onset suicide attempt. *Archives of General Psychiatry* 59: 801–7.

Butler, R., and M. Lewis. 1977. *Aging and Mental Health: Positive Psychosocial Approaches.* St. Louis: Mosby.

Chu, J. A., L. M. Frey, B. L. Ganzel, and J. A. Matthews. 1999. Memories of childhood abuse: Dissociation, amnesia and corroboration. *American Journal of Psychiatry* 156: 749–55.

Cicchetti, D., and F. A. Rogosch. 1996. Equifinality and multifinality in developmental psychopathology. *Development and Psychopathology* 8: 597–600.

Cohen, J. A., E. Deblinger, A. P. Mannarino, and R. A. Steer. 2004. A multisiter randomized controlled trial for children with sexual abuse-related PTSD symptoms.

Journal of the American Academy of Child and Adolescent Psychiatry 43, no. 4: 393–402.

Colarusso, C. A. 1993. Play in adulthood: A developmental perspective. *Psychoanalytic Study of the Child* 48: 225–48.

———. 1992. *Child and Adult Development: A Psychoanalytic Introduction for Clinicians.* New York: Springer.

———. 1990. The third individuation: The effect of biological parenthood on separation-individuation processes in adulthood. *Psychoanalytic Study of the Child* 45: 170–94.

Colarusso, C. A., and R. A. Nemiroff. 1981. *Adult Development: A New Dimension in Psychodynamic Theory and Practice.* New York: Plenum.

DeBellis, M. D., M. S. Keshevan, and D. B. Clark. 1999. Developmental traumatology, part II: Brain development. *Biological Psychiatry* 45: 1271–84.

Ehrenberg, D. 1987. Abuse and desire: A case of father-daughter incest. *Contemporary Psychoanalysis* 24: 553–604.

Eisenberg, M. E., D. M. Ackard, and M. D. Resnick. 2007. Protective factors and suicide risk in adolescents with a history of sexual abuse. *Journal of Pediatrics* 151: 482–87.

Emde, R. 1985. From adolescence to midlife: Remodeling and structure of adult development. *Journal of the American Psychoanalytic Association* 33: 59–112.

Erikson, E. H. 1963. *Childhood and Society,* 2d ed. New York: W.W. Norton.

———. 1956. The concept of ego identity. *Journal of the American Psychoanalytic Association* 4: 56–121.

Feiring, C., and L. S. Taska. 2005. The persistence of shame following sexual abuse: A longitudinal look at risk and recovery. *Child Maltreatment* 10, no. 4: 337–49.

Fergusson, D., M. Lynskey, and L. Horwood. 1996. Childhood sexual abuse and psychiatric disorder in young adulthood: Prevalence of sexual abuse and factors associated with sexual abuse. *Journal of the American Academy of Child and Adolescent Psychiatry* 35: 1355–64.

Finkelhor, D. 1993. Epidemiological factors in the clinical identification of child sexual abuse. *Child Abuse and Neglect* 17: 67–70.

Freud, S. 1923. *Ego and the Id,* standard ed. 19: 3–66.

Freud, S. 1905. *Three Essays on the Theory of Sexuality,* standard ed., 7: 125–243.

Gaensbauer, T. J., and L. Jordan. 2009. Psychoanalytic perspectives on early trauma. *Journal of the American Psychoanalytic Association* 57, no. 4: 920–47.

Galenson, E., and H. Roiphe. 1976. Some suggested revisions concerning early female development. *Journal of the American Psychoanalytic Association: Supplement, Female Psychology #5,* 24: 29–58.

Goin, M. 1990. Emotional survival and the aging body. In *New Dimensions in Adult Development.* Ed. R. Nemiroff and C. Colarusso. New York: Basic Books.

Green, A. H. 1995. Comparing child victims and adult survivors: Clues to the pathogenesis of child sexual abuse. *Journal of the American Academy of Psychoanalysis and Dynamic Psychiatry* 23: 655–70.

Gurwitt, A. 1982. Aspects of prospective fatherhood. In *Father and Child.* Ed. S. Cath, A. Gurwitt, and J. M. Ross, 275–300. Boston: Little Brown.

Hertzog, J. 1982. Pattern of expectant fatherhood: A study of the fathers of a group of premature infants. In *Father and Child.* Ed. S. Cath, A. Gurwitt, and J. M. Ross, 301–14. Boston: Little Brown.

Jay, S., and K. Dell'Angela. 2002. Somatic and psychological problems in a cohort of sexually abused boys: A six-year follow-up case-control study. *Journal of Pediatrics* 141, no. 3: 445.

Jung, C. 1933. *Modern Man in Search of a Soul.* New York: Harcourt, Brace.

Kestenberg, J. 1976. Regression and reintegration in pregnancy. *Journal of the American Psychoanalytic Association Supplement, Female Psychology #5,* 24: 213–50.

Kisiel, C. L., and J. S. Lyons. 2001. Dissociation as a mediator of psychopathology among sexually abused children and adolescents. *American Journal of Psychiatry* 158, no. 7: 1034–39.

Lab, D., J. Feigenbaum, and P. DeSilva. 2000. Mental health professionals' attitudes and practices toward male childhood sexual abuse. *Child Abuse and Neglect* 24: 391–409.

Leichsenring, F., and S. Rebring. 2008. Effectiveness of long-term psychodynamic psychotherapy. *Journal of the American Medical Association* 300, no. 13: 1551–65.

Levinson, D. J., C. N. Darrow, and E. B. Klein. 1978. *The Seasons of a Man's Life.* New York: Knopf.

Luyten, P., S. J. Blatt, B. Van Houdenhove, and J. Corveleyn. 2008. Equifinality, multifinality, and the rediscovery of the importance of early experiences: Pathways from early adversity to psychiatric and (functional) somatic disorders. *Psychoanalytic Study of the Child* 63: 27–60.

———. 2006. Depression research and treatment: Are we skating to where the puck is going to be? *Clinical Psychology Review* 26: 985–99.

Luyten, P., S. J. Blatt, and J. Corveleyn. 2005. Towards integration in the theory and treatment of depression? The time is now. In *The theory and treatment of depression: Towards a dynamic interactionism model,* ed. J. Corveleyn, P. Luyten, and S. J. Blatt, 265–96. Leuven/Mahwah, NJ: Leuven University Press/Erlbaum.

Mahler, M., F. Pine, A. and Bergman. 1975. *The Psychological Birth of the Human Infant.* New York: Basic Books.

Marcano, S. 2006. Sexual abuse: The abusive family unit. *The International Journal of Psychoanalysis* 87, no. 3: 853–57.

Maslow, A. 1968. *Toward a Psychology of Being.* New York: Van Nostrand.

Masters, W., and V. Johnson. 1966. *Human Sexual Response.* Boston: Little, Brown.

Meloy J. R. 2002. The polymorphously perverse psychopath: Understanding a strong empirical relationship. *Bulletin of the Menninger Clinic* 66, no. 3: 273–87.

———. 1997. The psychology of wickedness: Psychopathy and sadism. *Psychiatric Annals* 27, no. 9 (September): 630–33.

———. 1986. Narcissistic psychopathology and the clergy. *Pastoral Psychology* 35, no. 1: 50–55.

Nelson, E. C., A. C. Heath, and P. A. F. Madden. 2002. Association between self-reported childhood sexual abuse and adverse psychosocial outcomes. *Archives of General Psychiatry* 59: 139–45.

Neugarten, B. 1979. Time, age and the life cycle. *American Journal of Psychiatry* 136: 887–94.

Offer, D., and J. B. Offer. 1975. *From Teenage to Young Manhood: A Psychological Study.* New York: Basic Books.

Paolucci, E., M. Genuis, and C. Violato. 1995. A meta-analysis of the published research on the effects of child sexual abuse. *Journal of Psychology* 135: 17–36.

Pearson, G. 1958. *Adolescence and the Conflict of Generations.* New York: W. W. Norton.

Piaget, J. 1969. *The Psychology of the Child.* New York: Basic Books.

Pollock, G. H., and S. L. Greenspan, eds. 1998. *The course of life: Completing the journey,* vol. 7. Madison, WI: International Universities Press.

Price, L., A. Maddocks, and L. Griffiths. 2002. Somatic and psychological problems in a cohort of sexually abused boys: A six-year follow-up case-control study. *Archives of Disease in Childhood* 86: 164–67.

Putnam, F. W. 2003. Ten-year research update review: Child sexual abuse. *Journal of the American Academy of Child and Adolescent Psychiatry* 42, no. 3 (March): 269–78.

Putnam, F., and P. Trickett. 1997. The psychobiological effects of sexual abuse: A longitudinal study. *Annual of the New York Academy of Science* 821: 150–59.

Rangell, L. 1963. On friendship. *Journal of the American Psychoanalytic Association* 11: 3–11.

Saporta, J. 2003. Synthesizing psychoanalytic and biological approaches to trauma: Some theoretical proposals. *Neuro-psychoanalysis* 5: 97–110.

Saywitz, K. J., A. P. Mannanino, L. Berliner, and J. A. Cohen. 2000. Treatment for sexually abused children and adolescents. *American Psychology* 55: 1040–104.

Sedlak, A. J., and D. Broadhurst. 1996. *Executive summary of the third national incident study of child abuse and neglect (NIS-3).* U.S. Department of Health and Human Services, Administration for Children and Families, National Center for Child Abuse and Neglect.

Shedler, P. 2009. The efficacy of psychodynamic psychotherapy. *American Psychologist* 65, no. 2: 98–109.

Sobsey, D., W. Randall, and R. Parrila. 1997. Gender differences in abused children with and without disabilities. *Child Abuse and Neglect* 21: 707–20.

Spitz, R. 1965. *The first year of life.* New York: International Universities Press.

Stevens-Long, J. 1990. Adult development: Theories past and present. In *New Dimensions in Adult Development.* Ed. R. Nemiroff and C. Colarusso. New York: Basic Books.

Stoller, R. 1968. *Sex and Gender: On the Development of Masculinity and Femininity.* New York: Science House.

Summit, R. C. 1983. The child abuse accommodation syndrome. *Child Abuse and Neglect* 7: 177–93.

Terr C. 1991. Childhood traumas, an outline and overview. *American Journal of Psychiatry* 148: 10–20.

Tyson, P., and R. Tyson. 1990. *Psychoanalytic Theories of Development.* New Haven: Yale University Press.

U.S. Department of Health and Human Services. 1998. *Child maltreatment 1996: Reports from the states to the national child abuse and neglect data system.* Washington, DC: U.S. Government Printing Office.

Vaillant, G. 1977. *Adaptation to life.* Boston: Little, Brown.

Widom, C. S. 1999. Posttraumatic stress disorder in abused and neglected children grown up. *American Journal of Psychiatry* 156: 1223–29.

Widom, C. S., and M. Ames. 1994. Criminal consequences of childhood sexual victimization. *Child Abuse and Neglect* 18: 303–18.

Wonderlich, S. A., R. D. Crosby, J. E. Mitchell, J. A. Roberts, B. Haseltine, G. DeMuth, and K. M. Thompson. 2000. Relationship of childhood sexual abuse and eating disturbance in children. *Journal of the American Academy of Child and Adolescent Psychiatry* 39, no. 10: 1277–83.

Index

About the Author

Calvin A. Colarusso, MD, is a clinical professor of psychiatry at the University of California at San Diego and training and supervising analyst in adult and child psychoanalysis at the San Diego Psychoanalytic Institute. In private practice of adult and child psychiatry and psychoanalysis in San Diego since 1973, Dr. Colarusso is the author of fifty articles and five books on adult and child development. For the past thirty years he has served as an expert witness in civil suits, including approximately one hundred cases related to child sexual abuse.

Breinigsville, PA USA
14 December 2010
251438BV00002B/1/P